THE REVELS PLAYS

Founder Editor
Clifford Leech 1958–71

General Editors
F. David Hoeniger, E. A. J. Honigmann and J. R. Mulryne

THE JEW OF MALTA

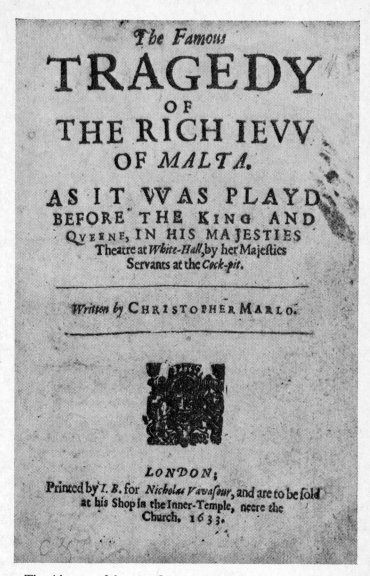

The Famous

TRAGEDY

OF

THE RICH IEVV

OF *MALTA*.

AS IT WAS PLAYD
BEFORE THE KING AND
QVEENE, IN HIS MAJESTIES
Theatre at *White-Hall*, by her Majesties
Servants at the *Cock-pit*.

Written by CHRISTOPHER MARLO.

LONDON;
Printed by *I. B.* for *Nicholas Vavasour*, and are to be sold
at his Shop in the Inner-Temple, neere the
Church. 1 6 3 3.

The title page of the 1633 Quarto, reproduced by courtesy of the
British Library

THE REVELS PLAYS

THE JEW OF MALTA

CHRISTOPHER MARLOWE

edited by

N. W. Bawcutt

MANCHESTER
UNIVERSITY PRESS

THE JOHNS HOPKINS
UNIVERSITY PRESS

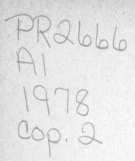

Introduction, apparatus criticus, etc, ©
N. W. Bawcutt 1978

Published by
Manchester University Press
Oxford Road, Manchester M13 9PL
ISBN 0 7190 1502 2

Published in the United States of America, 1978, by
The Johns Hopkins University Press
Baltimore, Maryland 21218
ISBN 0–8018–2084–7

Library of Congress Catalog Card Number 77–17261

British Library Cataloguing in Publication Data

Marlowe, Christopher, b. 1564
    The jew of Malta.—(The Revels plays).
    I. Title. II. Series. III. Bawcutt, N.
    822'.3   PR2666

    UK ISBN 0-7190-1502-2
    US ISBN 0-8018-2084-7

Printed in Great Britain
by W & J Mackay Ltd, Chatham

Contents

For
PRISCILLA

General Editor's Preface

The series known as the Revels Plays was conceived by Professor Clifford Leech. The idea emerged in his mind, as he tells us in the General Editor's Preface to the first of the Revels Plays, published in 1958, from the success of the New Arden Shakespeare. The aim of the series was, in his words, 'to apply to Shakespeare's predecessors, contemporaries, and successors the methods that are now used in Shakespeare editing'. We owe it to Clifford Leech that the idea has become reality. He planned the series, set the high standards for it, and for many years selected and supervised the editors. He aimed at editions of lasting merit and usefulness, that would appeal to scholars and students, but not to them alone; producers and actors were also much in his mind. 'The plays included should be such as to deserve and indeed demand performance.' And thus the texts should be presented in a form that is attractive and clear to the actor, with some space of the introduction devoted to records of productions, and some of the notes to comments on stage business.

The text of each Revels Play is edited afresh from the original text (in a few instances, texts) of best authority, but spelling and punctuation are modernised, and speech-headings silently normalised. The text is accompanied by collations and commentary, and in each volume the editor devotes one section of his introduction to a discussion of the provenance and trustworthiness of the 'copytext', the original on which he has based his edition, and to a brief description of particular aspects of his editorial method. Other sections of the introduction deal with the play's date and sources, its place in the work of the author, its significance as a dramatic work of literature in the context of its time and designed for a certain theatre, actors, and audience, its reputation, and its stage-history. In editions of a play by an author not previously represented in the series, it has been customary also to include a brief account of the author's life and career. Some emphasis is laid on providing available records of performances, early and modern.

Modernisation has its problems, and has to be practised with care and some flexibility if the substance of the original is not to be distorted. The editor emends, as distinct from modernising, the original text only in instances where error is patent or at least very probable, and correction persuasive. Archaic forms need sometimes to be retained when rhyme or metre demands them or when a modernised form would alter the required sense or obscure a play on words. The extent to which an editor feels free to adapt the punctuation will largely depend on the degree of authority he attributes to the punctuation of his copy. It is his task to follow the original closely in any dramatic or rhetorical pointing that can be trusted for good reason. Punctuation should do justice to a character's way of speaking, and to the interplay of dialogue.

In general, the manner of modernisation is similar to that in the Arden Shakespeare. Yet in the volumes since 1968, the '-ed' form is used for non-syllabic terminations in past tenses and past participles ('-'d' in Arden and earlier Revels volumes), and '-èd' for syllabic ('-ed' earlier). Act divisions are given only if they appear in the original text or if the structure of the play clearly points to them. Those act and scene divisions not found in the original are provided unobtrusively in small type and in square brackets. Square brackets are also used for any other additions to or changes in the stage directions of the original. But in no instances are directions referring to locale added to scene headings; for the plays (at least those before the Restoration) were designed for stages whose acting area was most of the time neutral and where each scene flowed into the next without interruption; and producers in our time would probably be well advised to attempt to convey this characteristic fluidity of scene on whatever stage they may have at their disposal.

A mixture of principles and common sense also governs the collations accompanying the text. Revels plays do not provide a variorum collation; only those variants which require the critical attention of serious textual students. All departures of substance from 'copy-text' are listed, including any relineation and those changes in punctuation which involve to any degree a decision between alternative interpretations; but not such accidentals as turned letters, nor necessarily additions to stage directions whose editorial nature is already made clear by the use of brackets. Press corrections in the 'copy-texts' are likewise included. Of later emendations of the text (or errors) found in seventeenth-century reprints of no authority or editions from the eighteenth century to modern times, in general only those are given which as alternative readings still deserve serious attention. Readings of a later text of special historical interest or influence are, in some instances, more fully collated.

One of the hallmarks of the Revels Plays is the thoroughness of their annotations. Besides explicating the meaning of difficult words and passages and alerting the reader to special implications, the editor provides comments on customs or usage, text or stage business—indeed on anything he judges pertinent and helpful. Glosses are not provided for words that are satisfactorily explained in simple dictionaries like the *Concise Oxford*. Each volume contains a Glossarial Index to the Commentary, in which particular attention is drawn to meanings for words not listed in *O.E.D.*

The series began with some of the best-known plays of the Elizabethan and Jacobean era, but has expanded to include also some early Tudor and some Restoration plays. It is moreover not our object to concentrate solely on well-known plays but also to make available some of the lesser known of whose merit as literature and as drama we are convinced.

Early 1976 saw a change in the publisher of the Revels Plays, from Methuen & Co. Ltd to Manchester University Press. Further, I am happy to announce that Professors Ernst Honigmann of the University of Newcastle and J. R. Mulryne of the University of Warwick have now joined me as general editors of the Revels Plays. These new arrangements should ensure that several volumes planned long ago will soon be published, and that the future direction of the series will be in able hands.

F. DAVID HOENIGER

Toronto, 1977

Preface

I have tried in this edition of *The Jew of Malta* to follow the normal principles and practices of the Revels series, as set forth in the General Editor's Preface. (One exception to this rule is in the presentation of asides, where, for reasons given in the introduction, I have followed the quarto's method of using italic type to indicate asides.) The commentary is probably fuller than in any previous edition; here I have put special emphasis on elucidating the political, historical, and religious allusions in the play, for if Marlowe is, as T. S. Eliot once described him, 'the most *thoughtful* and philosophical mind, though immature, among the Elizabethan dramatists', it is essential that we should know as much as possible about the background of his ideas. This particularly applies to the Prologue spoken by Machevil, which has demanded more detailed annotation than any other part of the play.

This edition was substantially completed in the spring of 1972, but publication has been delayed for various causes beyond my control. One effect of this has been that the textual side was prepared before the appearance of Fredson Bowers's old-spelling edition of Marlowe's *Works* in 1973. Professor Bowers is sceptical of the theory that the quarto is based upon foul papers, and prefers to derive it from the prompt-book. He also seems to believe that Heywood or someone else 'touched up' the play for the performances at court and at the Cockpit theatre. He gives, however, hardly any evidence for his case, and I have therefore not thought it necessary to alter the position expressed in my introduction.

The former general editor of the Revels Plays, Professor Clifford Leech, and the present general editor, Professor David Hoeniger, both read my original typescript with great care and pointed out numerous errors and weaknesses which I have tried to correct, though of course they must not be held responsible for those which remain. Professor Harold Jenkins criticised in detail the textual section of my introduction. Professor Richard Hosley discussed with me the problems of the original staging of the play, to the great benefit of Appendix C, but does not necessarily agree with all my conclusions. I am grateful to those librarians, especially in the British Library, the Bodleian Library, the National Library of Scotland, and the Harold Cohen Library of the University of Liverpool, who helped me to put together the material on which my edition is based. My wife has been a constant source of help and encouragement, and to her I dedicate this book.

N. W. BAWCUTT

Liverpool, 1975

Abbreviations

Bullen   *The Works of Christopher Marlowe*, ed. A. H. Bullen,
              vol. II (London, 1885).

Ellis   *Christopher Marlowe (The Mermaid Series)*, ed.
              Havelock Ellis (London, n.d. [1887]).

A. Wagner   *Marlowe's Werke: III The Iew of Malta*, ed. Al-
              brecht Wagner (Heilbronn, 1889).

Thayer   *The Best Elizabethan Plays*, ed. W. R. Thayer
              (Boston, 1890).

Perry   *The Jew of Malta . . . by Christopher Marlowe . . .
              Adapted acting version of the Williams College English
              Department*, ed. Lewis Perry (Williamstown, Mass.,
              1909).

Thomas   *The Plays of Christopher Marlowe (Everyman's
              Library)*, ed. Edward Thomas (London, 1909).

Brooke   *The Works of Christopher Marlowe*, ed. C. F. Tucker
              Brooke (Oxford, 1910).

Neilson   *The Chief Elizabethan Dramatists, Excluding Shake-
              speare*, ed. W. A. Neilson (Cambridge, Mass., 1911).

Phelps   *Christopher Marlowe (Masterpieces of the English
              Drama)*, ed. W. L. Phelps (New York, 1912).

Bennett   *The Jew of Malta and The Massacre at Paris*, ed.
              H. S. Bennett (London, 1931).

Brooke ii   *English Drama, 1580–1642*, ed. C. F. Tucker Brooke
              and N. B. Paradise (Boston, 1933).

Spencer   *Elizabethan Plays*, ed. Hazelton Spencer (Boston,
              1933).

Parks   *The English Drama: An Anthology, 900–1642*, ed.
              E. W. Parks and R. C. Beatty (New York, 1935).

Ridley   *Marlowe's Plays and Poems (Everyman's Library)*,
              ed. M. R. Ridley (London, 1955).

Kirschbaum   *The Plays of Christopher Marlowe*, ed. Leo Kirsch-
              baum (Cleveland, 1962).

Ribner   *The Complete Plays of Christopher Marlowe*, ed.
              Irving Ribner (New York, 1963).

Van Fossen   *Christopher Marlowe, The Jew of Malta (Regents
              Renaissance Drama Series)*, ed. R. W. Van Fossen
              (Lincoln, Nebraska, 1964).

Craik   *Christopher Marlowe, The Jew of Malta (The New Mermaids)*, ed. T. W. Craik (London, 1966).

Steane   *Christopher Marlowe: The Complete Plays*, ed. J. B. Steane (Harmondsworth, 1969).

Dean   *Twelve Great Plays*, ed. Leonard F. Dean (New York, 1970).

Gill   *The Plays of Christopher Marlowe*, ed. Roma Gill (Oxford, 1971).

Bowers   *The Complete Works of Christopher Marlowe*, ed. Fredson Bowers (Cambridge, 1973).

OTHER TEXTUAL ABBREVIATIONS

Brennan   C. Brennan, 'Marlowe', *Beiblatt zur Anglia*, XVI (1905), 207–9.

Brereton   J. Le Gay Brereton, 'Notes on the text of Marlowe', *Beiblatt zur Anglia*, XVI (1905), 203–7.

Brereton ii   J. Le Gay Brereton, 'Marlowe: some textual notes', *M.L.R.*, VI (1911), 94–5.

Broughton MS   Manuscript notes by James Broughton in his copy of Robinson, now in the British Library (shelfmark 11771. d. 4).

Collier MS   Manuscript notes by J. P. Collier in his copy of Dyce, now in the British Library (shelfmark 11771. bbb. 6).

Danchin   F.-C. Danchin, 'Trois Corrections au texte de Marlowe', *Revue Anglo-Américaine*, X (1933), 330.

Deighton   K. Deighton, *The Old Dramatists: Conjectural Readings* (London, 1896).

Elze   Karl Elze, *Notes on Elizabethan Dramatists* (Halle, 1889).

Holthausen   F. Holthausen, 'Zur Textkritik von Marlowe's *Jew of Malta*', *Englische Studien*, XL (1909), 395–401.

Kittredge   Conjectural readings by G. L. Kittredge recorded in Spencer.

Koeppel   E. Koeppel's review of Wagner in *Literaturblatt*

<table>
<tr><td></td><td>für germanische und romanische Philologie, XI (1890), 259–263.</td></tr>
<tr><td>Maxwell</td><td>J. C. Maxwell, 'How bad is the text of The Jew of Malta?', M.L.R., XLVII (1953), 435–8.</td></tr>
<tr><td>Mitford</td><td>Conjectural readings by J. Mitford recorded in Dyce.</td></tr>
<tr><td>Seaton</td><td>Ethel Seaton, 'Fresh sources for Marlowe', R.E.S., V (1929), 385–401.</td></tr>
<tr><td>Seaton ii</td><td>Ethel Seaton's review of Bennett in R.E.S., IX (1933), 328–32.</td></tr>
<tr><td>Steevens</td><td>Conjectural readings by George Steevens recorded in Reed.</td></tr>
<tr><td>W. Wagner</td><td>Wilhelm Wagner, 'Emendationen und bemerkungen zu Marlowe', Shakespeare-Jahrbuch, XI (1875), 70–7, 363.</td></tr>
</table>

PERIODICALS

E.L.H.	*English Literary History*
E.L.R.	*English Literary Renaissance*
H.L.Q.	*Huntington Library Quarterly*
J.E.G.P.	*Journal of English and Germanic Philology*
M.L.N.	*Modern Language Notes*
M.L.Q.	*Modern Language Quarterly*
M.L.R.	*Modern Language Review*
M.P.	*Modern Philology*
N. & Q.	*Notes and Queries*
P.M.L.A.	*Publications of the Modern Language Association*
R.E.S.	*Review of English Studies*
S.P.	*Studies in Philology*
T.J.H.S.E.	*Transactions of the Jewish Historical Society of England*
T.L.S.	*Times Literary Supplement*

MISCELLANEOUS

Abbott	E. A. Abbott, *A Shakespearian Grammar*, 3rd edition (London, 1874).

E.E.T.S. Early English Text Society.

Gentillet Innocent Gentillet, *A Discourse Upon the Meanes of Well Governing . . . A Kingdom* [translated by Simon Patericke] (London, 1602).

Hunter G. K. Hunter, 'The theology of Marlowe's *The Jew of Malta*', *Journal of the Warburg and Courtauld Institutes*, XXVII (1964), 211–40.

Kocher P. H. Kocher, *Christopher Marlowe: A Study of his Thought, Learning, and Character* (New York, 1962).

M.S.R. Malone Society Reprints.

O.E.D. *The Oxford English Dictionary.*

Tilley M. P. Tilley, *A Dictionary of the Proverbs in England in the Sixteenth and Seventeenth Centuries* (Ann Arbor, Mich., 1950).

Whiting B. J. Whiting, *Proverbs, Sentences, and Proverbial Phrases from English Writings mainly before 1500* (Cambridge, Mass., 1968).

Quotations from Marlowe's other writings are taken from Revels editions, except for *Tamburlaine* and *Edward II*, where I have used the editions of Una Ellis-Fermor (1930) and H. B. Charlton and R. D. Waller (1933). Biblical quotations follow the first edition of the Geneva Bible (Geneva, 1560). The titles of Shakespeare's plays are abbreviated as in Onions, *A Shakespeare Glossary* (Oxford, 1911); quotations are from Peter Alexander's single-volume edition of the *Works* (1951).

Introduction

I. DATE AND STAGE HISTORY

The Prologue to *The Jew of Malta* alludes to the death of the Duke of Guise, who was assassinated on 23 December 1588, and as Marlowe's way of referring to it ('And now the Guise is dead . . .') suggests a fairly recent event, most scholars have assumed that the play was written in 1589 or 1590.[1] It is possible, as A. Wagner suggested,[2] that the Prologue was written later than the play itself, but this seems to be an unnecessary complication. The earliest references to the play are in Henslowe's *Diary*, which records a total of thirty-six performances, mostly at the Rose theatre, and given by various companies, between February 1592 and June 1596.[3] Between February and June 1592 there were ten performances at intervals of less than a fortnight, all earning good sums of money. The theatres were then closed by the Privy Council because of an outbreak of plague, and apart from a brief reopening of just over a month at the beginning of 1593, during which *The Jew of Malta* was played three times, they remained closed until the end of 1593. Productions of *The Jew of Malta* began again in 1594, and Bakeless has suggested that the play's popularity was boosted by the excitement caused by the trial of the Queen's Jewish physician Dr Lopez, executed on 7 June 1594.[4] There were four performances in June 1594 and two in July, but in the second half of the year receipts fell off steeply, and no performances are recorded for 1595. There were, however, eight in the first six months of 1596.

Henslowe ceased to keep detailed records of individual plays after November 1597, but his papers contain two pieces of evidence that the play continued to be performed. An inventory of stage properties made on 10 March 1598 lists among its items 'j cauderm for the Jewe', presumably the cauldron into which

Barabas falls at the end of the play,[5] and on 19 May 1601 Henslowe
made the following entry in his diary:[6]

> lent vnto Robart shawe & mr Jube the 19 of ⎫
> maye 1601 to bye divers things for the Jewe of ⎬ v^{li}
> malta the some of   .   .   .   . ⎭
> lent mor to the littell tayller the same daye for ⎫ x^s
> more things for the Jewe of malta some of   ⎭

Some scholars have assumed that this indicates a revival of the
play, but there may simply have been a straightforward renewal of
costumes and stage properties worn out by use. It has also been
suggested, without justification from Henslowe, that the text of the
play was revised at this point.[7]

The Jew of Malta made a considerable impact on contemporary
audiences during the last decade of the sixteenth and the first
decade of the seventeenth centuries. Everard Guilpin imitated two
lines from it in the eighth epigram of his *Skialetheia* (1598)[8] and
there appear to be allusions to the title in two of Dekker's
pamphlets written in 1606[9] and also in an epigram by Sir John
Harington which cannot be precisely dated.[10] In *A Search for
Money* (1609) William Rowley portrays a repulsive usurer, 'an old
moth-eaten cap buttoned under his chinne, his visage (or vizard)
like the artificiall Jewe of Maltae's nose',[11] which suggests that the
actor playing Barabas wore a large false nose. *The Jew of Malta*
influenced Shakespeare's *The Merchant of Venice* and Ben Jonson's
Volpone, and there are echoes and borrowings in various lesser
plays of the period.[12]

The title page of the 1633 quarto, the only early edition, shows
that by this date the play had come into the possession of Queen
Henrietta's company, who played at the Cockpit or Phoenix
theatre. Heywood's prologue to the Cockpit production reveals
that Barabas was acted by Richard Perkins, and that the rôle had
originally been played by Edward Alleyn. The Queen's company
also presented *The Jew of Malta* at court in or before 1633;
Heywood's prologue and epilogue for this production are rather
apologetic in tone, as though the play was now regarded as old-
fashioned and unlikely to appeal to Charles I and his courtiers.
But it still had some popularity for less sophisticated audiences in

the years preceding the closure of the theatres in 1642, to judge by a comment of Edmund Gayton, who deplored the rowdiness of theatre audiences on public holidays:

> I have known upon one of these *Festivals*, but especially at *Shrove-tide*, where the Players have been appointed, notwithstanding their bils to the contrary, to act what the major part of the company had a mind to; sometimes *Tamerlane*, sometimes *Jugurth*, sometimes the Jew of *Malta*, and sometimes parts of all these, and at last, none of the three taking, they were forc'd to undresse and put off their Tragick habits, and conclude the day with the merry milk-maides.[13]

Gayton's use of the phrase 'parts of all these' is perhaps relevant to the fact that the 1663 quarto of Marlowe's *Doctor Faustus* contains a new scene which partly consists of badly garbled material from *The Jew of Malta*.[14] The play remained sufficiently well known in the mid-seventeenth century for allusions to its title to be made in an anonymous political ballad of 1647[15] and in II.iii of Cowley's *Cutter of Coleman Street*, 1663.[16]

The Jew of Malta seems to have been among the plays performed in Germany in the early seventeenth century by the troupe led by Robert Browne and John Green, and it may have been played at Passau in 1607, at Graz in 1608, at Halle in 1611, at Dresden in 1626, and at Prague in 1651; the surviving records are somewhat confusing, and it is not always clear whether the play in question was *The Jew of Malta*, *The Merchant of Venice*, or an adaptation put together from several plays.[17] Two manuscript copies exist of a play in German, probably written late in 1605 or in 1606, which appears to have a slight indebtedness to *The Jew of Malta*.[18]

The next English revival took place on 24 April 1818 at the Drury Lane theatre in London, with Edmund Kean as Barabas, in a version of the play rather clumsily adapted, and in places expanded, by Samson Penley, a minor dramatist of the time.

The earliest twentieth-century revival was in America, in a production by the English Department of Williams College, Massachusetts, in 1907, using Perry's abridged edition. In November 1923 the Phoenix Society gave two performances at Daly's theatre, London, with Balliol Holloway as Barabas, and the

Yale Dramatic Association played it in June 1940. In post-war years the play has been produced by the following companies: the Marlowe Players of Reading University (May 1954), with Ian Calder as Barabas; the Cambridge Theatre Group (1957); the Marlowe Theatre Company, Canterbury (February 1964), with Michael Baxter as Barabas; the Tavistock Repertory Company (March 1964); the Victoria Theatre Company, Stoke on Trent (March 1964), with Bernard Gallagher as Barabas; the Merseyside Unity Theatre, Liverpool (November 1964), with Jim Wiggins as Barabas; and the Marlowe Society of Chislehurst, Kent (October 1966), at the Toynbee Hall, London. Perhaps the outstanding production was that by the Royal Shakespeare Company (October 1964–March 1965), at the Aldwych theatre, London, with Clive Revill as Barabas, Tony Church as Ferneze, Michele Dotrice as Abigail, Ian Richardson as Ithamore, and Glenda Jackson as Bellamira. The producer was Clifford Williams, and the stage settings were by Ralph Koltai. In April 1965 this production was transferred to Stratford with a modified cast which included Eric Porter as Barabas, Tony Church again as Ferneze, Katherine Barker as Abigail, Peter McEnery as Ithamore, and Patsy Byrne as Bellamira.[19]

2. SOURCES

Our present knowledge suggests that in *The Jew of Malta* Marlowe did not draw upon a single narrative source but made his own combination of source material from a wide variety of backgrounds. It must be emphasised immediately that Marlowe often made comparatively brief use in the play of a plot-incident, historical event, or idea which can be repeatedly paralleled in earlier writers, so that it is impossible to say confidently that he followed any particular version. In addition, the play probably had dramatic sources or analogues which are now lost beyond recovery; Stephen Gosson, for example, mentioned a play called *The Jew*, shown at the Bull in 1579 or earlier, 'representing the greedinesse of worldly chusers, and bloody mindes of Usurers'.[20] The play has not survived, and we cannot tell whether it resembled *The Jew of*

Malta, though attempts have been made, perhaps rather rashly, to reconstruct the contents on the basis of Gosson's brief description.[21] Similarly, Henslowe recorded three productions of a play called '*matchavell*' between March and May 1592, the first occurring only a few days after the first recorded performance of *The Jew of Malta*.[22] The play is lost, and nothing more is known about it, but it could have been written earlier than *The Jew of Malta*, in which case Marlowe may not have been the first English dramatist to present the figure of Machiavelli on the stage.

Marlowe's first play, *Tamburlaine*, showed his fascinated interest in the geography of the Middle East, and he drew much of the material for *The Jew of Malta* from the writings of travellers and historians. The historical background is presumably the Turkish siege of Malta in 1565, though Marlowe's play bears little resemblance to what actually happened. Between May and September of 1565 the Christian Knights of Malta and their Maltese auxiliaries fought desperately against a substantially larger Turkish army until at last the Turkish troops, their morale broken by failure and disease, withdrew and sailed away.[23] Marlowe also alluded to the Turkish siege of Rhodes, the former headquarters of the Knights of Malta, in 1522, and gave the impression that the Christian defenders were wiped out:

> Small though the number was that kept the town,
> They fought it out, and not a man survived
> To bring the hapless news to Christendom.
> [II.ii.49–51]

In fact the Knights surrendered on terms and were allowed to leave by the Turks. There were literally dozens of accounts of these events available to Marlowe, in several languages, and he can hardly have failed to know the truth. He may have had that careless indifference to historical fact which is so often attributed to Elizabethan dramatists, or he may have reversed the truth because he needed a contrast in his play between a heroic past and a sordid and avaricious present. (Incidentally, the Knights of Malta never paid tribute to the Turks, although many rulers of the time did so.)

Mediterranean history in the sixteenth century is full of accounts of Turkish sieges of towns and small islands which may have provided hints and suggestions for incidents in the play. Barabas's trick of blowing up the Turkish troops in a monastery, for example, may have been inspired by an event during the Turkish siege of a small town in Hungary in 1543, which Marlowe could easily have read about in the account of Turkish history given by John Foxe in his *Actes and Monuments*:

> At the first beginning of the siege, there stoode a little without the munitions in the front of the citie, a certayne church or Monastery, whiche the Cittizens pretending to mayntayne and keepe agaynst the turkes, had priuily conueyed light matter easely to take flame, with pouder, in secret places therof, and had hid also fire withall. Which done, they (as agaynst theyr willes being driuen backe) withdrew themselues within the munitions, wayting the occasions, when this fire would take. Thus the turkes hauing the possession of the churche, sodenly the fire comming to the pouder, raysed vp the Churche, and made a great scatter and slaughter among the barbarous turkes.[24]

The way in which Barabas betrays Malta to the Turks has several historical analogues: Nicolas de Villegagnon, describing the siege of Tripoli (1551) in a work published in 1553, told how a renegade soldier fled to the Turks and told them where the walls defending the town were weakest, so that they were able to break them down by gunfire and capture the town. Another French writer, Nicholas Nicolay, borrowed the story from Villegagnon in a work which was translated into English in 1585.[25] The use of an underground tunnel as a means of capturing a city is briefly mentioned in Belleforest's *Cosmographie*, in his account of the siege of Rhodes,[26] but it is a common device in the history of war, and Kocher quotes references to it by Jean du Bellay and others.[27] Perhaps the closest parallel is with a siege in which the Turks were not involved, that of Naples in 1442, when Alphonso V of Aragon captured the city from René of Anjou:

> . . . a certain Aniello, having abandoned the city from hunger, came to Alfonso suggesting that the Aragonese could success-fully penetrate the city by means of an aqueduct through which he, if suitably rewarded, would guide them. And so it was decided that a body of two hundred men should attempt to make an entry by this means and occupy a point on the walls adjoining

the place where they would emerge from the aqueduct, where-
upon Alfonso, standing by with his troops outside the walls,
would attempt to scale them, whilst his men on the inside
impeded the Angevins from repulsing the assailants.[28]

This device was eventually successful, and is remarkably similar
to Barabas's plan at v.i.86–94.

There were few if any Jews in Malta in the later sixteenth
century, and certainly none as ostentatiously wealthy as Barabas,
the central and dominating character of the play.[29] It is possible,
however, that Marlowe knew something of a historical Jew who
achieved considerable notoriety in the sixteenth century and is still
not forgotten.[30] He was a Portuguese marano (a Jew whose
ancestors had been forcibly converted to Christianity), born c. 1520
and christened João Miguez.[31] His family was wealthy and well-
connected, and he lived for varying periods in a number of
western European cities. He arrived in Constantinople in 1554;
the Turks at this period were much more tolerant than the
Christians of Europe towards Jews, and he settled there, reverting
to his Jewish faith and taking the name of Joseph Nasi. He
continued his financial activities, becoming extremely wealthy, and
was ultimately an important and influential figure at the court of
the Turkish emperor Selim II. From 1536 the Duke of Naxos, a
small island in the Aegean, had paid tribute to the Turks, but in
1566 the Turks finally occupied the island, ejected the Christian
duke, and created Nasi Duke of Naxos in his place. Late in 1569
the Turks began the military campaign that ended in the conquest
of Cyprus, and it was widely believed that Nasi had vigorously
urged Selim to attack Cyprus, and had even hoped to become
King of Cyprus himself. He continued to live in Constantinople,
making only a brief visit to Naxos, and died in 1579.

The similarity between this story of a Jew made governor of a
Christian island by the Turks (a most unusual and remarkable
event at the time) and the plot of The Jew of Malta was first
pointed out by Leon Kellner.[32] Kellner had difficulty in finding
contemporary accounts of Nasi that Marlowe could have read, and
mentions only one, a historical work in Latin by Uberto Foglietta.[33] Foglietta gave a brief and decidedly hostile biography of

Nasi, and portrayed him as urging Selim to occupy Cyprus, at that time ruled by the Venetians. According to Foglietta, Selim promised to make Nasi ruler of Cyprus, and Nasi even made himself a flag bearing the words 'Joseph King of Cyprus'; but after the conquest Selim decided that it would be unfit to give this dignity to a Jew, and made him Duke of Naxos instead. (This, of course, is quite inaccurate; Nasi became Duke of Naxos some years before the Turks conquered Cyprus.)

Subsequently Miss Ethel Seaton showed that there are references to Nasi in works by Contarini, Balbi da Correggio, and Belleforest,[34] and Bakeless added to this list a work by Pietro Bizari.[35] Other allusions exist, hitherto unnoticed, most of which deal with Nasi as instigator of the Turkish attack on Cyprus.[36] These accounts vary in detail, but on the whole they tell the same story: on 13 September 1569 the Arsenal at Venice blew up (possibly by accident),[37] and there was simultaneously a shortage of food in the city. This news was passed on to Nasi by the Jews of Venice, and he advised Selim to take this favourable opportunity of attacking Cyprus. There are only one or two references to Nasi as Duke of Naxos; one may be found in Natalis Comes' *History of his own Times*.[38]

It is impossible to say precisely how much of this material was known to Marlowe; the basic situation of a wealthy Jew who assisted the Turks to conquer a Christian island may have been as much as he needed to stimulate his imagination. The contemporary accounts consistently describe Nasi as evil, cunning, and ambitious, though his modern biographers are much more sympathetic, presenting him as a generous patron of Jewish culture and explaining that any territorial ambitions he may have had sprang from a wish to create a refuge for his persecuted co-religionists. Clearly Marlowe had some idea of the ramifications of international Jewish finance: Barabas ranks himself among the leading wealthy Jews of his time (I.i.123–7) and he has dealings in the major European financial centres (IV.i.71–4). There were other Jews living in Constantinople who became notorious, such as David Passi and Alvaro Mendes,[39] but their careers have no detailed resemblances to Barabas's, and I have not discovered any printed allusions to them early enough for Marlowe to have read.

There are other Jewish elements in Barabas's character, though it is hard to tell how intensively Marlowe had studied the history of the Jews. The play contains a number of biblical allusions, especially to the Book of Job, and the references to the apocryphal Book of Maccabees (II.iii.156) and to the conquest of Jerusalem by Titus (II.iii.10) suggest that Marlowe had at least a superficial knowledge of the heroic period of Jewish history in the early Christian era. There were Jews living in England in the early Middle Ages, and the chronicles of Matthew Paris and later historians contain many accounts of heavy fines and forced levies imposed on the Jews, especially in the thirteenth century, which could have provided a model for Ferneze's behaviour in I.ii of *The Jew of Malta*.

Anti-semitism, on theological rather than racial grounds,[40] was very common in western Europe in the later Middle Ages, and Marlowe certainly knew two of the commonest accusations made against the Jews, that they crucified children and poisoned wells,[41] charges so frequently repeated that it would be pointless to look for a particular source. Medieval legends tell of Jewish fathers who try to kill their children when they become converts to Christianity, and some story of this kind may have influenced Barabas's treatment of his daughter.[42] There are also various tales of beautiful Jewesses loved by Christians, as Abigail is loved by Mathias and Lodowick, though I have not come across anything which is very close to Marlowe.[43] Jews are sometimes portrayed in medieval drama, and a parallel has been noted between Barabas's list of precious stones (I.i.25–32) and part of the opening speech of the Jew Jonathas in the late fifteenth-century Croxton *Play of the Sacrament*, in which he boastingly thanks Mahomet for making him wealthy:

> For I thanke the hayly that hast me sent
>   Gold, syluer, and presyous stonys,
> And abunddaunce of spycys thou hast me lent,
>   As I shall reherse before yow onys:
>   I have amatystys, ryche for the nonys,
> And baryllys that be bryght of ble;

> And saphyre semely, I may show yow attonys,
>   And crystalys clere for to se;
> I haue dyamantys derewourthy to dresse,
>   And emerawdys, ryche I trow they be,
> Onyx and achatys both more and lesse,
>   Topazyouns, smaragdys of grete degre,
>   Perlys precyous grete plente,
> Of rubes ryche I have grete renown;
>   Crepawdys and calcedonyes semely to se,
> And curyous carbunclys here ye fynd mown . . .[44]

The rest of the play, however, is based on a very common medieval legend which has no relationship to *The Jew of Malta*.

Recent criticism has stressed the similarities between Barabas and the figure of the Vice in the Tudor interludes.[45] Barabas's delight in his own cunning, his reluctance to let others know his plans, his treacherous playing on both sides (like the 'Ambidexter' figure of several interludes), his use of stage tricks such as feigned weeping, verbal plays and deliberate misunderstandings, his disguise as a foreigner using scraps of foreign languages, and even the enormous nose he wears,[46] can all be paralleled in one or more of the extant interludes. In several interludes the central theme is an attack on avarice, and Barabas's self-assertive soliloquies in the first scene of the play read to some extent like a much more elaborate and richly orchestrated version of the opening speech of 'Worldly Man' in William Wager's *Enough is as good as a Feast*:

> Because I am a man indewed with treasure,
> Therefore a worldly man men doo me call:
> In deed I haue riches and money at my pleasure,
> Yea, and I wil haue more in spight of them all.
>   A common saying better is enuy then rueth,
> I had rather they should spite then pitty me:
> For the olde saying now a dayes proueth trueth,
> Naught haue naught set by as dayly we see.
>   I wis I am not of the minde as some men are,
> Which look for no more then wil serue necessitie:
> No against a day to come I doo prepare,
> That when age commeth I may liue merily.[47]

Similar ideas occur in a later speech by 'Worldly Man':

> Oh, me thinks it is a very pleasant thing,
> To see a great heap of olde Angels and Crownes:

> When I haue store of money I can be mery and sing,
> For money as men say winneth bothe Citties and townes. [48]

The last line of this quotation reads like a very faint anticipation of the theme of *The Jew of Malta*, though the two plays are very different in plot structure.

The Jew of Malta opens with a prologue put into the mouth of Machiavelli, and the exact nature of the play's 'machiavellianism' has been much debated. [49] It seems to me, however, that some general clarifications must be made about Machiavelli's reception in Elizabethan England before Marlowe's play can be discussed profitably.

In a pioneering study Edward Meyer came to the conclusion that the Elizabethans knew little of Machiavelli at first hand, [50] and derived what knowledge they had of his doctrines from the simplified and distorted presentation of them in Innocent Gentillet's famous attack on him, first published anonymously in French in 1576. [51] But subsequent research showed more and more clearly that plenty of Elizabethans had access to Machiavelli's own writings, including the two most 'dangerous' works, *The Prince* and *Discourses*, in the original and in French or Latin translations; because of this Felix Raab dismissed what he called the 'myth of Gentillet'. [52] Irving Ribner tried to offer a compromise by arguing that two separate traditions of thought existed side by side, a scholarly response based on genuine knowledge of Machiavelli himself, and a popular distortion deriving from the attacks of Gentillet and others. [53] Ribner also argued that the Machiavellianism of *The Jew of Malta* is clearly of the second, popular kind.

There is some truth in this, but it is not an adequate explanation. Instead of thinking in terms of two separate strands, we might do better to imagine a whole spectrum of responses, ranging from extreme admiration at one end to violent hatred at the other, with various mixtures of feeling in between, and with varying degrees of accuracy and distortion. Many sixteenth-century readers were simultaneously fascinated and repelled by Machiavelli's ideas, and found it very difficult to make a satisfactory adjustment to them. Sometimes they plagiarised from his writings but were rude about him whenever they mentioned his name, as though

they were ashamed to admit to a liking, or, like John Case'
referred to him with hostility on some occasions and with what
seems to be approval at others.[54] One Elizabethan, Richard
Beacon, author of *Solon His Folly* (1595), quoted extensively from
the *Discourses* in a Latin translation, but never once mentioned
Machiavelli's name, perhaps thereby illustrating 'Machevil's'
claim in the prologue that 'such as love me guard me from their
tongues'. Indeed, when Marlowe made 'Machevil' say:

> Admired I am of those that hate me most:
> Though some speak openly against my books,
> Yet will they read me . . .
>
> [Prologue, ll. 9–11]

he was both shrewd and accurate.

The assumption has too readily been made that the writings of
Machiavelli and Gentillet are so incompatible that no Elizabethan
could have studied them both. John Case gave several accurate
and specific references to the works of both men, and a minor
Elizabethan, Simon Harward, quoted in two of his books from
Machiavelli in Italian and Gentillet in French.[55] A somewhat later
figure, William Drummond of Hawthornden, possessed Machiavelli's books in Italian and French as well as a copy of Gentillet
in French. Clearly it was possible for some Elizabethans to read
both Machiavelli and his opponents simultaneously. We should
also remember that Gentillet was not the only Frenchman to
discuss Machiavelli; the crisis of the French civil wars in the
second half of the sixteenth century provoked a great deal of
controversial writing in which Machiavelli's name often occurred,
and many of these books and pamphlets circulated in England or
were translated into English, and helped to influence English
opinion.[56]

This leads to a point which needs particular stress. The
Elizabethans did not read Machiavelli in isolation, but saw him in
the light of their own strongly developed traditions of thought.
Most modern scholars place Machiavelli's writing in the historical
context of an Italy disintegrating under the shock of foreign
invasion in the late fifteenth and early sixteenth centuries, a
desperate situation in which there was some excuse for desperate

remedies. But it would, I think, be true to say that none of
Machiavelli's opponents or admirers in the sixteenth century paid
any real attention to the Italian political situation during his lifetime. Instead they saw him straightforwardly as a writer on the art
of government at all times and seasons, and compared his ideas
with those of the standard treatises on the way a king should rule.
A traditional division had grown up between the good king, pious,
just, and concerned for his people, and the tyrant, faithless, cruel,
and selfish, and if the prince described by Machiavelli had to be
put into one of these categories there could be little doubt that he
belonged to the second. Indeed, from classical times onwards the
nature and methods of tyranny had been debated, and Case
accused Machiavelli of stealing his pernicious ideas from the list
given by Aristotle in his *Politics*, Book V, chapter 11, of means by
which the tyrant could maintain his power.[57]

A further complication was that most sixteenth-century writers
on Machiavelli made little attempt to be scrupulously accurate in
attributing ideas to him. Genuinely Machiavellian material was
blended and mingled with more or less similar material from
different origins, sometimes with the result that ideas were
attributed to Machiavelli which he had never expressed, and the
ideas he had expressed were ignored or distorted. The only slight
justification that could be made for this is that Machiavelli did
sometimes deal with stock topics that had been discussed by
earlier authors, and his readers confused him with what other men
had said. This, incidentally, helps to show the falsity of a neatly
divided 'learned' and 'popular' response; it was sometimes the
learned readers of Machiavelli, their heads full of Aristotle and
Seneca and the traditional concept of the tyrant, who most
violently distorted his doctrines.

By the time Marlowe came to write *The Jew of Malta* these
patterns of response to Machiavelli had become well established,
chiefly in works of political and religious controversy. There are
some indications that in the late 1580s knowledge of Machiavelli,
often at a very superficial level, began to percolate outwards from
the learned controversialists to a wider audience that would be
more likely to visit the theatre, so it is possible—though this is

only speculation—that Marlowe's flair for what was of topical interest led him to take advantage of this movement of opinion, and to create, perhaps for the first time, the figure of the 'Machiavel' on the English stage.

It must be admitted that the ideas and behaviour of the stage 'Machiavel' often bear very little resemblance to the actual writings of Machiavelli himself, but it would, I think, be possible to regard this as an extreme form of the blending and distorting approach already described. Sometimes we cannot tell whether a possible borrowing does in fact derive from Machiavelli. In Act v of *The Jew of Malta*, for example, Barabas invites Selim-Calymath to a banquet with the intention of treacherously killing him. This is very similar to a trick mentioned in chapter VIII of *The Prince*, where Machiavelli described in some detail how Oliverotto da Fermo invited the leading citizens of Fermo, including the uncle who had helped to bring him up, to a banquet, and then massacred them in order to secure control of the town. But there are plenty of other examples of what might be termed the 'treacherous banquet'; Marlowe presumably knew the Book of Maccabees, for example, and would have known that at the end of I Maccabees Ptolomeus used this trick to kill Simon Maccabee and two of his sons.

I should be surprised if it could be shown that Marlowe had no first-hand acquaintance with Machiavelli's writings, but there is nothing in *The Jew of Malta* to prove beyond doubt that he had read them. If Kocher is right, Marlowe had an extensive knowledge of the pamphlets inspired by the French civil wars;[58] the Prologue opens with a reference to the Duke of Guise, and Marlowe occasionally used ideas that were bandied about in these pamphlets.[59] He also knew something of classical tyrants like Phalaris (Prologue, 24) and Dionysius of Syracuse (v.iii.11). Some lines in the play may echo (rather faintly) ideas in Machiavelli which his opponents usually ignored;[60] a larger group of lines may echo ideas which Marlowe could have derived from Machiavelli himself or his adversaries or both (and it is as well to remember that Gentillet and other opponents did reproduce a number of Machiavelli's ideas with reasonable accuracy, even if they were torn from the context in which they appeared).[61] There may also be a couple of borrowings exclusively from Gentillet.[62] Machiavelli was notorious for his use of Cesare Borgia as an admirable example in chapter VII of *The Prince*, and Marlowe refers to Borgia (III.iv.98–9), but in terms of an anecdote which neither Machiavelli nor (rather surprisingly) Gentillet ever mentions.

It is, of course, the Prologue to the play which purports to give an exposition of Machiavellianism. The ideas contained in it are discussed in detail in the commentary of this edition, but a few remarks on it may be in place here. Clearly the Prologue is not, by modern standards, a scholarly and accurate presentation of Machiavelli's actual beliefs. Nor, for that matter, does it come from Gentillet or from a Latin poem by Gabriel Harvey.[63] But it has a certain connection with Machiavelli in that it deals with some of the fundamental issues that preoccupied him: how states and kingdoms should be founded and ordered, and by what means they should be strengthened and preserved. But these preoccupations may be found in dozens of other writers on politics, from Aristotle onwards, and it is hardly surprising, in view of what has just been said, that Marlowe, if he did in fact read Machiavelli, did not confine himself strictly to the attitudes and illustrations to be found in his works. Furthermore, on many of these issues it was possible to take up a variety of attitudes, and my impression is that Marlowe always chose the harshest and most cynical extreme, either because he wished to shock his audience or else because he genuinely believed, like many others in the sixteenth century, that Machiavelli gave his approval to the utmost extremes of human wickedness.

If my arguments are right it obviously becomes impossible to define precisely just how much of Machiavelli Marlowe knew at first hand, and this is partly due to the varied and sometimes muddled and even contradictory nature of the total Elizabethan response to Machiavelli. But it is clear that Marlowe had at least some knowledge of the political and religious controversial writings of his day, the context in which allusions to Machiavelli and discussions of him are most commonly found.

A few minor sources remain to be mentioned for various incidents in the play. The trick played on Jacomo with the corpse

of Bernardine is part of an old tale which Heywood later employed
in a more developed form in his play *The Captives* and his prose
work *Gynaikeion*.[64] P. H. Kocher has suggested an analogy
between Barabas's use of a poisoned pot of porridge to destroy the
nuns and his subsequent death in the cauldron and a historical case
of poisoning which occurred in late 1529 or early 1530, when
Richard Rose or Rouse poisoned some porridge cooked in the
Bishop of Rochester's kitchens, causing the death of several
members of the bishop's household and also of some poor people
to whom the porridge had been given as alms.[65] Because of this
Parliament passed an Act in 1530 (22 Henry VIII, c. 9) making
wilful poisoning an act of high treason for which the offender was
to be boiled to death; Rose and a few others actually suffered this
punishment, though in 1547 the statute was repealed and poisoning reverted to its old status as a form of murder. But the cauldron
used to punish Barabas could have originated in various ways:
Levin has pointed out that in one of Whitney's *Emblems* the boiling
cauldron is a symbol of overreaching ambition,[66] and Hunter has
shown that a boiling cauldron was among other things the traditional infernal punishment for usurers.[67] And as the Book of
Maccabees has already been mentioned, it could perhaps be noted
that in II Maccabees, 7, seven Jewish brothers are burnt to death
in 'pans and cauldrons'.

3. THE PLAY

Modern criticism of *The Jew of Malta* has been complicated by the
fact that many scholars have doubted whether the quarto of 1633
accurately represents the play as Marlowe first wrote it. But this
uncertainty has usually been caused not by clear linguistic or
bibliographical evidence but by a critical response, a belief that the
last three acts are so obviously inferior to the first two that the text
must have been seriously corrupted before publication in 1633,
probably because of revision by a different hand. Sometimes the
argument has been circular: the critical judgement has provoked
the textual assessment which has then been accepted as fact

(although merely an unproven hypothesis) and allowed in its turn to modify the critical judgement.

But in my opinion *The Jew of Malta*, while not an unqualified masterpiece, is far more of a unity than many earlier critics allow, and, as far as the text is concerned, the strictly textual analysis given at the end of this introduction suggests that the quarto of 1633 is derived from Marlowe's 'foul papers', with no signs of revision by a later dramatist, and therefore has considerable authority. Indeed, I ought to make it unmistakably clear that throughout this edition I have assumed that the quarto gives us substantially what Marlowe wrote, and the critical and editorial techniques adopted have been based on this assumption.

This does not mean, however, that *The Jew of Malta* is easy to interpret, and many problems remain to be considered. The title page and the prologue describe the play as a tragedy, but much of its content is hardly tragic in the usual sense, and even if we no longer bother very much about placing plays in their correct genre, now that we have grown accustomed to 'black comedy' and the theatre of the absurd, we may still find it difficult to decide just how seriously Marlowe intended the play. The earliest critics of *The Jew of Malta*, in the late eighteenth and early nineteenth centuries, were struck by its mixture of tones and were uncertain how to respond to it. In a letter to Southey written in 1798 Charles Lamb quoted the speeches of Barabas and Ithamore at II.iii.176–214, and commented on the 'mixture of the ludicrous and the terrible in these lines',[68] and in the first critical essay to be written on the play 'H.M.' (John Wilson), after giving a fairly detailed account of the plot, was not sure how the reader would react:

> We scarcely know how to speak of the character of such a drama as this, being so uncertain of the sympathies of our readers. If it fail to excite a kind of wild and fearful interest, it will probably seem to be a tissue of folly, madness, and extravagance.[69]

Perhaps not surprisingly, some early critics could see little in the play to compensate for its 'grotesque absurdities'.[70]

Yet in 1818 an anonymous reviewer of Kean's revival argued in opposition to most of his contemporaries that *The Jew of Malta* was Marlowe's best play, because of its consistency of tone:

> Not that we *like* it better than the Faustus or Edward II., but it is better *as a play*. There is more variety of character, and more of moral purpose, in the Edward II., and the Faustus exhibits loftier and more impassioned poetry; but neither of those plays possess, in so great a degree as the one before us, that rare, and when judiciously applied, most important quality, which we have called dramatic unity,—that tending of all its parts to engender and sustain the same kind of feeling throughout. In the Jew of Malta, the characters are all, without exception, wicked . . .[71]

Henry Hallam's judgement was partly favourable and partly unfavourable:

> The first two acts of the Jew of Malta are more vigorously conceived, both as to character and circumstance, than any other Elizabethan play, except those of Shakespeare . . . but the latter acts, as is usual with our old dramatists, are a tissue of uninteresting crimes and slaughter.[72]

This view of the play as broken-backed, half great tragedy, half ludicrous melodrama, was taken up by many later critics, and became to a large extent the standard attitude towards it.

Barabas himself has provoked a wide variety of responses. Among the earliest critics the debate centred on whether he was 'a mere monster brought in with a large painted nose to please the rabble', to use Lamb's phrase,[73] or a human being warped by persecution and injustice.[74] Later in the nineteenth century he tended to be seen as a smaller version of the aspiring and ambitious Renaissance man that Marlowe was thought to have portrayed in Tamburlaine and Faustus. In recent years he has been caught up in the controversy over the orthodoxy or otherwise of Marlowe's religious and political beliefs, and the extent to which Marlowe was personally involved in the attitudes of his central characters; for some critics the theological allusions in the play point to an implicit but clear condemnation of Barabas, while for others the most vital parts of *The Jew of Malta* are those in which Marlowe satirises Christian hypocrisy.

One consequence of these difficulties has been that many

scholars have sought for external evidence to justify their particular interpretations. Attempts have been made, for example, to construct a scheme or pattern of Marlowe's total development as a dramatist, in order to assess *The Jew of Malta* more easily by relating it to his other work. But the chronology of his plays is still very unsure—*The Jew of Malta* seems to come fairly soon after *Tamburlaine*, the first of his plays for the public theatre, but the relative position of the other plays, especially *Faustus*, is far from clear—and there are disagreements over the interpretation of all Marlowe's major plays, so that patterns of Marlowe's development tend to be neat constructions created by the critic rather than clear deductions from evidence.

Another approach has been to relate the play to its sources, on the assumption that Marlowe's attitude towards his central character can be determined by his use of traditional material, such as the stereotyped patterns of behaviour associated with the Jew, the Vice, and the Machiavellian. Certainly the play has its sources, but Marlowe's use of source material was not merely inert, and even if he took over a current stereotype he did not necessarily accept the moral outlook that usually went with it: the figure of Tamburlaine may be related to earlier portrayals of the conqueror and tyrant, but much of the excitement of the play comes from a deliberately outrageous celebration of kinds of behaviour usually condemned by orthodox moralists. In any case, Marlowe's indebtedness to sources must not be exaggerated: Barabas owes something to the Vice, but his plotting is infinitely more inventive and elaborate than that of the usual Vice, and although there had been a fair amount of discussion of Machiavelli prior to *The Jew of Malta*, Marlowe may have been the first to portray in imaginative terms a character explicitly presented as a disciple of Machiavelli. In other words, Marlowe himself did not merely borrow, but *created* stereotypes in his plays which later dramatists copied, developed from, or sometimes parodied.

If this is the case, all we can hope to do, it seems to me, is to respond to the play itself as fully and sensitively as we can, with as few preconceptions as possible. And while it is perfectly legitimate to bring in external evidence as an aid to understanding, we should not allow that evidence to restrict or simplify our response as human beings to the drama in front of us.

As we have seen, a common criticism of the play is that it breaks down into melodrama after the first two acts, and various theories have been put forward to account for this collapse.[75] An opinion held over a long period by many acute and sensitive critics must be treated with respect, and although I would prefer to argue for the essential unity of the play, I must concede that its most impressive parts, with the richest verse and the most subtle character analysis, are found in the first two acts. A reader who feels that the last three acts are grossly inferior will simply have to accept that Marlowe did not consistently write at his best—not a very revolutionary or implausible conclusion. It does not follow, however, that the text has been tampered with, and F. P. Wilson surely exaggerated when he argued that the disparity between the two halves of the play was so great that they cannot have been written by the same hand.[76]

The view of the play as broken-backed may perhaps be caused by a failure to see it in perspective. Wilson was obviously impressed by Barabas's soliloquies in I.i describing his activities as a merchant, and he analysed them enthusiastically and perceptively. But these soliloquies, splendid though they are, should not be regarded as a kind of norm by which the rest of the play must be judged. (If anything can be said to set the tone of the play, it is surely the prologue spoken by Machevil.) The portrait of Barabas as a sixteenth-century tycoon, involved in international commerce and ordering his subordinates about with immense self-confidence, is extremely vivid, but to argue that Marlowe should have continued to present him consistently in this way is to ask for a completely different play from the one Marlowe wrote. Barabas himself, of course, would like to stay as he is; he recognises that the Jews will never achieve political power, and wants a 'peaceful rule' by the Christians (I.i.133) which will allow trade to go on unhindered. Ironically his downfall comes when he does in fact reach a position of authority, and foolishly tries to sell it for cash so that he can revert to his original status. But the whole point of the play is that he is not allowed to go on peacefully making money; the

Knights of Malta have neglected to pay their tribute regularly to
the Turks, and the resulting political and financial crisis, into
which Barabas is drawn against his will, sparks off the action of the
play.

The soliloquies themselves need to be read with caution.
Certainly Barabas's character becomes harder and more ruthless
as the play progresses, but even at the beginning he is shown as
lacking wide human sympathies, and some details suggest that
Marlowe did not view the pursuit of wealth with naïve approval.
One critic quotes I.i.106–10:

> What more may heaven do for earthly men
> Than thus to pour out plenty in their laps,
> Ripping the bowels of the earth for them,
> Making the sea their servant, and the winds
> To drive their substance with successful blasts ?

and finds in the passage 'the intoxication of expanding empire
which Elizabethans could experience in the exploits of Hawkins or
Drake'.[77] But the phrase 'earthly men' should make us pause
(compare 'Worldly Man' in Wager's *Enough is as Good as a Feast*),
and Marlowe's lines seem to me to echo Ovid's descriptions of the
coming of the cruel and treacherous Iron Age, when men first
sailed the seas in search of gain, and ripped open the bowels of the
earth for precious metals.[78]

There is also in these soliloquies an element of self-deception
which can be paralleled, I think, in the opening soliloquies of
Faustus, who promises himself benefits from his use of magic
which never materialise. Barabas enjoys gloating over his wealth,
and boasts that even one of his precious stones

> May serve in peril of calamity
> To ransom great kings from captivity . . .
> [I.i.31–2]

but in fact his status is that of a despised alien living on sufferance,
whose wealth is stripped from him with contemptuous ease, and
who illustrates Machiavelli's dictum that 'the unarmed riche man,
is a bootie to the poore souldiour'.[79] In taking his money away
from him Ferneze does make some pretence at politeness, even if

it is hypocritical, by requesting Barabas's 'aid', but when Barabas tries to get out of a difficult situation by pretending to mis-understand:

> Alas, my lord, we are no soldiers;
> And what's our aid against so great a prince?
> [1.ii.50–1]

the First Knight brutally strips away any pretence:

> Tut, Jew, we know thou art no soldier;
> Thou art a merchant, and a moneyed man,
> And 'tis thy money, Barabas, we seek.
> [52–4]

and at a nod from Ferneze Barabas is left, as far as the knights are aware, totally destitute.

In the opening scene Barabas is repeatedly shown as utterly self-centred, and indifferent to the fate of Malta so long as he himself comes to no harm. He has no links with any group of human beings (not even his fellow Jews), and while this attitude leaves him free to pursue his own interests, it has the great disadvantage that in times of danger he has no allies to support him. This helps to explain why he resorts to various forms of trickery and deceit: no other weapon is available to him. Like a guerilla faced by a large army, he cannot mount a frontal attack, but must try to find out where his enemy is weak and unsuspect-ing. One of the few ways in which he can deal with his opponents is to split them into opposing factions and play them off against each other; he does this on a small scale with Lodowick and Mathias and the two friars, and on a large scale with the Christians and Turks.

Another of Barabas's techniques for dealing with his enemies is to feign emotions and attitudes which are deliberately intended to confuse and deceive. This device of rôle-playing is used in a fairly primitive form by the Vices of the Tudor interludes, and there may have been some influence from this direction on Marlowe. But it is used much more elaborately and inventively in *The Jew of Malta*, and is in any case a psychologically plausible weapon for a man in Barabas's position. His disguise as a French lute-player at the end of Act IV may seem merely absurd, and the way he shams dead at the beginning of Act V may not be very convincing, but we are clearly meant to see them as extreme examples of the kind of transformation we are shown in Act I. After his money has been stripped from him and Barabas is left with the other Jews, he adopts the manner of an Old Testament prophet lamenting disaster, but as soon as the other Jews go out he abruptly changes to a contemptuous and arrogant schemer who has foreseen precisely this event and made arrangements for it. The news that his house has been confiscated for use as a nunnery is a temporary setback, but he soon devises an expedient which he helps along by posing as a devoted father outraged by his daughter's desertion.

Obviously the rôle Barabas most enjoys playing is that of wealthy merchant, but he knows perfectly well that he must not assume that he can continue with it undisturbed: in times of emergency other rôles will be needed, and Barabas the merchant should not be regarded as the 'real' Barabas of whom Barabas the lute-player is a crude travesty. Indeed, Barabas changes so rapidly, with one rôle undercutting another, that it is sometimes hard to know whether the attitude behind one of his speeches is real or assumed. Is the catalogue of crimes he recites to Ithamore at II.iii.176–202 a piece of genuine autobiography to be taken at face value, or a pretence designed to indicate to Ithamore what kind of behaviour is expected from him, or a kind of bravura display that hovers on the borders of fact and fantasy? Marlowe leaves us wondering, and if we take into account how other characters in the play collapse or alter under the pressure of a sudden crisis—like the two friends Lodowick and Mathias when they become rivals in love, or the two friars at the prospect of acquiring great wealth—or say one thing but do another, like the blandly hypocritical Ferneze, we may sense that underlying the play is a sombre awareness of the deceptiveness of appearances and the instability and weakness of human nature.

So far I have tried to suggest that the second half of the play does not simply break away from the first half, but develops from it, and I shall say more about this later, in discussing the dramatic and stylistic techniques of the play. What has been said already clearly indicates that our reaction to Barabas himself is the main factor in our reaction to the play as a whole, in which he is over-whelmingly the dominating figure.[80]

Barabas may strike us as a very strange mixture. Even his Jewishness takes a variety of forms: he is in turn the large-scale merchant proud of belonging to a small set of wealthy Jewish international financiers, the despised alien who responds to the hypocritical confiscation of his money with a kind of parody of Job's behaviour, and the medieval bogey-man who improves on his predecessors who murdered children and poisoned wells by killing his own daughter and a convent of nuns in one act of mass poisoning. He has something in him of the Vice, the usurer, and the Machiavellian, and it is hardly surprising that H. S. Bennett should see *The Jew of Malta* as 'a challenge to our powers of assimilation'.[81] A less sympathetic critic might suggest that the onus of assimilating the material was on Marlowe himself, and some readers may feel that the different elements of Barabas's character do not completely coalesce.

Yet this objection may result from a simplified idea of how human beings can be expected to behave; the history of the tycoons and millionaires of the nineteenth and twentieth centuries shows that rich men, especially if they have made their own fortunes as Barabas has, can sometimes swing to the wildest extremes of behaviour, and it would be naïve to assume that cunning, hypocrisy, secretiveness, and deliberate deception do not frequently play a part in the acquisition of large sums of money. Some aspects of Barabas's character suggest that Marlowe had a fairly shrewd understanding of the economic developments of his age; R. H. Tawney, drawing on the ideas of Pirenne, contrasts

> . . . the outlook of the medieval bourgeoisie, intent on the conservation of local and corporate privileges, with that of the new plutocracy of the sixteenth century, with its international ramifications, its independence of merely local interests, its triumphant vindication of the power of the capitalist to dispense with the artificial protection of guild and borough and to carve his own career. Naturally the creed of these economic *conquistadores* was an almost modern individualism.[82]

Obviously Tawney has in mind international bankers and money-lenders like the Fuggers; Barabas is more a merchant in valuable commodities, but his outlook has interesting similarities to theirs.

Barabas's selfishness may also help to explain his Machiavellianism, since for some Elizabethans Machiavelli's doctrines were ultimately based on a principle of complete selfishness:

> And *Machiavel* whose workes are so highly esteemed of many states-men at this day; doth he teach any other gouerment, then that which proceedeth from the principles of this law, to wit from self loue and particular interest ?[83]

The unscrupulous adventurer in economics parallels the Machiavellian in politics; both reject traditional ethical systems which call for submission to divine laws and a respect for one's fellow human beings. A key term in the play is 'policy',[84] which had a wide range of meanings in sixteenth-century English, sometimes favourable ('a praiseworthy skill in public affairs'), sometimes highly unfavourable ('deliberate cunning and deception'), though by the end of the century the unfavourable meaning came to predominate. In two allegorical interludes from the middle of the sixteenth century, *Respublica*, probably by Nicholas Udall, and Wager's *Enough is as Good as a Feast*, the chief of the evil characters, Avarice or Covetousness, disguises himself under the name of 'policy', here used in a favourable sense, and in George Wapull's *The Tide Tarrieth No Man* (printed 1576) the association between 'policy' (here used pejoratively) and avarice is demonstrated in a symbolic tableau.[85] The financial implications of 'policy' (cunning used to acquire wealth) were probably still current in Marlowe's day, and may have helped to unify *The Jew of Malta* for its earliest audiences.

How did Marlowe intend us to respond to his central character ? By any normal standards of human decency Barabas is a monster of egotism who destroys without compunction anyone who has injured him or seems likely to, including his own daughter. His unpleasant end in the boiling cauldron he has prepared for others is an appropriate and satisfying example of the biter bit, the engineer hoist with his own petard. But if this were all the play was about—the villain who gets the punishment he deserves—it would not have aroused the controversy it has, and might have made no more impact on us than a fourth-rate tragedy like Preston's *Cambyses*. Marlowe has shaded his portrait with ironies and qualifications, and to assess their exact weight and significance is among the major critical problems we face in dealing with the play.

Even a villain can have his attractive qualities (if evil were simply repulsive there would be no problem in dealing with it), and Elizabethan and Jacobean drama is full of clever villains whose ingenuity we are forced to admire even if we ultimately condemn them on moral grounds. Barabas is among the earliest of a group that includes Shakespeare's Richard III and Jonson's Volpone, and may well have influenced his successors. They came into existence partly because the Elizabethan audience delighted in them, to judge from one of Gosson's complaints:

> . . . in the Theaters they generally take vp a wonderfull laughter, and shout altogether with one voyce, when they see some notable cosenedge practised, or some slie conueighance of baudry brought out of Italy. Wherby they showe them selues rather to like it then to rebuke it.[86]

And Barabas is not merely ingenious, but has a resilience, a desire to fight back against adversity, that commands some degree of respect for him, so that his claim to be 'framed of finer mould than common men' (I.ii.221) does not seem merely arrogant.

In addition, Barabas has a kind of honesty in his villainy which cannot be found in the behaviour of his opponents. He deceives and betrays, but makes sharp conscious choices which involve no self-deception, and his sudden shifts of attitude have an underlying consistency. To his mind it is no worse to begin with deception than to begin with ideals and then to lapse away completely from them:

> As good dissemble that thou never mean'st
> As first mean truth, and then dissemble it.
>   [I.ii.290–1]

The Christians never show this kind of insight into themselves, and their lack of self-consciousness has the effect of making

Barabas seem both more perceptive and more complex than they are.

Even if his savagely destructive response is out of proportion to his injury, Barabas is shown as having been unjustly treated by the Christians who appropriate his money; when Abigail agrees to take part in a revenge plot against those

> That have so manifestly wrongèd us
> [I.ii.275]

the force of 'manifestly' suggests that the sympathy of the audience is meant to flow towards the persecuted Jew and his daughter. And I do not feel, despite the arguments of G. K. Hunter,[87] that the persecution of Barabas is given any real theological justification in the play; the Knights may use theological arguments to justify their contempt for Barabas, at I.ii.63–5 and 108–10, but this merely makes it easier for them to confiscate his money—and they do not even use the money for the purpose for which it was ostensibly collected. A simpler and perhaps more honest version of the Knights' attitude is found in Ithamore's remark:

> To undo a Jew is charity, and not sin
> [IV.iv.80]

and I cannot believe that Marlowe simply intended the audience to endorse wholeheartedly this casual piece of brutality.

Marlowe's themes are sharply emphasised. The world of the play is dominated by avarice:

> The wind that bloweth all the world besides,
> Desire of gold.
> [III.v.3–4]

The Knights of Malta, though under a religious vow to dedicate themselves to attacking the enemies of Christianity, have bought off the Turks by paying tribute, so that even del Bosco is rather shocked:

> Will Knights of Malta be in league with Turks,
> And buy it basely, too, for sums of gold?
> [II.ii.28–9]

But del Bosco himself has commercialised war, since his motive in coming to Malta was to sell off his prisoners as slaves, and the slave market itself, where human beings are treated like cattle and 'Every one's price is written on his back' (II.iii.3), seems to emphasise that this is a society in which everything can be bought and sold. Lodowick begins to woo Abigail not directly, but through her father, as though he were buying a diamond, and his enquiries culminate in the essential question, 'what's the price?' (II.iii.65).

The only genuine and disinterested love in the play is Abigail's love for her father and Mathias. Of her two lovers Lodowick is arrogant, snobbish, and treacherous to his friend, and Mathias, though his affection is sincere, is unsure of himself and subservient to his mother, and their rivalry in love turns to a bitter jealousy which destroys them both. Shakespeare's Shylock looks back to his dead wife Leah with affection, but the only love affair Barabas can remember is a case of 'fornication', casually shrugged aside:

> But that was in another country:
> And besides, the wench is dead.
> [IV.i.41–2]

Ithamore's attempts to act the romantic lover, in his infatuation with the tawdry prostitute Bellamira, are merely ridiculous, and it is probable that Marlowe himself deliberately parodied his own graceful lyric, 'Come live with me and be my love', in Ithamore's speech at IV.ii.94–104.

In this atmosphere of greed and selfishness traditional morality has little power to assert itself. Organised religion, in the shape of the two friars, is merely venal and lecherous. Moral affirmations are undercut because often they seem unconvincingly tacked on at the end of a sordid calculation. In II.ii, for example, Ferneze is at first reluctant to risk offending the Turks by letting del Bosco sell his prisoners, but when promised aid from Spain his attitude alters, and he defies the Turks in phrases that ring completely hollow:

> Claim tribute where thou wilt, we are resolved;
> Honour is bought with blood, and not with gold.
> [II.ii.55–6]

This kind of hypocrisy is neatly parodied at the end of IV.i in the remarks addressed to Friar Jacomo by Barabas and Ithamore, when they ironically assume the rôle of complacent moralists.

The supernatural is muted; the word 'God', that echoes through *Tamburlaine* and *Faustus*, is not found in *The Jew of Malta*,[88] and though an equivalent, 'Heaven', does occur sixteen times, Ferneze's attempts to assert that divine providence is at work seem weak and unconvincing:

> Wonder not at it, sir, the heavens are just.
> [v.i.55]
> What greater misery could heaven inflict ?
> [v.ii.14]
> O villain, heaven will be revenged on thee!
> [v.ii.25]

This is largely because we have been shown only too clearly that the events of the play have occurred not by chance or divine intervention but through human machinations. The most striking use of this effect is of course Ferneze's final couplet:

> So, march away, and let due praise be given
> Neither to fate nor fortune, but to heaven.
> [v.v.122–3]

Spoken by a man who has just broken his word and double-crossed his opponent, it comes as a resounding anti-climax, a final touch of hypocrisy rather than a stirring recall to moral order.

The key-words of the play fall into groups which can be defined fairly clearly. The first group relates to religious denominations ('Jew', 'Christian', 'Turk'), the second to various synonyms for riches ('gold', 'wealth', 'money'), and the third and relatively smallest to the values men live by, and the attitudes they adopt in their dealings with other men ('policy', 'profession', 'promise').[89] Several key-words are ambiguous in relating either to morality and religion or to worldly activities: 'profession' can mean 'profession of belief' or 'occupation', 'promise' can refer to God's promise to his chosen people, or to a human vow or commitment, and 'faith' can mean 'creed' or 'trustworthiness'.[90] This ambiguity is part of a major theme in the play, the relationship of theory and practice, the values men claim to live by and those that actually govern their behaviour. The repetition of a word like 'Jew' or 'Christian' in all sorts of contexts subjects it to an intense scrutiny: insistently the question is implied, what in fact does this label mean?

The main function of the prologue spoken by Machevil is to generalise the sceptical attitude implicit in the play as a whole, and to give a kind of bird's eye view of history ranging from Greek tyrant and Roman dictator to the French politician who has only just died. The lesson of history is consistent: in practice men scorn idealism and morality, and rely on force, or come to grief if they do not do so. Admittedly Machevil's maxims are only vaguely related to the genuine doctrines of Machiavelli, but they are still a reasonably accurate reflection of the impact these doctrines made on many sixteenth-century readers, who saw Machiavelli as the most extreme incarnation of the iconoclasts who ignored divine sanctions and relied on human power and ingenuity. And Machiavelli is a good patron for Barabas in that both men, as Professor Bradbrook points out,[91] are hated and scorned in public by men who secretly imitate them.

Machevil is very conscious that he is addressing an audience of Englishmen, and in its relation to England *The Jew of Malta* has the ambiguity of many Elizabethan and Jacobean tragedies which present scenes of exotic and glamorous villainy set in a remote country, but hint with varying degrees of openness at a relevance to the contemporary audience.[92] Challenged that his play was unorthodox, Marlowe could have replied that his Christians were after all Catholics, and a good Protestant would naturally regard a country populated with Catholics, Jews, and Turks as a hotbed of evil. But the Prologue makes it clear, with grim humour, that Machevil, who has come to 'frolic with his friends', is well established in England. Machevil launches into his list of maxims, but then suddenly restrains himself:

> But whither am I bound? I come not, I,
> To read a lecture here in Britany . . .
>
> [28-9]

perhaps with the implication that he is wasting his time because the audience already knows what he has to teach. Barabas himself uses direct address to the audience, after he has sold Malta back to Ferneze:

> Now tell me, worldlings, underneath the sun
> If greater falsehood ever has been done.
>
> [v.v.49–50]

The spectators are not allowed to be detached, but are drawn into the world of the play, and treated as fellow connoisseurs of villainy.

The dramatic technique of the play deserves more attention than it has so far received. *The Jew of Malta* dates from the late 1580s, at the very beginning of the great period of Elizabethan-Jacobean drama, and while some aspects of its technique seem crude in comparison to the mature masterpieces of Shakespeare and the great Jacobeans, in other respects its technique is extra-ordinarily sophisticated when compared to the lumbering attempts at tragedy that preceded Marlowe. The plot construction, for ex-ample, is remarkably neat: Marlowe uses a kind of chain pattern, in which one incident or episode provokes the next, as the hero-villain pursues his machinations or tries to prevent the truth leak-ing out, a pattern which was to be imitated in Jonson's *Volpone* and Tourneur's *The Revenger's Tragedy*. (And as far as we know the overall shape of the play was Marlowe's own invention.) The soliloquies do not simply hand over an undigested lump of useful information, as so often happens in the interludes, but flow spontaneously out of the action, and the interplay of characters in discussion and argument is more plausible and effective than in any earlier play. Even in an exchange of single lines:

> *First Jew.* Alas, my lord, the most of us are poor!
> *Fern.* Then let the rich increase your portions.
> *Bar.* Are strangers with your tribute to be taxed?
> *Sec. Knight.* Have strangers leave with us to get their wealth?
>
> [1.ii.57–60]

there is little trace of the self-conscious stichomythia of Kyd's *The Spanish Tragedy*.

Asides are strikingly frequent in *The Jew of Malta*. One recent critic has attacked them as merely a crude and heavy-handed underlining of the character's intention which is obvious enough

from the context.[93] Certainly Marlowe's use of asides cannot compare for subtlety with Shakespeare's in *Othello* or Middleton and
Rowley's in *The Changeling*, but he seems to have been the first
English dramatist to explore at length the possibilities of the aside,
and a few clumsy touches can be forgiven. Furthermore, Marlowe
may have felt that an audience not accustomed to such an extensive
use of asides might be baffled by Barabas's sudden changes of
attitude without some signposting.[94] The comic possibilities of
rapid alternation between direct speech and aside are brilliantly
exploited in Barabas's pseudo-rejection of Abigail at 1.ii.342–63;
elsewhere the repeated asides form a sinister running commentary
which gives an added dimension to the play, as in Barabas's
discussion with Lodowick at ii.iii.36–96. At times there is even a
multiple use of asides, as in the later part of ii.iii, where at first one
pair and then another out of a group of characters are anxious to
communicate without letting the others know, and this gives a
kaleidoscopic effect of different perspectives suddenly opening up.

Asides are particularly appropriate in a work which deals so
much in concealed purposes and deceptive appearances. Sometimes this is emphasised by asides that end abruptly with a phrase
that completely contradicts what has gone before:

> Assure yourselves I'll look—*unto myself*.
> [1.i.172]

This forms a neat verbal equivalent for Barabas's device of arous-
ing expectations he has no intention of fulfilling. These sudden
shifts of tone are very characteristic of *The Jew of Malta*: sometimes a character who has embarked on a somewhat pompous
speech is interrupted and deflated (as at 1.ii.4–5 and 42–3), or a
speech is begun by one character and then taken over by another
so that its meaning changes, the most inventive example of this
occurring at iv.i.28–45, where Bernardine breaks off his accusations because he doesn't want Jacomo to share his knowledge,
Jacomo echoes Bernardine's phrases but cannot add to them because of his ignorance, and Barabas supplies relatively innocuous
conclusions that are not what Bernardine meant, until at last
Bernardine is forced to become more explicit.

As we should expect, the blank verse is not as flexible as in the mature Shakespeare. Most lines are end-stopped; sense units are commonly linked together by simple conjunctions like 'And' and 'But'; and when particular emphasis is needed, the line often begins with a crude signal for attention like 'Now' or 'Know':

> Now then, here know that it concerneth us—
> [I.ii.42]

But within these limitations Marlowe achieves impressive results: the soliloquies of Barabas are splendid and sustained paragraphs of blank verse, and the unctuous nature of Ferneze is emphasised by the skilful modulation of his lines.

Marlowe uses some of the repetitions and rhetorical devices popular at the time the play was written. Alliteration is common; when used most effectively it falls on the significant words and gives an impression of crisp, decisive statement:

> Fie, what a trouble 'tis to count this trash!
> [I.i.7]
> The needy groom that never fingered groat
> Would make a miracle of thus much coin.
> [I.i.12–13]

Syntactical forms are often repeated in successive lines:

> Why stand you thus unmoved with my laments?
> Why weep you not to think upon my wrongs?
> Why pine not I, and die in this distress?
> [I.ii.172–4]

Frequently a significant single word is picked up and repeated, as though the character using it has suddenly seen a new facet of its meaning:

> Excess of wealth is cause of covetousness:
> And covetousness, O, 'tis a monstrous sin!
> [I.ii.124–5]
> Was this the pursuit of thy policy,
> To make me show them favour severally,
> That by my favour they should both be slain?
> [III.iii.40–2]
> And naught is to be looked for now but wars,
> And naught to us more welcome is than wars.
> [III.v.35–6]

Where a word at the end of one line is used again near the beginning of the next, the repetition becomes the rhetorical figure known as anadiplosis, as at I.i.149–51 and III.iii.47–9.

Sometimes within a single line one word echoes another with an effect almost like internal rhyme, or a faint pun:

> This is the ware wherein consists my wealth:
> [I.i.33]
> The hopeless daughter of a hapless Jew,
> [I.ii.316]
> And was my father furtherer of their deaths?
> [III.iii.25]

At times a pun is clearly intended:

> For whilst I live, here lives my soul's sole hope.
> [II.i.29]

This brings us to the word-play in *The Jew of Malta*, which deserves a fuller analysis than I can give it here. The heaviest concentration is in II.iii; most of the puns are spoken by Barabas, and express, with harsh irony, his bitter resentment at the hypocrisy of the Christians. Elsewhere Marlowe plays with some of the traditional metaphors of Christianity as ferociously as Swift does in *A Tale of a Tub*, particularly in the group of puns attacking the lecherous behaviour of the nuns at II.iii.79–91. Words like 'fruits' and 'profit' are ambiguous in various ways—theological, financial, and sexual—and by sardonically exploiting these ambiguities Marlowe sharpens his portrayal of human hypocrisy and inconsistency.[95]

A related characteristic of the play's style is the use of biblical allusions and proverbs, which cannot be neatly separated into two distinct categories for the simple reason that many proverbs are biblical in origin.[96] We could say, at the risk of over-simplification, that the Bible represents spiritual values, and proverbs represent worldly wisdom, but they are played off against each other so that both are seen in an ironic light. Hunter and other scholars have argued that the biblical allusions act as a kind of moral standard by which Barabas is decisively condemned, but this depends on an assumption that Marlowe accepted the Bible literally and uncritically, and documents like the Baines note or Kyd's

letter to Sir John Puckering[97] strongly suggest the contrary,
though they obviously need to be treated with caution. Barabas
can be seen as a kind of parody or inversion of Job, but, as J. B.
Steane points out,[98] this does not simply mean that we must
condemn Barabas for not imitating Job. The first hint of the Job
comparison occurs in Ferneze's line to Barabas:

> Be patient, and thy riches will increase.
> [I.ii.123]

In the circumstances we can hardly blame Barabas if he finds the
advice intolerably condescending.

Although I have not made detailed comparative studies, I
suspect that many of the features just discussed—asides, word-
play and puns, biblical allusions and proverbs—are used more
frequently in *The Jew of Malta* than in Marlowe's other plays, and
Marlowe may to some degree have developed a special style for the
play, in which the verbal discontinuities and shifts of level reflect
the hypocrisy and double standards of Maltese society. What
subtlety there is in the play does not come from patient
introspection and self-discovery but from ironic clashes and juxta-
positions. These can sometimes generate a complex response:
when Abigail dies after the words 'And witness that I die a
Christian' (III.vi.40) and Bernardine comments, 'Ay, and a virgin,
too, that grieves me most', the brutality of his reply does not, I
think, merely make Abigail ridiculous, but intensifies the pathos
and difficulty of her attempt to live decently.[99]

If my view of what Marlowe was trying to do is correct, there
was no sudden change of focus or alteration of technique in the
play as a whole in its second half, though there may have been
some loss of subtlety. There are certainly many local changes of
tone or sudden reversals of direction, but this is a basic characteristic of the play's technique which is consistently applied, and
Marlowe is always in control—indeed, we would perhaps be more
justified in seeing the play as too tightly controlled, too systematic
in its patterning, than in seeing it as loose and disorganised. Even
the scenes involving Bellamira and Pilia-Borza, which have usually
been regarded as the weakest part of the play, fit so neatly into its

organisation that they cannot be seen just as crude comic relief. Ferneze may look down on Bellamira and her bully ('Away with her, she is a courtezan', v.i.8), but the prostitute and thief, both of them blackmailers, are not much worse morally than the upper levels of Maltese society, though they reveal their greed and selfishness more crudely and blatantly. Their treatment of Barabas shows his true status: even the dregs of the Christian population feel free to persecute him. Most of Act IV is in prose; scholars in the past tended to assume that this was a clear pointer to textual corruption, but Marlowe wrote prose in some of his other plays,[100] and in my opinion he shows in *The Jew of Malta* a mastery of direct colloquial dramatic prose which is equalled among his contemporaries only by Shakespeare.

If the analysis made so far is valid, the answer to the question posed earlier in this introduction—how seriously did Marlowe intend his play?—may well be that *The Jew of Malta* is a deeply pessimistic work in which, like Abigail, we discover that

> there is no love on earth,
> Pity in Jews, nor piety in Turks.
> [III.iii.50–1]

The conclusion does not bring about a resumption of moral order; all that has happened is that the less imaginative hypocrites have managed to hang on until the clever rogue overreaches himself and plays into their hands. This may mean, of course, that there is a constricted quality about the play which prevents it from being ranked among the greatest tragedies, where there is some kind of affirmation of human greatness even in the middle of destruction.

It is possible that Marlowe deliberately intended to expose the ultimate sterility of 'policy', the emptiness and destructiveness of a world devoted to greed and egotism,[101] and if we argue that the play has nothing coherent to offer by way of a political philosophy, the answer may be that such a philosophy is impossible in a society where altruism barely exists. This interpretation would bring Marlowe's attitude closer to that of an orthodox moralist like John Case, who clearly felt that Machiavelli's principles were intended to destroy order and religion. But in Marlowe's play the negative and pessimistic view predominates, and although G. K.

Hunter has drawn our attention to various theological allusions and symbols I cannot feel that these are substantial or powerful enough to function as a moral positive. If we are to make a theological interpretation, the emphasis must remain on fallen man, with no intervention of divine grace.

It may be felt that my approach neglects an important element in the play. *The Jew of Malta* is often very funny indeed, and it would be possible to regard it simply as a brilliant theatrical entertainment intended to make us laugh rather than think. Certainly it would be foolish to read the play in too solemn a fashion; the problem here is to maintain the right balance of the 'ludicrous' and the 'terrible', to use Lamb's terms. T. S. Eliot was aware of this problem; even though he preferred to classify the play as a farce rather than as a tragedy, he was careful to emphasise that its humour was 'terribly serious'.[102]

My own feeling is that the comedy (which is theatrically very effective, as modern productions show)[103] is a harsh and disturbing comedy, near to ridicule, not the cheerful laughter which relaxes and heals. It should not distract us from the play's seriousness, but intensify it, by making us aware of the ludicrous instability of our attitudes and the absurdity of our pretensions to moral superiority. The play may seem at times a parody of normal human behaviour; even so, it is the kind of parody that is uncomfortably close to reality.

Whatever our final judgement may be, it is clear that *The Jew of Malta* has been more fully and more sympathetically discussed by critics during the past twenty years than at any time since it was written, and producers have seized on it as a play with exciting and unexplored possibilities. The popularity of such a cynical and unromantic work may tell us something about the mood of our time. Until that mood changes radically *The Jew of Malta* will continue, I believe, to be regarded as one of the best and most interesting of the non-Shakespearian Elizabethan plays.

4. THE TEXT

The Jew of Malta was entered in the Stationers' Register on 17

May 1594 for Nicholas Ling and Thomas Millington, but if an
edition was printed at this time no copy of it has yet been traced.
It is of course true that editions of some Elizabethan plays, including the 1604 text of Marlowe's own *Doctor Faustus*, survive in
only one copy, and it would be possible for a complete edition to
have perished, but Heywood's dedication to the 1633 quarto
reads as though the play was reaching print for the first time, and I
suspect that no earlier edition was printed. Why the play was
entered but not apparently published can only be conjectured; it
seems unlikely that the entry was a 'blocking entry' designed to
prevent publication, for Ling and Millington were not particularly
scrupulous, and both of them published 'bad quartos' of plays.[104]
The day before, 16 May 1594, a ballad called *The murtherous life
and terrible death of the rich Jew of Malta* was entered in the
Register for John Danter; this appears to derive from the play but
no copy of it survives.

The play was re-entered in the Register on 20 November 1632
for Nicholas Vavasour, and printed by John Beale soon after-
wards. Beale also printed Ford's *Love's Sacrifice* in 1633, and it
does not seem to have been noticed that the running-title on A3*v*
of *The Jew of Malta* ('*The Epistle Dedicatory.*') can also be found
on A[2]*v* of Ford's play, in such an exactly identical form that the
phrase must unquestionably have been kept in standing type.
Presumably one play was set soon after the other, though I do not
know which came first.

The 1633 quarto of *The Jew of Malta* is a very ordinary piece of
book production, with about fifty trivial and obvious misprints
involving single letters, the omission of several single words, and
anything between sixty and a hundred words requiring emendation. But in most cases the alteration needed is obvious enough,
and there are few serious textual cruces. One set of running-titles
was used for sheets B and C; a second was introduced on D outer,
and the two sets alternate regularly for the rest of the play. The
four pages of sheet K were printed by half-sheet imposition, using
the outer-forme skeleton. The spelling characteristics of the
quarto are uniform, and I have not discovered any evidence which
points to more than one compositor. It has been argued from the

pattern in which identifiable damaged letters recur that the quarto was set by formes, the inner first.[105] At times the repetition of certain speech-prefixes exhausted the supply of italic capitals, and the compositor was forced to use roman instead; the pattern of these substitutions, though sometimes ambiguous, tends to support the suggestion that setting was by formes. If this was so it would help to explain some of the oddities of layout and lineation of the quarto: the compositor was forced to squash together or space out a fixed amount of copy to make it fill a page of type.

For the present edition fourteen copies of the quarto were collated.[106] This collation revealed isolated press corrections on A4*r* and H1*r*, and six corrections scattered over the four pages of E outer, but they are all obvious corrections of trivial misprints which have no textual significance. The many uncorrected errors remaining in the quarto indicate that press correction was sporadic and unsystematic.

As I have already mentioned, the authenticity of the quarto text has been a matter of acute controversy. Bullen first suggested that the play was not exclusively by Marlowe,[107] and Fleay argued that the collaborator was Thomas Heywood:

> In the Court Epilogue, 'what others write', I think, indicates a second author; and I have no doubt that the Bellamira part was inserted by Heywood to bombast out Marlowe's short play. This is III.i; IV.iv, v; v.i. The prose shows it not to be Marlowe's, and the story is that of the friars in *The Captives*.[108]

Tucker Brooke, writing in 1910, was even more pessimistic:

> Undoubtedly the 1633 quarto presents the tragedy in a form sadly corrupted and altered from that in which it left the hands of Marlowe. Beside the incidental impurities due to very bad printing and to the casual changes of actors during many decades, it is probable that the extant text incorporates the results of at least two separate revisions; the first carried out before the revival in 1601, to which Henslowe alludes, the second that which must have been necessary before so old a work could be presented at Court and at the Cock-pit.[109]

Brooke agreed with Fleay that the author of this second revision was probably Heywood, though he did not accept that the plot similarities between *The Captives* and *The Jew of Malta* proved that Heywood wrote the friar scenes in *The Jew of Malta*, and he believed that the last three acts of *The Jew of Malta* preserved, though in a debased form, Marlowe's original conception of the play, 'bare of the imaginative humanizing which the earlier acts received'.[110] This might seem to be a slight modification of the pessimism of his opening sentence, but it was the more hostile parts of Brooke's argument which were taken over by the majority of later scholars as the orthodox attitude to the play. A. M. Clark tried to reconstruct in some detail the way in which, as he saw it, the play had been tampered with by Heywood.[111]

Other scholars, however, have defended the quarto. Margarete Thimme examined the stylistic characteristics of the play, and could find nothing which pointed to revision.[112] And R. F. Welsh has shown that when the play is studied in the light of certain distinctive spelling forms which Heywood liked to use, the evidence contradicts any theory of revision by him.[113]

The problem involved here has two aspects which need to be kept separate. In the first place, does the 1633 quarto represent Marlowe's original version of the play, or a version revised by Heywood or another dramatist? Secondly, how faithfully does the quarto transmit the text, whether revised or not? The second question can be soon answered. No one has ever suggested that the 1633 text of *The Jew of Malta* is a 'bad quarto' in the same way as the only surviving version of *The Massacre at Paris*, where the text has been seriously corrupted in the process of transmission,[114] and indeed there is no evidence for such a hypothesis.[115] We are clearly dealing with a 'good' quarto; what we have to determine is whether or not it was revised.

My own belief is that the quarto, though somewhat carelessly printed, is in fact a good and reliable text of Marlowe's original version, unrevised either by the actors or by another dramatist. It does indeed show certain peculiarities, but these can, I think, be convincingly explained on other grounds than revision. It might be best, however, to look first at the external evidence for revision and then to examine the quarto itself.

The external evidence is very flimsy. The fact that Henslowe had new costumes made in 1601 is no proof whatever that the text was revised, and Henslowe's mention of a cauldron to be used as a stage property in the play suggests, as several scholars have remarked, that the ending of the play in the quarto is basically the same as the ending of the earliest stage version. The case for Heywood as reviser is open to serious objection. His phrase 'what others write' was obviously, seen in its context, a generalisation about the relationship between actors and authors, and not a specific reference to *The Jew of Malta*. In his prefatory material Heywood spoke of Marlowe with great respect ('so worthy an author', 'the best of poets in that age') and described himself merely as an usher who had provided the play with prologues, epilogues, and a dedication. There is no hint in this that he has tampered with the text, and I do not see why we should not take him at his word. His use of the friar plot in two of his works is striking, but it certainly does not prove that he wrote the similar episode in *The Jew of Malta*, especially as the story is a common one.[116]

In addition, Heywood's prologues both refer to the play as an old-fashioned work which may not please the audience, and the Epilogue at Court even reads as though the actors were prepared in advance for the play to be a failure. This does not suggest that any attempt was made to bring the play 'up to date', and in any case it is hard to believe that Heywood could have made the play more popular with a sophisticated Caroline audience by introducing into it crude scenes of melodrama. A more tentative point is suggested by the Prologue and Epilogue to the Cockpit production, which imply that the audience might be disposed to compare Perkins's portrayal of Barabas with Alleyn's original creation of the rôle; it could be argued that a comparison of this kind would be difficult to make if the two men were acting in widely differing versions of the play.[117]

The internal evidence is more complex, and since no editor except Van Fossen has attempted a full analysis of the quarto's formal characteristics, I shall need to go into the matter in some detail.[118]

1. *Variations in characters' names and speech-prefixes.* These

reveal themselves in a variety of ways. Barabas has the speech-prefix '*Iew.*' in I.i, but from then on is '*Bar.*', except for three instances of '*Iew.*' at v.i.18.1, 31, and 96. The followers of Caly-math are called 'Bassoes' in I.ii, but 'Bashaws' in III.v and v.i. Sometimes the characters alternate in speech-prefixes between names and numbers; the three Jews are simply '1.', '2.', and '3.' in I.i, but become '1 *Iew.*' and '2 *Iew.*' in I.ii. The two friars are '1 *Fry.*' and '2 *Fry.*' in I.ii and III.vi, but in III.iii, where he appears by himself, Jacomo is simply '*Fry.*'. In IV.i they first appear as '2 *Fry.*' and '1 *Fry.*', at lines 24–5, but immediately switch to '2.' and '1.'. When Bernardine goes out and Jacomo is left by himself he is called '*Fry.*' (lines 109–13), but when the position is reversed and Bernardine reappears by himself, to meet his death, he too is simply '*Fry.*'. When Jacomo makes his last appearance, and strikes down the corpse of Bernardine, at lines 160–200, he has the pre-fix '*Ioco.*'. There are sometimes trivial variants in the spelling of characters' names. Abigail appears as '*Abigaile*' at I.ii.231 and '*Abigail*' at I.ii.238; elsewhere she is '*Abigall*', except for a few cases of '*Abigal*'. Ithamore appears thus only twice in the play, at III.iii.55 and III.iv.116 (and there are three examples of the speech-prefix '*Itha.*' at II.iii.115 and 131, and IV.i.0.1); elsewhere he is '*Ithimore*', with a few instances of '*Ithimer*', with the speech-prefixes '*Ith.*' and '*Ithi.*'. Friar Jacomo never appears in precisely this form, but as '*Iacomi*' at III.iii.71, '*Iocome*' at IV.i.108, and '*Iocoma*' at IV.i.116, 159, 159.1, and 174, while Bernardine once appears as '*Barnardine*' at IV.i.99 (I do not know why editors prefer the latter form). What is presumably 'Jaques' appears as 'Iaynes' (III.iii.31) and '*Iagues*' (III.iv.76). The courtesan is called '*Bella-mira*' at IV.ii.33 and 133, but '*Allamira*' at IV.ii.59; the mother of Mathias is '*Katherin*' at III.ii.16, but '*Katherina*' at III.ii.36; and the governor's son, usually '*Lodowicke*' in the quarto, has his name in the form '*Lodovicoes*' at III.iv.8. Finally, when characters appear in groups (Knights, Officers, Carpenters), the quarto sometimes uses an abbreviated speech-prefix ('*Kni.*', '*Off.*', '*Carp.*') which could refer either to an individual or to the group as a whole. Editors since Dyce have assumed that the '*Reader*' who suddenly appears at I.ii.68 is one of the officers.

2. *Use of generic character-names*. Ferneze is always called '*Governor*' in stage directions, and has the speech-prefix '*Gov.*'; Bellamira is always '*Curtezane*' and '*Curt.*'; and Katherine, the mother of Mathias, is always '*Mater*'. Other characters, like Barabas and Friar Jacomo, alternate between individual and generic speech-prefixes.

3. *Misattribution of speeches*. This occurs at I.ii.306 and 312, II.iii.115–24, III.ii.3–4, IV.i.84 and 100–1, and IV.iv.5. I.ii.137 has been re-assigned to Ferneze and IV.i.90 to Friar Jacomo by all recent editors, but the changes are not accepted in the present edition.

4. *Omission of entries*. There are ten omissions of entries in the play, mostly for minor characters like the officers. There are, however, two double entries, for Barabas at II.iii.4–6 and for Abigail at III.vi.0.1–6.1.

5. *Omission of exits*. The present edition has nineteen exits which are not marked in the quarto, some of which occur at the end of a scene when the stage needs to be cleared.

6. *Omission of stage directions*. Many essential stage directions are incomplete or omitted.

7. *Asides inconsistently marked*. The quarto uses a variety of devices to mark asides; sometimes the aside is printed in italic, sometimes the word '*Aside.*' is placed in the margin, and sometimes both are used together. At some points where '*Aside.*' is used it is difficult to know exactly how much of the text is intended to be spoken aside. Numerous lines and speeches are obviously asides but are not marked at all, and II.iii.64 is marked as an aside though this seems unnecessary.

8. *Plot confusions and inconsistencies*. At III.i.1 Bellamira describes Malta as besieged by the Turks, though strictly speaking the siege does not begin until after III.v, when Ferneze refuses to pay tribute. The arrangements for the challenge that leads to the duel between Lodowick and Mathias are somewhat confused (see III.ii.3 n.), and in IV.i it is not clear whether the murder of Bernardine and the trick played on Jacomo are parts of a plan prepared in advance which Ithamore knows about or are simply a sudden inspiration of Barabas (see IV.i.117–18 n.).

How can we interpret this evidence? Or, to be more specific, what kind of manuscript lay behind the quarto? Clearly it was an authentic playhouse manuscript, released by the actors and supplied with a dedication by one of the company's leading dramatists. Equally clearly, it was not a prompt-copy; the quarto has far too many confusions and omissions in speech-prefixes and stage directions to be acted as it stands. The answer is suggested, I think, by recent work on the texts of Shakespeare's plays. Several Shakespearian texts, both quarto and folio, display some of the features listed above for *The Jew of Malta*, and it was once customary to attribute these features to revision. But in two important papers R. B. McKerrow argued that companies might very well have two copies of a play, the author's rough draft, or 'foul papers', and a transcript prepared for use as a prompt-copy, and that in releasing the play for publication the company might prefer to retain the prompt-copy because of its importance to them and to send off the foul papers to be printed.[119] One sign of foul papers would be inconsistencies in speech-prefixes, since an author might regard a character in different ways in different parts of the play, whereas the prompter would insist on uniformity.[120] Following on from McKerrow, later scholars analysed the characteristics of 'foul papers' texts with increasing refinement.[121]

The quarto of *The Jew of Malta* is, I would argue, a foul papers text of high authority.[122] The alternation between '*Iew.*' and '*Bar.*' is like the alternation between '*Iew.*' and '*Shylock.*' in Q1 of *The Merchant of Venice* (1600), which also fails to provide entries for minor characters.[123] The use of a generic name like '*Curtezane*' for Bellamira can be compared to Shakespeare's use of '*Whoore*' for Doll Tearsheet in v.iv of the quarto of *Henry IV, Part II*, and the use of '*Reader*' at I.ii.68–76 is very like Shakespeare's use of '*Interpreter*' in IV.i and IV.iii of *All's Well That Ends Well* for the soldier who helps to interrogate Parolles. G. K. Hunter's Arden edition of *All's Well* (1959) contains twenty-three exits not in the Folio text, and the 1600 quarto of *Much Ado About Nothing* is similarly deficient. Finally, the use of numbers instead of names for certain characters is paralleled in quartos of two plays by Middleton which derive from foul papers.[124]

When we turn to Marlowe's other plays some interesting similarities become evident. In *Tamburlaine* entries for minor characters and exits, sometimes at the ends of scenes, are frequently omitted; there are trivial variants in the spellings of characters' names; and the speech prefix for Usumcasane, which is usually 'Vsum.', at four points occurs in the form 'Cas.'. It is not surprising that a recent editor of the play has conjectured that the text derives from foul papers.[125] *Edward II* has a number of textual oddities, particularly in the naming of characters; some of these have been usefully listed by W. W. Greg,[126] but there are others he does not mention. Entries for minor characters and exits are frequently omitted, and the speech-prefix for Edmund Earl of Kent alternates between '*Edm.*' and '*Kent.*'. Both plays contain characters (Magnetes in *Tamburlaine* and Trussel in *Edward II*) who suddenly appear without any entry provided, and are given abbreviated speech-prefixes ('*Mag.*' and '*Tru.*') whose full form never appears in the plays and has had to be supplied by modern editors. It is true that Greg argued that *Edward II* is based on 'a playhouse manuscript [which] had undergone some kind of revision for the stage',[127] but he was writing in 1925, before the characteristics of foul papers texts had been analysed, and it is much more plausible to see the confusions in the play as authorial tangles which had not yet been sorted out.

In contrast, the bad quarto of *The Massacre at Paris*, though it omits a few entries and exits (but never at the end of a scene), is consistent in its naming of characters and in speech-prefixes, and has detailed and accurate stage directions. Admittedly evidence of this kind can sometimes be interpreted in different ways, but it is surely significant that the formal characteristics of *The Jew of Malta* link it with the two plays by Marlowe that have always been regarded as existing in good and reliable texts. The 1633 quarto has so often been described as a very dubious version of Marlowe's original play that some scholars may be reluctant to accept this approach; it seems to me, however, the best way of accounting for the facts. I find it much easier to see most of the confusions in the play as authorial mistakes and inconsistencies than as the blunders of a remarkably incompetent reviser. (It would also be odd if evidence that points in one direction for Shakespeare and Middleton points in a different direction for Marlowe.) Furthermore, if it should seem improbable that Marlowe's foul papers survived intact for more than forty years after the play was written, it may be noted that *The Comedy of Errors*, one of the most striking of Shakespeare's foul papers texts, and one in which recent editors detect no signs of revision by another hand, was probably written by about 1593 but not printed until thirty years later in the First Folio.

To say that the play derives from foul papers does not, of course, immediately account for every difficulty. Some minor confusions (e.g. in the spelling of names) may well be compositorial blunders. In any case, some problems have been exaggerated: the plot confusions listed above are not very serious, and can easily be paralleled in Shakespearian plays whose authenticity has never been doubted. The only spelling variant that divides neatly between the first two and last three acts is 'Bassoes' / 'Bashaws', but one word hardly seems a secure foundation for a theory of multiple authorship.[128]

The term 'foul papers' can cover a variety of manuscripts, from the most tangled rough drafts to a reasonably tidy version that could be converted into prompt copy, and it looks as though the manuscript behind *The Jew of Malta* came nearer to the latter end of the scale. Fredson Bowers has argued that dramatists might be required to supply the company with a tidy and legible transcript of their foul papers that could then be written out again for use as a prompt copy;[129] the existence of such intermediate transcripts has been questioned, but the text of *Tamburlaine*, which obviously derives from a very neat and carefully written manuscript, might lend support to the theory. The manuscript behind *The Jew of Malta* was obviously not as tidy as this, but all the same the spoken text of the play is remarkably clean (particularly in the major soliloquies), with only one or two slight confusions that could suggest the presence of revisions by Marlowe himself.[130] The manuscript behind the quarto may thus have been Marlowe's own fair copy of his foul papers.

At this point we might ask whether the play contains any indication that the book-keeper had begun to annotate the text for use in the playhouse. The quarto is divided into acts, but recent discussions have argued that the marking of acts in Elizabethan plays is often an authorial feature which is sometimes deleted by a playhouse annotator, and it would be perfectly reasonable to regard the act division as by Marlowe himself.[131] W. T. Jewkes has drawn attention to imperative stage directions such as '*Fight.*' at IV.i.96 and '*Kisse him.*' at IV.ii.134; he notes that part of the stage direction at V.ii.0.1, 'Alarmes.', is in roman type, whereas the rest is in italic, which might imply that it was a later insertion in a different hand, and suggests that the comparatively long stage direction at V.v.62.1, which is crowded into the margin of the quarto, may be a stage-adaptor's note.[132] We should also perhaps take into account the double entries at II.iii.4–6 and III.vi.0.1–6.1. This evidence, however, is hardly conclusive: we should need to assume that the book-keeper added an odd word or phrase here and there (mostly in the later part of the play), and then broke off with most of his work still to do. It is equally possible that Marlowe himself made a few last-minute insertions during the preparation of his manuscript.[133]

If these arguments are accepted, certain conclusions follow for the editor of the play. He may not always be able to sort out the tangles and confusions of the text, but he can reasonably try to make sense of it, and can refer to other parts of the text and other plays by Marlowe to justify emendation at a particular point. He can also correct certain readings on the assumption that they are slips of the pen by Marlowe himself.[134] For the most part, however, his job will be very similar to that of the book-keeper who first received the manuscript from Marlowe's hands: he will need to introduce sufficient clarity and consistency for the play to be performed by actors and understood by readers. I have therefore regularised the characters' names and speech-prefixes, and substituted individual names for generic. I have followed the commonly accepted forms of Ithamore and Abigail, but have preferred to use Bernardine rather than Barnardine. I have also added stage directions when they seemed necessary to elucidate the action, usually in the form, though not always in the wording, of earlier editors.

The lineation of the play presents some difficulty, as at several points it is not clear whether the quarto is supposed to be read as prose or verse.[135] Barabas's speeches, for example, are mostly in verse, with a small amount of prose; for Ithamore the opposite seems to be true. In cases of difficulty my principle has been to re-line the quarto text as verse only when this could be done easily and naturally, without verbal emendation, and elsewhere to arrange it as prose. Metrically the play contains various irregularities—alexandrines, lines of nine or fewer syllables, and lines with additional extra-metrical syllables—but I have heeded Tucker Brooke's warning that these are characteristic features of Marlowe's style, even in an early play like *Tamburlaine*,[136] and have ignored most of the attempts of late nineteenth-century scholars to bring about metrical regularity. I have not added words to short lines merely to fill them out, except in a few cases where the awkwardness of the syntax indicated fairly clearly that something was missing.

The treatment of asides presented a special problem, partly because of the quarto's inconsistent methods of marking asides (see above, p. 43), and partly because several speeches in the play alternate frequently between aside and direct speech. The use of the normal modern method of indicating asides would have produced a text heavily cluttered with stage directions; it would also have been difficult sometimes to record economically the quarto's reading in the collation. In the end it seemed to me that the neatest and least cumbersome way of marking asides was to follow Bennett in retaining and extending the quarto's use of italic for this purpose.

It should therefore be clearly understood that in the present edition italic is used only for asides; quotations, letters, and so on are put in inverted commas. I have also introduced the word '*Aside.*' in square brackets, usually in the margin, at those points where the quarto does not already have it.[137]

I have tried to collate all previous editions of the play which are not merely reprints. The five editions published in 1810 and 1818 have been rather neglected by modern editors (only Bowers, for example, has made use of Broughton's edition),[138] but despite some silly and unnecessary emendations, not recorded here, they deserve attention, and give interesting readings which I have sometimes adopted.

Certain omissions have been made from the collation in order to keep it within reasonable bounds. Departures from the lineation of the quarto are all recorded separately in Appendix B. The information given earlier in this section (pp. 41–3, 1 and 2) about variations in characters' names and speech-prefixes, and the use of generic character-names, is not repeated in the collation, except where the quarto is ambiguous (e.g. '*Kni.*' at v.i.6) and editors have interpreted it in different ways. Except for those at I.ii.347–59, all indications of the character to whom a speech or aside is addressed (e.g. '*to Ith.*' at II.iii.137) are modern editorial insertions which are not individually collated.

One other feature of this edition deserves mention. In the quarto of 1633 Heywood's dedication, and his two sets of prologues and epilogues, are placed at the beginning. This material, however, was written forty years later than *The Jew of Malta*, and I see no reason why it must necessarily stand between the reader and what after all is Marlowe's play. It has undoubtedly helped to foster the assumption that Heywood tampered with the text, and I have preferred to remove it to an appendix.

NOTES

[1] See the list given in John Bakeless, *The Tragical History of Christopher Marlowe* (Cambridge, Mass., 1942), I, 329–30.

[2] A. Wagner, p. iv.

[3] *Henslowe's Diary*, ed. R. A. Foakes and R. T. Rickert (Cambridge, 1961), pp. 16–47.

[4] Bakeless, *op. cit.*, I, 361–6. Bakeless tends to argue that the popularity of the play fluctuated wildly according to external circumstances; no doubt these had an influence, but the total evidence suggests to me that the play was more continuously popular than Bakeless allows.

[5] *Ed. cit.*, p. 321.

[6] *Ibid.*, p. 170. Henslowe records buying 'divers things' for various plays, with sums ranging from five shillings to fifteen pounds. The 'little tailor', whose name was Radford (*ibid.*, pp. 169, 184), worked frequently on costumes for Henslowe between 1597 and 1601.

[7] See the textual introduction, p. 39.

[8] See the commentary on II.i.1–2.

[9] *The Seven Deadly Sinnes of London* and *Newes from Hell* (*Non-dramatic Works of Thomas Dekker*, ed. A. B. Grosart, London, 1885, II, 31 and 142).

[10] *The Letters and Epigrams of Sir John Harington*, ed. N. E. McClure (Philadelphia, 1930), p. 236.

[11] W. Rowley, *A Search for Money*, Percy Society Publications (London, 1840), p. 19.

[12] See Bakeless, *op. cit.*, I, 367–75. Bernard Spivack, *Shakespeare and the Allegory of Evil* (New York, 1958), p. 354, suggests an indebtedness in Chettle's *Tragedy of Hoffman*, probably written in 1602.

[13] E. Gayton, *Pleasant Notes Upon Don Quixot* (London, 1654), p. 271.

[14] Reprinted in Tucker Brooke's edition of the *Works* (1910); see *Doctor Faustus*, ed. J. D. Jump, Revels Plays, 1962, p. lxii.

[15] Thomason Tracts, 19 June 1647; reprinted in *Political Ballads Published in England during the Commonwealth*, ed. Thomas Wright, Percy Society Publications (London, 1841), p. 28.

[16] *Essays and Plays of Abraham Cowley*, ed. A. R. Waller (Cambridge, 1906), p. 284.

[17] See E. K. Chambers, *The Elizabethan Stage* (Oxford, 1923), II, 281–6.

[18] For an account of this play, and an English translation, see Ernest Brennecke, *Shakespeare in Germany, 1590–1700* (Chicago, 1964), pp. 105–89. Hermann Sinsheimer has argued (*Shylock: The History of a Character or the Myth of the Jew*, London, 1947, pp. 58–61) that this play is a debased version of a lost early play which was a source both for *The Jew of Malta* and *The Merchant of Venice*, but this is mere hypothesis, and it seems very much more probable that the German dramatist simply put together bits of English plays which had proved popular in Germany.

[19] Much of this information is taken from James L. Smith, 'The Jew of Malta in the Theatre', in *Christopher Marlowe (Mermaid Critical Commentaries)*, ed. Brian Morris (London, 1968), pp. 1–23. Smith provides a lively discussion of productions from Kean onwards, together with reactions from contemporary reviewers, in greater detail than would be possible in this introduction.

[20] Stephen Gosson, *The Schoole of Abuse*, 1579, f. C6v.

[21] See the sensible comments of E. A. J. Honigmann, 'Shakespeare's "lost source-plays"', *M.L.R.*, XLIX (1954), 297–8.

[22] Henslowe, *ed. cit.*, pp. 16–18.

[23] There is a vivid account in Ernle Bradford, *The Great Siege: Malta 1565* (London, 1961).

[24] John Foxe, *Actes and Monuments*, 1583, I, 754. See my note in *N. & Q.*, CCXIII (1968), 250.

[25] *Navigations . . . made into Turkie by Nicholas Nicolay*, trans. T. Washington, 1585, p. 22v. Both Villegagnon and Nicolay are quoted by Bakeless, *op. cit.*, I, 343–6.

[26] F. de Belleforest, *Cosmographie Universelle* (Paris, 1575), II, 747.

[27] P. H. Kocher, *Christopher Marlowe: A Study of His Thought, Learning, and Character* (Chapel Hill, 1946), pp. 260–1.

[28] This summary is from J. D. Moores, 'New light on Diomede Carafa', *Italian Studies*, XXVI (1971), 1–2. Moores gives references to accounts by sixteenth-century historians.

[29] Cecil Roth, 'The Jews of Malta', *T.J.H.S.E.*, XII (1928–31), 187–251.

[30] There have been four full-length biographies of Miguez, or Nasi, since 1859; the most recent is by Cecil Roth, *The House of Nasi: The Duke of Naxos* (Philadelphia, 1948).

[31] His name is found in various forms, Miguez, Miques, Miches, etc.

[32] L. Kellner, 'Die Quelle von Marlowe's *Jew of Malta*', *Englische Studien*, X (1887), 80–111.

[33] U. Foglietta, *De Sacro Foedere in Selimum Libri Quattuor* (Genoa, 1587), pp. 2–3; quoted in Kellner, *op. cit.*, pp. 97–8.

[34] Ethel Seaton, 'Fresh sources for Marlowe', *R.E.S.*, V (1929), 390–1. Miss Seaton points out that Contarini's allusion was translated into Latin in P. Lonicerus, *Chronicorum Turcicorum Tomi Duo* (Frankfurt, 1584), II, 3, but does not mention that in the same work (II, 153–61) Lonicerus reprinted a letter in Latin by the father of the Duke of Naxos supplanted by Nasi, signed from Naxos and dated 1537, which describes in some detail how the Duke was forced to agree to pay tribute to the Turks by a powerful Turkish fleet and army which threatened to invade him if he refused. This has some affinity with I.ii and III.v of the play.

[35] Bakeless, *op. cit.*, I, 339.

[36] E. M. Manolesso, *Historia Nova della guerra Turchesca* (Padua, 1572), ff. 8–8v; F. Angelo Calepio, *Narratione del successo dell'espugnatione, & defensione del Regno di Cipro*, printed in F. Steffano Lusignano, *Chorograffia, et Breve Historia Universale dell'Isola de Cipro* (Bologna, 1573), p. 93 (translated into French as *Description de Toute L'Isle de Cypre*, Paris, 1580, ff. 238v–239); Hieronymo de Torres y Aguilera, *Chronica, y Recopilacion de varios successos de Guerra* (Saragossa, 1579), ff. 6–6v; F. Sansovino, *Historia Universale dell'origine, et Imperio de' Turchi* (Venice, 1582), f. 439v; and Giovambatista Adriani, *Istoria de' suoi tempi* (Florence, 1583), p. 848.

[37] In a book which Marlowe could not have seen, Faminius Strada's *De Bello Belgico* (Rome, 1632), p. 172, it is stated that (according to authorities not named by Strada) the arsenal was blown up by agents of Nasi himself. If Marlowe saw an earlier version of this story it could have helped to prompt Barabas's use of the device of blowing up Selim's soldiers.

[38] Natalis Comes, *Universae Historiae Sui Temporis Libri Triginta* (Venice, 1581), pp. 386–7, 442. Comes has an ironical description of how the former Duke went to Constantinople with a sum of money, hoping to bribe the Turks to restore his dukedom. The attempt was pathetically unsuccessful (the Turks merely confiscated the money) but the story could have suggested to Marlowe, if he read it, the scheme by which Ferneze buys Malta back from Barabas. Comes also bluntly refers to the Jews as spies for the Turks (*cf. The Jew of Malta*, v.i.69–71).

[39] For Passi, see Tucker Brooke, 'The prototype of Marlowe's Jew of Malta', *T.L.S.*, 8 June 1922, p. 380, and, for Mendes, Lucien Wolf, 'Jews in Elizabethan England', *T.J.H.S.E.*, XI (1924–7), 24–9.

[40] This distinction is stressed by G. K. Hunter, 'The theology of Marlowe's *The Jew of Malta*', *Journal of the Warburg and Courtauld Institutes*, XXVII (1964), 214 ff.

[41] See III.vi.49 and II.iii.178.

[42] One example is printed and discussed by Beverley Boyd, *The Middle English Miracles of the Virgin* (San Marino, 1964), pp. 38–43, 117–18; she refers to a full survey of the story by Eugen Wolter, *Der Judenknabe* (Halle, 1879).

[43] See Beatrice D. Brown, 'Mediaeval prototypes of Lorenzo and Jessica', *M.L.N.*, XLIV (1929), 227–32.

[44] *Non-cycle Plays and Fragments*, ed. Norman Davis, E.E.T.S. (London, 1970), p. 63; noted independently by Arthur Freeman, 'A Source for *The Jew of Malta*', *N. & Q.*, CCVII (1962), 139–40, and M. C. Bradbrook, 'The inheritance of Christopher Marlowe', *Theology*, LXVII (1964), 349–50.

[45] Spivack, *Shakespeare and the Allegory of Evil*, and D. M. Bevington, *From Mankind to Marlowe* (Cambridge, Mass., 1962).

[46] T. W. Craik, *The Tudor Interlude* (Leicester, 1958), pp. 51, 132. Craik points out that the Devil often has a large nose in mystery plays and interludes, and suggests that Barabas's nose would help the audience to identify him as an incarnation of the devil. See also III.iii.10 n.

[47] London, ?1565, f. Aiii–Aiiiv. (I have used S. de Ricci's facsimile edition, New York, 1920.)

[48] Ibid., f. Bi.

[49] The following section is a much abbreviated version of my article 'Machiavelli and Marlowe's *The Jew of Malta*', *Renaissance Drama*, N.S. III (1970), 3–49, which gives fuller evidence to support the arguments put forward.

[50] Edward Meyer, *Machiavelli and the Elizabethan Drama* (Weimar, 1897), pp. ix–x.

[51] *Discours sur les moyens de bien gouverner et maintenir . . . un Royaume ou autre Principaute . . . Contre Nicholas Machiavel Florentin* (n.p., 1576); Latin translation (n.p., 1577); English translation by Simon Patericke (London, 1602). It should be noted that Patericke's dedication is not his own work but a translation of the Latin dedication of 1577, written by an anonymous Huguenot who translated Gentillet into Latin for the benefit of English readers.

[52] F. Raab, *The English Face of Machiavelli* (London, 1964), pp. 56–7.

[53] Irving Ribner, 'Marlowe and Machiavelli', *Comparative Literature*, VI (1954), 348–56.

[54] Case's *Sphaera Civitatis* (1588), written in Latin, is probably the most elaborate discussion of Machiavelli by an Elizabethan Englishman.

[55] See my article, 'Some Elizabethan allusions to Machiavelli', *English Miscellany*, XX (1969), 62–4.

[56] A useful list is given in Appendix A of J. M. H. Salmon's *The French Religious Wars in English Political Thought* (Oxford, 1959).

[57] Case, *op. cit.*, pp. 495 ff.

[58] P. H. Kocher, 'Francois Hotman and Marlowe's *The Massacre at Paris*', *P.M.L.A.*, LVI (1941), 349–68, and 'Contemporary pamphlet

backgrounds for Marlowe's *The Massacre at Paris*', *M.L.Q.*, VIII (1947), 151–73, 309–18.

⁵⁹ See notes on Prologue, 20, and II.iii.313.

⁶⁰ See notes on Prologue, 23–4, 26 (*petty wights*), I.i.130–1, I.ii.147–9, and V.ii.27.

⁶¹ See notes on Prologue, 22, I.ii.209 (cf. II.iii.19), I.ii.281–2, and V.ii.113–14.

⁶² See notes on Prologue, 32, and IV.i.54.

⁶³ Meyer, *op. cit.*, pp. 22–3, argued that Marlowe's Prologue was inspired by Harvey's 'Epigramma in effigiem Machiavelli: Machiavellus ipse loquitur', *Gratulationum Valdinensium Libri Quatuor* (London, 1578), Liber II, p. 9. Ribner (*op. cit.*, p. 352) and others repeat the assertion, but a close examination of the two passages reveals no similarities either of tone or of content.

⁶⁴ Heywood's sources are discussed by Emil Koeppel, 'Zur Quellenkunde des Stuart-Drama', *Archiv*, XCVII (1896), 323–9, and G. L. Kittredge, 'Notes on Elizabethan plays', *J.E.G.P.*, II (1898), 13; a more general survey is in Archer Taylor, 'Dane Hew, Munk of Leicestre', *M.P.*, XV (1917–18), 221–46.

⁶⁵ P. H. Kocher, 'Legal history in Marlowe's *Jew of Malta*', *H.L.Q.*, XXVI (1962–63), 155–63.

⁶⁶ Harry Levin, *Christopher Marlowe: The Overreacher* (London, 1965), p. 98; Geoffrey Whitney, *A Choice of Emblems* (London, 1586), p. 216.

⁶⁷ Hunter, pp. 233–5.

⁶⁸ *The Letters of Charles and Mary Lamb*, ed. E. V. Lucas (London, 1935), I, 133.

⁶⁹ 'H.M.', 'Analytical essays on the early English dramatists, No. III: *Jew of Malta.*—Marlowe', *Blackwood's Edinburgh Magazine*, II (1817), 265.

⁷⁰ *The Monthly Review; or Literary Journal*, LXVII (1812), 434. Cf. the comments on the play in 'The early English drama', *The Retrospective Review*, IV (1820), 153.

⁷¹ 'Marlowe's Jew of Malta', *Blackwood's Edinburgh Magazine*, III (1818), 209.

⁷² Henry Hallam, *Introduction to the Literature of Europe* (London, 1839), II, 375–6.

⁷³ Charles Lamb, *Specimens of English Dramatic Poets* (London, 1808), p. 31.

⁷⁴ Compare Lamb with Hazlitt, *Lectures on the Dramatic Literature of the Age of Elizabeth*, in *Works*, ed. A. R. Waller and Arnold Glover (London, 1902), V, 209–10, Leigh Hunt, *Dramatic Criticism, 1808–1831*, ed. L. H. and C. W. Houtchens (London, 1950), pp. 195–7, and the writers in *Blackwood's Edinburgh Magazine*, II (1817), 265–6, and III (1818), 209.

⁷⁵ See, for example, M. C. Bradbrook, *Themes and Conventions of Elizabethan Drama* (Cambridge, 1935), p. 158, and Spivack, *Shakespeare and the Allegory of Evil*, p. 348.

⁷⁶ *Marlowe and the Early Shakespeare* (Oxford, 1953), p. 65.

⁷⁷ Irving Ribner, 'Marlowe's "Tragicke Glasse"', in *Essays on Shakespeare and Elizabethan Drama*, ed. R. Hosley (London, 1963), p. 102.

78 See Ovid, *Metamorphoses*, I, 127–40, and Marlowe's own translation of *Amores*, III.vii, especially ll. 35–44, and *cf*. I.i.108 n.

79 *The Arte of Warre*, trans. Peter Whitehorne, 1560; ed. H. Cust, The Tudor Translations (London, 1905), p. 224.

80 According to Harry Levin (*The Overreacher*, London, 1954, p. 211) Barabas speaks 49 per cent of the lines in the play, a higher percentage than for any of Marlowe's other characters.

81 Bennett, p. 19.

82 Thomas Wilson, *A Discourse Upon Usury*, ed. R. H. Tawney (London, 1925), Introduction, p. 134.

83 Thomas Fitzherbert, *The First Part of a Treatise concerning Policy and Religion* (Douay, 1606), p. 109.

84 See Howard S. Babb, '*Policy* in Marlowe's *The Jew of Malta*', *E.L.H.*, XXIV (1957), 85–94.

85 This point is discussed at greater length in my article '"Policy", Machiavellianism, and the earlier Tudor drama', *E.L.R.*, I (1971), 195–209.

86 Stephen Gosson, *Plays Confuted in Five Actions* (London, [1582]), f. C8v–D1.

87 In the article mentioned above, n. 40.

88 Except in forms like 'God-a-mercy' and 'godfathers'. The word may possibly have been censored from the text because of the Act of 1606 against profanity in plays; this apparently happened to some extent in the 1616 text of *Faustus* (see Greg's parallel-text edition of *Faustus*, 1950, pp. 85–6), though twenty-five instances of 'God' remained unaltered. I have not found any evidence that censorship did take place in *The Jew of Malta*.

89 One way of distinguishing the unique quality of *The Jew of Malta* in Marlowe's work as a whole is to note that several of its key-words are not found in the same concentration in his other plays. In the following list of usages, which includes inflected forms, the first figure is for *The Jew of Malta* and the figure in brackets for all the other plays combined: 'wealth', 26 (16); 'crown' (in the sense of 'gold coin'), 25 (4); 'money', 22 (9); 'policy', 13 (6); 'promise', 9 (10); 'price', 8 (3); 'merchant', 8 (3); 'profession', 7 (4); 'dissemble', 5 (6); 'riches', 5 (6) and 'coin', 5 (2). For some other words the discrepancy is less marked, but *The Jew of Malta* still has a higher total than any other play; this applies to 'Christian', 35 (*cf*. the two parts of *Tamburlaine*, 29), and 'gold', 33 (the two parts of *Tamburlaine*, 28). The commonest key-word is 'Jew' (72 as against 3 elsewhere) but this is perhaps to be expected. These statistics are based on Charles Crawford, *The Marlowe Concordance* (Louvain, 1911–32).

90 There are also deliberate puns on words that have discordant religious and secular meanings; see below, p. 34.

91 *Themes and Conventions*, p. 156.

92 A crude example of this technique is Lodge and Greene's *A Looking-Glass for London and England* (*c*. 1592). This is set in Nineveh, but at intervals Oseas draws the moral of events explicitly for a London audience.

93 See Wilbur Sanders, *The Dramatist and the Received Idea* (Cambridge, 1968), p. 39.

94 This could apply within the play itself; Sanders attacks 'I must

dissemble' at IV.i.47, but Barabas may be signalling to Ithamore, not to the audience, that he is about to put on an act.

⁹⁵ Puns or similar plays on words are glossed at the following points in the commentary: I.ii.334–5; II.iii.57–8, 84, 85, 86, 120–1, 134–5, 243–4, 307; III.i.2; III.iii.35, 68; III.iv.112; IV.i.21; IV.ii.49, 52, 86, 88; and IV.iv.50.

⁹⁶ See the Index to Annotations, under 'Biblical allusions' and 'Proverbs and proverbial phrases'. To judge from Tilley, Marlowe was the first to introduce a number of proverbs into the drama, though caution is necessary as so many earlier plays are lost (and see the supplement to Tilley in F. P. Wilson, *Shakespearian and Other Studies*, Oxford, 1969, pp. 158–75).

⁹⁷ Which says of Marlowe that 'it was his custom . . . in table talk or otherwise to iest at the devine scriptures'.

⁹⁸ J. B. Steane, *Marlowe: A Critical Study* (Cambridge, 1965), p. 181 n. The author of *Tamburlaine* does not seem to have admired submission and self-abnegation, and in his *Discourses*, II, 2, Machiavelli criticised Christianity for over-valuing humility, thereby making good men an easy prey to the wicked, a doctrine which scandalised many of his opponents. We should get a wildly distorted view of the Elizabethans if we assumed that we could deduce what they all felt merely from the opinions of orthodox theologians and moralists.

⁹⁹ I would suggest to producers that Abigail should be played as realistically and sympathetically as possible; if she is guyed, one dimension of the play is lost.

¹⁰⁰ Fleay's comment, 'the prose shows it not to be Marlowe's' (quoted below, p. 39), shows how Marlowe has been the prisoner of his reputation; the poet of the 'mighty line', he *cannot* have written prose.

¹⁰¹ As far as I know this was first suggested by Una Ellis-Fermor, *Christopher Marlowe* (London, 1927), pp. 101–2.

¹⁰² 'Christopher Marlowe', in *Selected Essays* (London, 1932), p. 123.

¹⁰³ So much so that if producers are not careful they will give us simply the 'ludicrous' and trivialise the play. Much of *The Jew of Malta* is concerned with loss and suffering, which should not be made to appear merely ridiculous. See James L. Smith's perceptive comments in his article cited above, n. 19.

¹⁰⁴ See the accounts of Ling and Millington by Leo Kirschbaum, *Shakespeare and the Stationers* (Columbus, Ohio, 1955), pp. 305–8. Possibly Ling and Millington were about to publish a 'bad quarto' of the play but were somehow prevented from doing so.

¹⁰⁵ R. F. Welsh, as cited by Van Fossen, p. xxvii.

¹⁰⁶ In the following libraries: the British Library (three copies), the Bodleian Library (three copies), the Dyce collection in the Victoria and Albert Museum (two copies), Worcester College, Oxford (two copies), the National Library of Scotland (two copies), Trinity College, Cambridge, and the Senate House Library, the University of London. Van Fossen (p. xxvi) collated seven American copies but reported only the press variants in sheets A and H. Bowers records only one of the six variants on E outer.

[107] Bullen, I, xli.

[108] F. G. Fleay, *A Biographical Chronicle of the English Drama, 1559–1642* (London, 1891), I, 298, and II, 61–2.

[109] Brooke, pp. 231–2.

[110] *Ibid.*, p. 233.

[111] A. M. Clark, *Thomas Heywood* (Oxford, 1931), pp. 290–4.

[112] *Marlowe's 'Jew of Malta': Stil- und Echtheitsfragen* (Halle, 1921).

[113] 'Evidence of Heywood spellings in *The Jew of Malta*', *Renaissance Papers 1963* (Durham, North Carolina, 1964), pp. 3–9.

[114] See H. J. Oliver's account in his Revels edition (1968), pp. lii–lx.

[115] In 'How bad is the text of *The Jew of Malta*?', *M.L.R.*, XLVIII (1953), 435–8, J. C. Maxwell has defended the quarto by pointing out that, for all their rudeness about it, editors have not needed to make an unusually large number of emendations to the text; this is not, however, a conclusive argument by itself, as even a bad quarto, with a debased and simplified text, need not necessarily contain numerous textual cruces requiring emendation.

[116] See the discussion of sources, p. 16 above, n. 64.

[117] Jonson's satirical portrayal in the Induction to *Cynthia's Revels* of the playgoer who refers to *The Spanish Tragedy* 'as it was first acted' indicates that theatregoers could be expected to know when a play had been revised. R. C. Bald has shown that earlier plays were sometimes revised in the 1630s ('The foul papers of a revision', *The Library*, 4th series, XXVI (1945–46), 43), but the two examples he gives have the words '*new Vampt*' in their titles to show that they have been revised.

[118] I have assembled this information here so that it can be seen as a whole, but I have not thought it necessary to repeat all the details in the textual collation.

[119] 'The Elizabethan printer and dramatic manuscripts', *The Library*, 4th series, XII (1931–32), 253–75.

[120] 'A suggestion regarding Shakespeare's manuscripts', *R.E.S.*, XI (1935), 459–65.

[121] See for example Shakespeare's *Henry IV, Part II*, ed. M. A. Shaaber, Variorum Shakespeare (Philadelphia, 1940), pp. 488–94.

[122] This view has already been put forward very briefly by Kirschbaum, *The Plays of Christopher Marlowe* (Cleveland, Ohio, 1962), p. 464.

[123] See J. R. Brown's Arden edition of *The Merchant of Venice* (1955), p. xiv, n. 3.

[124] *Your Five Gallants* (?1608) and *A Trick to Catch the Old One* (1608); see R. C. Bald, *op. cit.*, p. 38, and G. R. Price, 'The early editions of *A Trick to Catch the Old One*', *The Library*, 5th series, XXII (1967), 208. Both plays are strikingly deficient in entries and exits.

[125] *Tamburlaine*, ed. J. D. Jump, Regents Renaissance Drama Series (Lincoln, Nebraska, 1967), p. xxv.

[126] *Edward II*, ed. W. W. Greg, M.S.R. (Oxford, 1925), pp. ix–xii. See also Bowers's discussion in his edition (*Works*, II, 8–11).

[127] *Op. cit.*, p. xii.

[128] Bowers (*Works*, I, 256) notes that in Acts III to V the use of italic for proper names differs slightly from that in Acts I and II, but this purely

typographical distinction carries little weight in the absence of stronger evidence.

[129] Fredson Bowers, *On Editing Shakespeare and the Elizabethan Dramatists* (Pennsylvania, 1955), pp. 12 ff.

[130] See commentary on IV.i.160–3. I am aware of not having dealt with one important point. If, as I argue, *Tamburlaine*, *Edward II*, and *The Jew of Malta* are all foul papers texts, how do I account for the fact that in all sorts of minute details the three texts are far from uniform? I can only plead that to attempt to answer this would involve an extremely thorough examination of the texts of all Marlowe's plays (and also of the practices of the various printers who set them) which I have felt unable to make. I only hope that my arguments will provoke further investigation.

[131] See W. T. Jewkes, *Act Division in Elizabethan and Jacobean Plays 1583–1616* (Hamden, Conn., 1958), pp. 26, 28–9, 82–3, and 302.

[132] *Ibid.*, p. 302.

[133] Stage directions in the imperative and a double entry can be found in Q1 of *The Merchant of Venice*, but J. R. Brown (*op. cit.*, p. xv) does not believe that they indicate playhouse annotation.

[134] E.g. at II.ii.11 and 38.

[135] For further discussion of the problem of lineation see Appendix B.

[136] 'Marlowe's versification and style', *S.P.*, XIX (1922), 191–205. See also Bakeless, *op. cit.*, II, 185–9 and 196–9.

[137] An important distinction in the collation should be noted. '*Aside not in Q*' means that Q gives no indication of any kind that an aside is intended; '*Italic not in Q*' means that Q prints '*Aside*' in the margin, but does not indicate by italic how much of the speech is aside.

[138] It is No. 3684 in C. J. Stratman, *A Bibliography of English Printed Tragedy, 1565–1900* (Carbondale, Illinois, 1966). I have used microfilms of a copy in the University of Michigan Library. No editor's name is given, and Bowers refers to it by the printer's name as the 'Chappell' edition; for proof that the editor was James Broughton see my note, 'James Broughton's edition of Marlowe's plays', *N. & Q.*, CCXVI (1971), 449–52.

THE FAMOUS TRAGEDY OF
THE RICH JEW OF MALTA

DRAMATIS PERSONAE

MACHEVIL, *speaker of the Prologue.*
BARABAS, *the Jew of Malta.*
FERNEZE, *the Governor of Malta.*
ITHAMORE, *slave to Barabas.*
SELIM-CALYMATH, *son of the Emperor of Turkey.*   5
CALLAPINE, *a Bashaw.*
DON LODOWICK, *the Governor's son.*
DON MATHIAS, *his friend.*
MARTIN DEL BOSCO, *Vice-Admiral of Spain.*
FRIAR JACOMO.   10
FRIAR BERNARDINE.
PILIA-BORZA, *a thief, in league with Bellamira.*
ABIGAIL, *the Jew's daughter.*
KATHERINE, *Mother of Mathias.*
BELLAMIRA, *a Courtezan.*   15
Abbess.
Nun.
Two Merchants; Three Jews; Knights of Malta; Bashaws, Officers, Slaves, Citizens of Malta, Turkish soldiers (Janizaries), Messenger, Carpenters.   20

The Scene: *Malta.*

DRAMATIS PERSONAE] This ed., based on Reed; not in Q.

The Jew of Malta

[Prologue]

[*Enter*] MACHEVIL.

Mach. Albeit the world think Machevil is dead,
    Yet was his soul but flown beyond the Alps;
    And now the Guise is dead is come from France,
    To view this land and frolic with his friends.
    To some perhaps my name is odious,   5
    But such as love me guard me from their tongues;

Prologue] *Broughton.*   0.1. *Enter*] *Reed.*   *Machevil*] Q (*Macheuil*);
Machiavel Reed.   1. *Mach.*] *Reed; not in Q.*

0.1. Machevil] It seems unnecessary to emend to 'Machiavel'; *cf.* Heywood's rhyming of 'still' and 'Machevill' in the Prologue at Court, ll. 7–8.

1–4.] The anonymous Huguenot who translated Gentillet into Latin in 1577 did so in order that Machiavelli's pernicious influence should not reach into England (Gentillet, 'The Epistle Dedicatorie', f. ¶ iv), and similarly Case, *Sphaera Civitatis*, p. 3, described with horror the spread of Machiavellianism from Italy to France, and hoped it would not penetrate to England. 'Machevil' gloatingly makes it clear that he is very much alive and has now got to England ('this land').

3. *the Guise*] Henry, third Duke of Guise, was assassinated on 23 December 1588 by order of the French king Henry III, an event dramatised by Marlowe himself in scene xxi of *The Massacre at Paris*. Guise was a bitter enemy of the Huguenots, who regarded him as evil and ambitious, but I have not come across contemporary accusations that he was a disciple or reincarnation of Machiavelli as Marlowe seems to imply.

5–6.] The real disciples of Machiavelli make use of his doctrines, but avoid mentioning his name in order not to alarm the conventionally minded. (For an example see Introduction, p. 12.) *Cf.* also the reluctance of evil characters in the interludes to be known by their true name, as in

And let them know that I am Machevil,
And weigh not men, and therefore not men's words.
Admired I am of those that hate me most:
Though some speak openly against my books,   10
Yet will they read me, and thereby attain
To Peter's chair; and when they cast me off
Are poisoned by my climbing followers.
I count religion but a childish toy,
And hold there is no sin but ignorance.   15
Birds of the air will tell of murders past?

16. past ?] *Kirschbaum;* past; *Q.*

---

the opening speech of Avarice in Udall's *Respublica*, ll. 73–4: 'For though
to moste men I am founde Commodius / yet to those that vse me my name
is Odius'.

7. *them*] the true followers of Machiavelli.

8. *weigh not*] attach no value to, am not impressed by. Presumably
'Machevil' has no respect for traditional authorities (*cf.* his contempt for
learning at l. 23).

9. *Admired*] According to *O.E.D.* 'admire' at this time usually meant
'marvel, wonder at', but could also sometimes imply 'esteem, value
highly'. Possibly both meanings are present here. The paradoxical love–
hate relationship described in this line is found repeatedly in 16th c.
discussions of Machiavelli; see Introduction, p. 11.

12. *Peter's chair*] Elizabethan writers were commonly deeply hostile to
the Papacy; Kocher, p. 197, quotes from *The Restorer of the French Estate*
(London, 1589), p. 71 'As for the Popes, most of them haue clymbed up
to the Holy See by lyes, hypocrisie, guiles and deceipt, by money, armes,
massacres, poysonings and Magicall arts'. But they do not seem to accuse
the Popes explicitly of being disciples of Machiavelli. Marlowe may be
thinking of Pope Alexander VI, father of Cesare Borgia (see III.iv. 98–9 n.).

14.] See I.ii.281–2 n., and *cf. The Massacre at Paris*, ii.63–6. Machiavelli did not in fact dismiss religion in this way (see *Discourses*, I, 11–15),
but his 16th c. opponents frequently described him as an atheist, or (with
some justification) as one who believed in religion simply as a political
tool (e.g. Hooker, *Of the Laws of Ecclesiastical Polity*, Book V, 1597, p. 7).
toy] trifle.

15. *ignorance*] either 1. ignorance of the rules for worldly success, or 2.
the kind of superstition jeered at in ll. 16–17.

16–17.] Bennett cites the classical legend of the cranes which revealed

I am ashamed to hear such fooleries!
Many will talk of title to a crown:
What right had Caesar to the empery?
Might first made kings, and laws were then most sure   20
When like the Draco's they were writ in blood.

19. empery] *Reed;* Empire *Q.*   21. the] *Q;* to *Broughton.*   Draco's]
Reed; Drancus Q.

---

the murder of Ibycus. One source for the story is Plutarch's *Moralia*, in
the essay called *De Garrulitate*, and in *De Sera Numinis Vindicta* Plutarch
tells the story of the swallows which revealed Bessus' murder of his father.
In *The First Part of a Treatise concerning Policy and Religion* (Douay,
1606), pp. 262, 441–2, Thomas Fitzherbert quoted both anecdotes as
proof of God's providence and justice, but 'Machevil' ridicules the idea;
murder can remain hidden. *Cf.* also *Macbeth*, III.iv.122–6.

18–19.] One of the stock characteristics of a tyrant was that he had no
legal right to his power, and it was debated from classical times onwards
whether Julius Caesar, who had no legal right to rule, ought to be regarded as a tyrant or not. (For the debate in the Italian renaissance see
Hans Baron, *The Crisis of the Early Italian Renaissance* (Princeton, 2nd
edn, 1966), pp. 48 ff.) Machiavelli describes Caesar as a tyrant who seized
power by force in the *Discourses*, I, 29, and Marlowe may have been
influenced by the hostile portrayal of Caesar in Lucan's *Pharsalia*.

19. *empery*] Both 'empire' and 'empery' were commonly used in
Marlowe's time to mean 'rule, dominion'. I have emended for three
reasons: 1. the confusion is easily made (*cf. Faustus*, i.74, where AI reads,
correctly, 'treasury', while other texts read 'treasure'); 2. Marlowe
several times elsewhere uses 'empery' at the end of a line, but never 'empire';
3. I assume that metrical regularity is more called for in the formal speech
of a prologue than in the rest of the play. *Cf.* 'Britany' in l. 29 below.

20. *Might . . . kings*] It was long debated whether kingship originated
through the violent seizure of rule by the most powerful, or through the
voluntary surrender of power by the community to the man most fitted to
rule. Machiavelli himself leant towards the second theory (*Discourses*,
I, 2), but Jean Bodin strongly advocated the theory of force (*The Six Books
of a Commonweal*, trans. R. Knolles, 1606, p. 47; earliest French edition,
1576). A plagiarised version of Bodin is in P. de la Primaudaye, *The
French Academy*, trans. T. Bowes, 1586, pp. 585–6. See Kocher, pp. 198–9.

21. *Draco*] the Athenian legislator who in 621 B.C. reformulated the
Athenian legal code. His severity became proverbial, and the orator
Demades said that his laws were written in blood. Machiavelli did not
mention Draco, but frequently discussed lawgivers like Moses, Lycurgus,
and Solon.

Hence comes it that a strong-built citadel
Commands much more than letters can import:
Which maxima had Phalaris observed,
He'd never bellowed in a brazen bull   25

---

24. maxima] *This ed.;* maxime *Q.*   had] *Q;* had but *Scott.*   25. He'd]
Dyce; H'had *Q;* He had *Reed.*

---

22. *citadel*] Machiavelli's attitude to citadels or fortresses was complicated, even contradictory, and can be only briefly summarised here. In
The Art of War, ch. 7, he gave detailed instructions for building fortresses
and besieging them; in *The Prince,* ch. 20, he argued that princes should
build citadels to protect themselves against their own subjects if they are
hostile, but should not rely on them for protection against a foreign
invader; in the *Discourses,* II, 24, he attacked the use of fortresses under
any circumstances. But fortresses were traditionally used by tyrants to
awe their subjects, and Gentillet, who saw Machiavelli's writings as a
handbook for tyrants, distorted and simplified his ideas to this effect
(Bk III, Maxim 33, pp. 347–9).

23–4. *letters . . . Phalaris*] For a commentary on these lines see A.
D'Andrea, 'Studies on Machiavelli and his reputation in the sixteenth
century: I. Marlowe's Prologue to *The Jew of Malta*', *Medieval and
Renaissance Studies,* V (1960), 214–48. The allusion is almost certainly to
the *Letters of Phalaris,* a series of letters in Greek long attributed to the
notorious Sicilian tyrant Phalaris (6th c. B.C.). It was not until 1697 that
Richard Bentley proved them to be spurious. The allusion must be related
to the Renaissance debate on whether too much concern for letters and
learning weakened the military effectiveness of a State (see, e.g., the
conclusion of Montaigne's essay 'Of Pedantisme', *Essays,* I, 24). For
Erasmus (*The Education of a Christian Prince,* trans. L. K. Born, New
York, 1936, p. 201), Phalaris' love of letters was his one redeeming
feature; for 'Machevil' it was his fatal weakness, and he would have done
better to behave like a true tyrant and rely on a strong citadel. Machiavelli expressed contempt for Phalaris (*Discourses,* I, 10), but he did rebuke
the Italian princes of his day for paying too much attention to verbal
subtlety in writing at the expense of military skill (*The Arte of Warre,*
trans. P. Whitehorn, 1560, ed. H. Cust, 1905, p. 230).

import] perhaps in *O.E.D.*'s sense 9, 'to obtain, win a victory'; i.e.
letters cannot command obedience like a fortress.

24. *maxima*] common in the late 16th c. as an alternative form of
'maxim' (see *O.E.D.*). This simple emendation provides metrical regularity.

25. *brazen bull*] a device used by Phalaris to burn his victims alive. The
story that its inventor, Perillus, was the first to perish in it is very common, but as Andrea points out (*op. cit.,* pp. 220, 242), the only early writer
to suggest that Phalaris himself died in it is Ovid, in his *Ibis,* ll. 439–40.

Of great ones' envy; o' the poor petty wights
Let me be envied, and not pitied!
But whither am I bound? I come not, I,
To read a lecture here in Britany,
But to present the tragedy of a Jew,   30
Who smiles to see how full his bags are crammed,
Which money was not got without my means.
I crave but this, grace him as he deserves,
And let him not be entertained the worse

---

26. ones'] *Dyce;* ones *Q;* one's *Robinson.*   wights] *Reed;* wites *Q;* wits
Shone.   29. Britany] *Bullen; Britaine Q.*

---

26. *Of*] because of.

great ones] I do not know why Marlowe implies that Phalaris was brought down by the 'great ones'; probably the most widely known account of his downfall, in Cicero's *De Officiis,* Book II, asserts that he perished in a general uprising of the people of Agrigentum.

petty wights] common people of no importance. Q's 'wites' is ambiguous, but 'wights', often used contemptuously at the time (see *O.E.D., sb.* 2), fits the context better than 'wits'. Andrea, *op. cit.,* pp. 227 ff., argues that the 'petty wights' are Marlowe's personal literary enemies, but I find this quite unconvincing. In *The Prince,* ch. 9, Machiavelli discussed whether a legitimate ruler should rely most on the great men (the 'grandi') or the people. His arguments are complicated and not easily summarised; 'Machevil', however, brutally asserts that with a strong citadel Phalaris could have protected himself from all his subjects.

27.] 'It is better to be envied than pitied' is proverbial (Tilley, E 177). *Cf.* Seneca's *Hercules Furens,* l. 353, 'ars prima regni est posse invidiam pati' ('the first art of ruling is to be able to endure envy'). Many political writers, including Machiavelli (*The Prince,* ch. 17), discuss whether a ruler should make himself feared or loved, but this is not quite the same point. See also I.i.113–14.

28. *whither . . . bound*] i.e. 'Where am I going?'; 'Machevil' has let his tongue run away with him.

29. *lecture*] apparently used in *O.E.D.*'s sense 6, 'an admonitory speech, esp. one delivered by way of reproof or correction'; but obviously ironical, since he has been giving lessons in villainy.

Britany] Britain: a form widely used in Elizabethan English. *Cf. Edward II,* II.ii.42, 'Unto the proudest peer of Britainy'.

32.] possibly influenced by Gentillet, who lays more stress on avarice as an attribute of Machiavelli's followers than any other opponent of him.

33. *grace*] show favour to.

34. *entertained*] received, accepted.

Because he favours me.   [*Exit.*]   35

[I.i]

> *Enter* BARABAS *in his counting-house,*
> *with heaps of gold before him.*

Bar. So that of thus much that return was made:
  And of the third part of the Persian ships,
  There was the venture summed and satisfied.
  As for those Samnites, and the men of Uz,
  That bought my Spanish oils and wines of Greece,   5
  Here have I pursed their paltry silverlings.
  Fie, what a trouble 'tis to count this trash!

35. *Exit.*] *Broughton.*

I.i] *Scene-divisions throughout the play added by Broughton; not in Q.*   4.
Samnites] *Broughton; Samintes Q; Sabans Bullen; Samarites conj.*
Koeppel; Samiotes conj. Brennan; Scaenites conj. Seaton.   6. silverlings]
conj. Steevens; siluerbings Q.

---

35. *favours*] Most editors gloss this as 'resembles' (*O.E.D., v.* 8). But
the more probable meaning is 'takes my part, is on my side' (*O.E.D., v.* 4).

I.i.0.1. Barabas] The murderer (Mark, xv.7, Luke, xxiii.19) and robber
(John, xviii.40) released to the Jews by Pilate in place of Christ. Hunter
shows, pp. 213–14, that in biblical glosses and patristic tradition Barabas
was seen as a type of Antichrist.

1 ff.] For the staging of this scene see Appendix C.

3. *summed and satisfied*] reckoned up and paid off.

4. *Samnites*] Q's 'Samintes' appears to be meaningless (unless it was
invented by Marlowe himself), and I have chosen the simplest emendation among several conjectures. Bullen objected that there was no connection between the Samnites (a central Italian tribe conquered by the
Romans, after a long struggle, in 295 B.C.) and the men of Uz (Job i.1),
and it would be preferable for the line to be consistently biblical, but no
conjecture made so far is fully convincing. The Sabans, or inhabitants of
Sheba, were wealthy, not poor, and I can find no evidence that the form
'Samarites' ever existed; all early translations into English of the New
Testament consistently describe the inhabitants of Samaria as 'Samari-
tans'. Miss Seaton's conjecture, adopted by some recent editors, can be
found in *O.E.D.*, which glosses 'scenite' as 'a member of a nomad tribe
dwelling in tents', but it seems too learned and specialised for the context.

6. *silverlings*] 'Silverling' is used in early 16th c. translations of the
Bible as an equivalent for the shekel, a Jewish coin.

Well fare the Arabians, who so richly pay
The things they traffic for with wedge of gold,
Whereof a man may easily in a day   10
Tell that which may maintain him all his life.
The needy groom that never fingered groat
Would make a miracle of thus much coin:
But he whose steel-barred coffers are crammed full,
And all his lifetime hath been tired,   15
Wearing his fingers' ends with telling it,
Would in his age be loath to labour so,
And for a pound to sweat himself to death.
Give me the merchants of the Indian mines,
That trade in metal of the purest mould;   20
The wealthy Moor, that in the eastern rocks
Without control can pick his riches up,
And in his house heap pearl like pebble-stones;
Receive them free, and sell them by the weight,
Bags of fiery opals, sapphires, amethysts,   25
Jacinths, hard topaz, grass-green emeralds,
Beauteous rubies, sparkling diamonds,

16. Wearing] *Reed;* Wearying *Q.*

---

8. *Well fare*] a widely used optative phrase ('May they prosper', 'Good
luck to them!'); *cf.* v.i.61. It could also be read as a simple inversion ('the
Arabians fare well, thrive'), but this gives a weaker sense.

9. *traffic*] carry on trade.

11. *Tell*] reckon up.

12. *groat*] See IV.ii.121 n.

13.] 'Would think it miraculous to see so much money gathered together'.

16. *Wearing*] Q's 'Wearying' is tautologous after 'tired' in the previous
line, which probably gave rise to a compositorial misreading. One can
hardly weary the fingers' *ends*, and Marlowe is clearly thinking of someone who rubs away the skin of his fingertips through continually counting
small change.

19. *Indian mines*] Bennett compares *1 Tamburlaine*, II.v.41, 'Then will
we march to all those Indian mines'. Miss Seaton, *R.E.S.*, v (1929), 397,
gives a background for the next dozen lines in contemporary books of
travel and geography. The 'eastern rocks' of l. 21 are probably the Arabian
desert, parts of which were thought to be fabulously rich in precious
stones.

22. *Without control*] freely, without restraint.

25 ff.] See Introduction, p. 9.

And seldseen costly stones of so great price
As one of them indifferently rated,
And of a carat of this quantity,　　　　　　　　30
May serve in peril of calamity
To ransom great kings from captivity.
This is the ware wherein consists my wealth:
And thus, methinks, should men of judgement frame
Their means of traffic from the vulgar trade,　　35
And as their wealth increaseth, so enclose
Infinite riches in a little room.
But now how stands the wind?
Into what corner peers my halcyon's bill?

---

28. *seldseen*] seldom seen, rare.

29. *As*] That.
indifferently rated] valued impartially. *Cf.* I.ii.187.

30. *carat*] 'A measure of weight used for diamonds and other precious stones, originally $\frac{1}{144}$ of an ounce . . . but now equal to about $\frac{1}{150}$ of an ounce troy' (*O.E.D.*).

32.] 'Worth a king's ransom' is a stock comparison; *cf.* John Heywood's *Witty and Witless*, '. . . a thing / Of price to pay the ransom of a king' (*Dramatic Writings*, ed. Farmer, 1905, p. 194). See also *Faustus*, vi. 163–4, and Whiting, K 47.

33. *ware wherein*] See Introduction, p. 34, and *cf.* l. 118 below and I.ii.254–5 and 316, II.i.29, and III.iii.25.

34. *frame*] arrange.

35. *from*] in a different way from.

37.] Hunter argues, pp. 221–5, that this line parodies the traditional imagery, of patristic origin, used to describe Christ in the womb of the Virgin. Tilley, however, quotes the line to illustrate the proverb, 'Great worth is often found in things of small appearance (in little boxes)' (W 921). This is often applied to precious ointments in small boxes; an early example, not in Tilley, is l. 591 of Heywood's *The Four PP* (?1544), 'Here lieth much riches in little space'. With other writers the idea seems to be purely financial; *cf.* Stephen Gosson, Dedication to *The School of Abuse*, 'Little Chestes may holde greate Treasure' (London, 1579), [A] 4. Whatever its origin, Marlowe expressed the concept so memorably that later poets imitated this line (e.g. Chapman, *Ovid's Banquet of Sense*, stanza 49 (London, 1595), C3*v*).

39. *halcyon's bill*] Sir Thomas Browne disproved by experiment the ancient superstition that if hung up the body of a halcyon or kingfisher would act as a weather-vane and turn in the direction of the wind (*Vulgar Errors*, Book III, ch. 10).

Ha, to the east ? Yes: see how stands the vanes!   40
East and by south; why then, I hope my ships
I sent for Egypt and the bordering isles
Are gotten up by Nilus' winding banks:
Mine argosy from Alexandria,
Loaden with spice and silks, now under sail,   45
Are smoothly gliding down by Candy shore
To Malta, through our Mediterranean sea.

Enter a Merchant.

But who comes here ? How now ?
Merch. Barabas, thy ships are safe,
Riding in Malta road; and all the merchants   50
With all their merchandise are safe arrived,
And have sent me to know whether yourself
Will come and custom them.
Bar. The ships are safe, thou say'st, and richly fraught ?
Merch. They are.
Bar.   Why then, go bid them come ashore   55
And bring with them their bills of entry;
I hope our credit in the custom-house
Will serve as well as I were present there.
Go send 'em threescore camels, thirty mules,
And twenty waggons to bring up the ware.   60
But art thou master in a ship of mine,

40. stands] *Q;* stand *Reed.*   46. Are] *Q;* Is *Shone.*   47.1. *Enter a*
Merchant.] *This ed.; after l. 48 in Q.*   50. road] *Reed;* Rhode *Q (and at
ll. 86, 146).*   51. all their] *conj. Maxwell;* other *Q.*

---

44. *argosy*] a very large merchant ship. The syntax of ll. 41–7 is slightly
confused; presumably 'Mine argosy' depends on 'I hope' in l. 41 and
governs 'Are' in l. 46, though *O.E.D.* gives no example of 'argosy' used
with a plural meaning.

46. *Candy*] Crete.

50. *road*] roadstead, or sheltered piece of water where ships can lie at
anchor. *Cf. Dido,* v.i.89.

51. *all their*] Maxwell suggests that 'al ther' in the manuscript was misread by the compositor as 'other'.

53. *custom*] pay the customs duties.

54. *fraught*] laden with goods.

58. *as I*] as if I.

    And is thy credit not enough for that?
Merch. The very custom barely comes to more
    Than many merchants of the town are worth,
    And therefore far exceeds my credit, sir.   65
Bar. Go tell 'em the Jew of Malta sent thee, man;
    Tush, who amongst 'em knows not Barabas?
Merch. I go.
Bar. So then, there's somewhat come.
    Sirrah, which of my ships art thou master of?   70
Merch. Of the Speranza, sir.
Bar.   And saw'st thou not
    Mine argosy at Alexandria?
    Thou couldst not come from Egypt, or by Caire,
    But at the entry there into the sea,
    Where Nilus pays his tribute to the main,   75
    Thou needs must sail by Alexandria.
Merch. I neither saw them, nor enquired of them.
    But this we heard some of our seamen say,
    They wondered how you durst with so much wealth
    Trust such a crazèd vessel, and so far.   80
Bar. Tush, they are wise, I know her and her strength.
    But go, go thou thy ways, discharge thy ship,
    And bid my factor bring his loading in.   [*Exit* Merchant.]
    And yet I wonder at this argosy.

Enter a Second Merchant.

70. master of] *Reed;* Master off *Q.*   82. But] *Shone;* By *Q.*   83. *Exit*
Merchant.] *Reed.*

---

  63. *The very custom barely*] even the customs duties alone.
  69. *there's somewhat come*] at least something has arrived safely.
  70. *Sirrah*] Usually in Elizabethan English this term implies an
assumption of superiority, or a certain degree of contempt, on the part of
the speaker. *Cf.* III.iii.37 n. and IV.ii.78 n.
  73. *Caire*] Cairo.
  80. *crazéd*] unsound, not seaworthy.
  81. *they are wise*] sarcastic: 'they think they know a lot about it'.
  82. *But*] Bullen suggests that Q's 'By' could mean 'goodbye'; this is
surely very unconvincing in the context.
  83. *factor*] commercial agent.
  loading] bill of lading.

Sec. Merch. Thine argosy from Alexandria,   85
    Know, Barabas, doth ride in Malta road,
    Laden with riches, and exceeding store
    Of Persian silks, of gold, and orient pearl.

Bar. How chance you came not with those other ships
    That sailed by Egypt?

Sec. Merch.   Sir, we saw 'em not.   90

Bar. Belike they coasted round by Candy shore
    About their oils, or other businesses.
    But 'twas ill done of you to come so far
    Without the aid or conduct of their ships.

Sec. Merch. Sir, we were wafted by a Spanish fleet   95
    That never left us till within a league,
    That had the galleys of the Turk in chase.

Bar. O, they were going up to Sicily. Well, go,
    And bid the merchants and my men dispatch,
    And come ashore, and see the fraught discharged.   100

Sec. Merch. I go.   *Exit.*

Bar. Thus trolls our fortune in by land and sea,
    And thus are we on every side enriched;
    These are the blessings promised to the Jews,
    And herein was old Abram's happiness.   105
    What more may heaven do for earthly men

106. men] *Shone;* man *Q.*

---

88. *orient*] rich, brilliant.

95. *wafted*] convoyed, escorted.

100. *fraught*] freight, cargo.

102. *trolls*] comes 'rolling in' abundantly.

fortune . . . by land and sea] Bennett compares the title of Heywood's play, *Fortune by Land and Sea* (*c.* 1608). The phrase sounds proverbial, but Tilley has nothing like it.

104–5.] a reference to the covenant made between God and Abraham in Genesis, xvii.1–22. See also Exodus, vi.1–8, and Galatians, iii.16 ('Now to Abraham and his sede were the promises made . . .'), and *cf.* II.iii.48. Hunter, pp. 216–18, shows how Christian theologians transferred God's promise from the Jews to the Christians.

106. *men*] I have adopted the reading of Shone (and also of Broughton and Oxberry) for two reasons: 1. the rest of the passage is consistently in the plural, 2. a similar crux exists in *Faustus*, i. 24, where A1 reads 'man' but A3 and B correctly read 'men', and all texts have 'them' in the next line.

Than thus to pour out plenty in their laps,
Ripping the bowels of the earth for them,
Making the sea their servant, and the winds
To drive their substance with successful blasts?   110
Who hateth me but for my happiness?
Or who is honoured now but for his wealth?
Rather had I, a Jew, be hated thus,
Than pitied in a Christian poverty.
For I can see no fruits in all their faith   115
But malice, falsehood, and excessive pride,
Which methinks fits not their profession.
Haply some hapless man hath conscience,
And for his conscience lives in beggary.

---

109. sea] *Q;* seas *Broughton.*   servant] *Shone;* seruants *Q.*   118.
Haply] *Broughton;* Happily *Q (and at l. 161).*

---

108. See Introduction, p. 21. The phraseology is fairly common; *cf.*
Spenser, *Faerie Queene,* II.vii.17. Kyd's *The Spanish Tragedy,* III.xii.71,
and Milton, *Paradise Lost,* I, 687.

109. *sea their servant*] There are three possibilities here: 1. that Q's 'sea
their seruants' is correct; 2. that both nouns should be plural; 3. that both
should be singular. I am not convinced that Q is right (although it is true
that this kind of inconsistency is common enough in the period), and have
emended 'servants' because Q has false plurals elsewhere (see I.ii.0.1 n.).

110. *substance*] wealth, carried in merchant ships.
successful] bringing success, propitious.

111. *happiness*] good fortune, prosperity.

112.] Several proverbs make the same point, though none is identical in
form; *cf.* Whiting, M 180 and 265, N 143, P 295 and 335, and R 108, and
Tilley, N 270 and P 468.

113–14. *hated . . . pitied*] See Prologue, l. 27 n.

115. *fruits . . . faith*] a common New Testament image (e.g. Matthew,
vii.16–20, John, xv.1–16, Romans, vi.21–2, and Galatians, v.22). See also
II.iii.85 n., and Kocher, pp. 124–5.

117. *profession*] professed religious faith. See Introduction, p. 29.

118. *Haply*] Perhaps.
hapless] unfortunate.

119.] possibly proverbial, though not in Tilley; in Robert Wilson's *The
Three Lords and Three Ladies of London* (1590), D4, Fraud refuses to
dwell 'with such a beggar as Conscience', and Usury comments, 'Who
cares for Conscience but dies a beggar?' The Second Murderer in *R3,*
I.iv.141–2, says of conscience that 'it beggars any man that keeps it', and
cf. also Barnabe Barnes, *The Devil's Charter* (1607), B4: 'And they that
liue puling vpon the fruits / Of honest conscience, starue on the Common'.

They say we are a scattered nation;   120
I cannot tell, but we have scambled up
More wealth by far than those that brag of faith.
There's Kirriah Jairim, the great Jew of Greece,
Obed in Bairseth, Nones in Portugal,
Myself in Malta, some in Italy,   125
Many in France, and wealthy every one:
Ay, wealthier far than any Christian.
I must confess we come not to be kings.
That's not our fault: alas, our number's few,
And crowns come either by succession,   130
Or urged by force; and nothing violent,

124. Bairseth] *Q;* Beirut *conj. Koeppel, Thayer.*

---

120. *scattered nation*] The fact that the Jews were widely dispersed
among other nations was sometimes taken as proof that they had angered
God and suffered the curse of Deuteronomy, xxviii.25.

121. *scambled up*] This is quoted by *O.E.D.* to illustrate sense 6 of
'scamble', *v.*, 'to collect in a haphazard or irregular manner, to "scrape"
together, up', but it surely has some flavour of sense 1 also, 'to struggle in
an indecorous and rapacious manner in order to obtain something'.

123. *Kirriah Jairim*] As Koeppel suggests, this may be a misunder-
standing of I Chronicles, ii.50–3, where the city of Kiriath-iearim (Geneva
version) is mentioned in such a way that it looks like a personal name.

124. *Obed*] There were several biblical figures with this name; the most
famous was the son of Boaz and father of Jesse (Ruth, iv. 17–22), also
mentioned in I Chronicles, ii.12.

Bairseth] not identified; possibly a distortion of a biblical name such as
Baaseiah (I Chronicles, vi.40).

Nones] The Nunez family were Portuguese Maranos (see Introduction,
p. 7). Hector Nunez (1521–91) was a physician and merchant, head of
the Marano community in London, who provided the Elizabethan government with military and diplomatic information from his agents on the
continent. See Lucien Wolf, 'Jews in Elizabethan England', *T.J.H.S.E.*,
XI (1924–7), 8–9.

130–1. *crowns . . . force*] possibly a faint echo of the early chapters of
The Prince, where Machiavelli distinguishes between hereditary princi-
palities and those acquired by force.

131–2. *nothing . . . permanent*] a very common proverb (Whiting, T 195,
Tilley, N 321), deriving ultimately from Aristotle's *Physics*. It is sometimes used by political writers in the same way as Marlowe, to support the
idea that tyrannical kingdoms established by force cannot be long-lasting;
see Gentillet, pp. 13, 200, and 316, and Case, *Sphaera Civitatis*, p. 491.

Oft have I heard tell, can be permanent.
Give us a peaceful rule, make Christians kings,
That thirst so much for principality.
I have no charge, nor many children,   135
But one sole daughter, whom I hold as dear
As Agamemnon did his Iphigen:
And all I have is hers. But who comes here?

Enter three Jews.

First Jew. Tush, tell not me 'twas done of policy.
Sec. Jew. Come therefore, let us go to Barabas,   140
For he can counsel best in these affairs;
And here he comes.
Bar.   Why, how now, countrymen?
Why flock you thus to me in multitudes?
What accident's betided to the Jews?
First Jew. A fleet of warlike galleys, Barabas,   145
Are come from Turkey, and lie in our road;
And they this day sit in the council-house
To entertain them and their embassy.
Bar. Why, let 'em come, so they come not to war;
Or let 'em war, so we be conquerors.   150
Nay, let 'em combat, conquer, and kill all,   Aside.
So they spare me, my daughter, and my wealth.
First Jew. Were it for confirmation of a league,
They would not come in warlike manner thus.

151–2.] *Italic not in* Q.

---

134. *principality*] supreme authority; Bennett compares *1 Tamburlaine*,
II.vii.12, 'The thirst of reign and sweetness of a crown . . .'.
135. *charge*] financial burden.
137.] a dramatic irony, since Agamemnon, the leader of the Greek army
in the Trojan war, was forced to appease the goddess Artemis by sacrific-
ing his daughter Iphigeneia to her.
138. *all . . . hers*] perhaps biblical; *cf.* Luke, xv.31, 'Sonne, thow art euer
with me, and all that I haue, is thine'.
147. *they*] the Knights of Malta.
148. *embassy*] the ambassador of the Turks and his retinue.

Sec. Jew. I fear their coming will afflict us all.   155
Bar. Fond men, what dream you of their multitudes?
    What need they treat of peace that are in league?
    The Turks and those of Malta are in league.
    Tut, tut, there is some other matter in 't.
First Jew. Why, Barabas, they come for peace or war.   160
Bar. Haply for neither, but to pass along
    Towards Venice by the Adriatic sea,
    With whom they have attempted many times,
    But never could effect their stratagem.
Third Jew. And very wisely said; it may be so.   165
Sec. Jew. But there's a meeting in the senate-house,
    And all the Jews in Malta must be there.
Bar. Hum; all the Jews in Malta must be there?
    Ay, like enough; why then, let every man
    Provide him, and be there for fashion sake.   170
    If anything shall there concern our state,
    Assure yourselves I'll look—*unto myself*.   *Aside.*
First Jew. I know you will. Well, brethren, let us go.
Sec. Jew. Let's take our leaves; farewell, good Barabas.
Bar. Do so; farewell, Zaareth, farewell Temainte.   175
                                [*Exeunt* Jews.]

---

168. Hum] *Reed;* Vmh *Q.*   172. look—*unto myself*] *Dyce (but no italic);*
looke vnto my self *Q;* look unto myself ('*Aside.*' omitted) *Scott;* look unto't
myself *conj. Collier;* look unto—myself *Broughton.*   175. Do so.] *Q;*
omitted *Shone.*   175.1. *Exeunt* Jews.] *Reed.*

---

  156. *Fond*] foolish, credulous.
  163. *With*] against.
  attempted] attacked, assaulted.
  164. *effect*] bring about, accomplish.
  170. *Provide him*] prepare, get himself ready.
  for fashion sake] as a mere formality.
  172.] Q does not indicate how much is aside, and editors have treated
the line in different ways. Clearly Barabas intends the Jews to think that
he means something like 'I'll look into it, deal with it', but at the last
minute twists his meaning to 'I'll look after my own interests'.
  175. *Do so*] Dyce justified the omission of this phrase on the grounds
that it was a stage direction telling the three Jews to go out which had
crept into the text. But this would be a very abnormal usage, and as the

And, Barabas, now search this secret out,
Summon thy senses, call thy wits together:
These silly men mistake the matter clean.
Long to the Turk did Malta contribute,
Which tribute, all in policy, I fear,   180
The Turks have let increase to such a sum
As all the wealth of Malta cannot pay,
And now by that advantage thinks, belike,
To seize upon the town; ay, that he seeks.
Howe'er the world go, I'll make sure for one,   185
And seek in time to intercept the worst,
Warily guarding that which I ha' got.
'Ego mihimet sum semper proximus.'
Why, let 'em enter, let 'em take the town!   [*Exit.*]

---

181. Turks have] *Q;* Turk hath *Broughton;* Turk has *Robinson.*   188.
proximus] *Reed; proximas Q.*   189. *Exit.*] *Reed.*

---

phrase occurs twice later in the play (II.iii.347 and V.ii.109) we should let it
stand. *Cf.* also Kyd's *The Spanish Tragedy*, II.iii.24.
Zaareth . . . Temainte] Of Job's three comforters (Job, ii.11), Eliphaz was
a Temanite, and 'Zaareth' may echo Zophar the Naamathite.

177.] Perhaps imitated by Barnabe Barnes in *The Devil's Charter*, 1607,
F4: 'Now *Caesar* Muster vp thy wittes together, / Summon thy Sences
and aduance thy selfe' (and *cf.* also 'call thy wits together', E4*v*).
178. *silly*] simple, foolish.
clean] completely.
181. *Turks have*] Broughton's emendation is plausible, as the singular
is used in ll. 179 and 183–4.
185.] possibly proverbial; see Tilley, O 50 ('It is good to save one'),
citing *Jacob and Esau* (1568), C4*v*, 'I tolde you at the fyrst, I woulde
prouide for one', and Tilley, M 112 ('Every man for himself'), citing *2H6*,
IV.viii.33, 'For me, I will make shift for one'.
188. *Ego . . . proximus*] 'I am always nearest to myself', i.e. 'I always
put my own interests first'; ultimately from Terence's *Andria*, IV.i.12,
'Proximus sum egomet mihi'. Bennett sees it as an inappropriate display
of classical learning on Marlowe's part, but in slightly varying forms the
tag is common in English and Latin as a proverbial expression of selfishness
(Tilley, N 57).

[I.ii]

Enter [FERNEZE,] *Governor of Malta*, Knights[, *and*
Officers,] *met by* Bashaws *of the Turk*, [*and*] CALYMATH.

Fern. Now, bashaws, what demand you at our hands ?
First Bas. Know, Knights of Malta, that we came from
    Rhodes,
    From Cyprus, Candy, and those other isles
    That lie betwixt the Mediterranean seas—
Fern. What's Cyprus, Candy, and those other isles   5
    To us, or Malta ? What at our hands demand ye ?
Calym. The ten years' tribute that remains unpaid.
Fern. Alas, my lord, the sum is over-great;

[I.ii] 0.1. *Ferneze*] *Dyce.*   *Governor*] *Shone; Gouernors Q.   and*
Officers] *Penley.*   0.2. Bashaws] *Reed; Bassoes Q (and at l.1).*   2. *First*
Bas.] *Dyce; Bass. Q (and at l. 22).*   came] *Q;* come *Cunningham.*   4.
seas—] *Scott;* seas. *Q.*   6. us, or] *Q;* us of *conj. W. Wagner.*

1.ii.0.1. Ferneze] The Grand Master of the Knights during the siege of
Malta was Jean de la Valette. Marlowe's name, as Bennett suggests, may be
a version of the Italian family name 'Farnese'; one of its best-known members, Alessandro Farnese, Prince of Parma, is mentioned in *Faustus*, i.92.

Governor] Q has the plural form 'Gouernors' here and at five other
points in this scene. Bennett suggests that Marlowe began the play with
the assumption that Malta had a ruling body of 'Governors', one of whom
acted as spokesman. But there are, I think, three reasons for emending:
1. a very superficial study of history would have taught Marlowe that the
Knights of Malta had a single governor (the Grand Master of the Order);
2. there may be false plurals elsewhere in the play (see notes on III.v.1,
IV.i.135 and V.v.85), and some of Shakespeare's plays have a clearly
incorrect 's' at the end of a word (see Abbott, § 338); 3. from II.ii onwards
there is clearly a single Governor who is leader of the Knights, and if we
are going to make Q consistent we should adopt Marlowe's second
thoughts rather than his first.

0.2. Bashaws] Q has 'Bassoes' here and in l. 1, but 'Bashaws' elsewhere.
This in itself is hardly enough to prove revision; both forms are common
in the period, and Marlowe may simply have been uncertain which to use.
I have adopted what is presumably the later form, as it may represent a
change of mind on Marlowe's part. Both words are equivalents of the
Turkish 'pasha', a senior military officer.

4. *seas*—] The Bashaw's pompous allusions to Rhodes and Cyprus, both
conquered by the Turks in the 16th c., may irritate Ferneze, who interrupts his speech.

I hope your highness will consider us.

Calym. I wish, grave governor, 'twere in my power   10
    To favour you, but 'tis my father's cause,
    Wherein I may not, nay I dare not, dally.

Fern. Then give us leave, great Selim-Calymath.

Calym. Stand all aside, and let the knights determine,
    And send to keep our galleys under sail,   15
    For happily we shall not tarry here.
    Now, governor, how are you resolved?

Fern. Thus: since your hard conditions are such
    That you will needs have ten years' tribute past,
    We may have time to make collection   20
    Amongst the inhabitants of Malta for 't.

First Bas. That's more than is in our commission.

Calym. What, Callapine, a little courtesy!
    Let's know their time, perhaps it is not long;
    And 'tis more kingly to obtain by peace   25
    Than to enforce conditions by constraint.
    What respite ask you, governor?

Fern.   But a month.

Calym. We grant a month, but see you keep your promise.
    Now launch our galleys back again to sea,

---

10. governor] *Shone;* Gouernours *Q* (*and at ll. 17, 27, 32, and 129*).
17. how] *Q;* say, how *Penley.*

---

9. *consider*] be considerate towards.

10. *grave*] a common form of respectful address; *cf.* ll. 129 and 313 below, III.iii.55, and V.iv.10.

13. *give us leave*] 'A polite request for privacy for consultation' (Bennett). *Cf.* l. 38 below, and J. Dover Wilson's note to II.ii.170 of his edition of *Hamlet.*

Selim-Calymath] During the siege of Malta Turkey was ruled by the emperor Soliman the Magnificent. His son Selim ruled from 1566 to 1574.

16. *happily*] with good luck, if things go well.

17. *how . . . resolved?*] What have you decided?

22. *commission*] instructions, authority as ambassadors.

23. *Callapine*] possibly borrowed, as Bennett suggests, from *2 Tamburlaine*, where it occurs as the historically accurate name of Bajazeth's son.

25–6.] *Cf.* such proverbs as 'It is better to obtain by love than force' (Tilley, L 487).

Where we'll attend the respite you have ta'en,   30
And for the money send our messenger.
Farewell, great governor, and brave knights of Malta.
Fern. And all good fortune wait on Calymath.

Exeunt [CALYMATH *and* Bashaws].

Go one and call those Jews of Malta hither:
Were they not summoned to appear to-day?   35
First Officer. They were, my lord, and here they come.

Enter BARABAS *and three* Jews.

First Knight. Have you determined what to say to them?
Fern. Yes: give me leave; and Hebrews, now come near.
From the Emperor of Turkey is arrived
Great Selim-Calymath, his highness' son,   40
To levy of us ten years' tribute past;
Now then, here know that it concerneth us—
Bar. Then, good my lord, to keep your quiet still,
Your lordship shall do well to let them have it.
Fern. Soft, Barabas, there's more longs to 't than so.   45
To what this ten years' tribute will amount,
That we have cast, but cannot compass it
By reason of the wars, that robbed our store;
And therefore are we to request your aid.
Bar. Alas, my lord, we are no soldiers;   50
And what's our aid against so great a prince?
First Knight. Tut, Jew, we know thou art no soldier;
Thou art a merchant, and a moneyed man,
And 'tis thy money, Barabas, we seek.
Bar. How, my lord, my money?

33.1. *Exeunt*] *Dyce; after l. 32 in Q.*   *Calymath and* Bashaws] *Broughton.*
36. *First Officer*] *Dyce; Officer Q.*   42. us—] *Cunningham; us: Q.*

---

30. *attend*] await.
43. *quiet*] peaceful state of affairs.
still] always, continually.
45. *longs*] belongs, pertains; 'there's more to it than that'.
47. *cast*] calculated.
compass] achieve, accomplish.

Fern.   Thine and the rest.   55
    For to be short, amongst you 't must be had.
First Jew. Alas, my lord, the most of us are poor!
Fern. Then let the rich increase your portions.
Bar. Are strangers with your tribute to be taxed?
Sec. Knight. Have strangers leave with us to get their wealth?   60
    Then let them with us contribute.
Bar. How, equally?
Fern.   No, Jew, like infidels.
    For through our sufferance of your hateful lives,
    Who stand accursèd in the sight of heaven,
    These taxes and afflictions are befallen,   65
    And therefore thus we are determinèd:
    Read there the articles of our decrees.
Officer (reads). 'First, the tribute-money of the Turks shall
    all be levied amongst the Jews, and each of them to pay
    one-half of his estate.'   70
Bar. How, half his estate? *I hope you mean not mine.*   [*Aside.*]
Fern. Read on.
Officer (reads). 'Secondly, he that denies to pay shall straight
    become a Christian.'
Bar. How, a Christian? *Hum, what's here to do?*   [*Aside.*]   75
Officer (reads). 'Lastly, he that denies this shall absolutely
    lose all he has.'
All Three Jews. O, my lord, we will give half!

---

57. *First Jew*] Broughton; *Iew* Q; *Barabas* Reed.   68. *Officer (reads).*]
Dyce; Reader. Q (*which has* 'Read.' *at ll. 73 and 76.*)   71.] *Thayer; aside*
not in Q.   75.] *Thayer; aside not in* Q.

---

58. *increase your portions*] give money to the poor people to bring their
contributions to the required size.
    59. *strangers*] aliens, foreigners.
    64.] because of their responsibility for the death of Christ; see note on
l. 108 below.
    66. *are determinèd*] have concluded, decided.
    73. *denies*] refuses.
straight] immediately.
    75. what's . . . do?] What shall I do about this?

Bar. O earth-mettled villains, and no Hebrews born!
    And will you basely thus submit yourselves   80
    To leave your goods to their arbitrament?
Fern. Why, Barabas, wilt thou be christened?
Bar. No, governor, I will be no convertite.
Fern. Then pay thy half.
Bar. Why, know you what you did by this device?   85
    Half of my substance is a city's wealth.
    Governor, it was not got so easily;
    Nor will I part so slightly therewithal.
Fern. Sir, half is the penalty of our decree;
    Either pay that, or we will seize on all.   90
Bar. Corpo di Dio! Stay, you shall have half;
    Let me be used but as my brethren are.
Fern. No, Jew, thou hast denied the articles,
    And now it cannot be recalled.
              [*Exeunt* Officers, *on a sign from* FERNEZE.]
Bar. Will you then steal my goods?   95
    Is theft the ground of your religion?
Fern. No, Jew, we take particularly thine
    To save the ruin of a multitude:
    And better one want for a common good
    Than many perish for a private man.   100

---

85. did] *Q; do Shone.*   91. Dio] *Collier; deo Q.*   94.1. *Exeunt . . . Ferneze.*] *Dyce; after l. 90 in Bennett.*

---

79. *earth-mettled*] having an earthy nature or temperament; dull, phlegmatic (not in *O.E.D.*).

81. *arbitrament*] decision, control.

85. *did*] Craik suggests that this may be a misreading of 'doe' (= 'do'), and that the line echoes Luke, xxiii.34 ('Father, forgiue them: for they knowe not what thei do').

88. *slightly*] easily, readily.

91. *Corpo di Dio!*] By God's body! As Bennett comments, we should not expect a Jew to use this oath, but possibly Barabas intends it sarcastically.

96. *ground*] basis, fundamental principle.

99. *want*] lack something, go without.

99–100.] Bennett and Hunter (p. 236) see this as an echo of John, xi.50, 'it is expedient for vs, that one man dye for the people, and that the whole nacion perish not'. We should note, however, that the idea became

Yet, Barabas, we will not banish thee,
But here in Malta, where thou got'st thy wealth,
Live still; and if thou canst, get more.
Bar. Christians, what, or how can I multiply?
    Of naught is nothing made.   105
First Knight. From naught at first thou camest to little
        wealth,
    From little unto more, from more to most;
    If your first curse fall heavy on thy head,
    And make thee poor and scorned of all the world,
    'Tis not our fault, but thy inherent sin.   110
Bar. What! Bring you scripture to confirm your wrongs?
    Preach me not out of my possessions.
    Some Jews are wicked, *as all Christians are*:   [*Aside.*]
    But say the tribe that I descended of
    Were all in general cast away for sin,   115
    Shall I be tried by their transgression?
    The man that dealeth righteously shall live:

113.] *This ed.; aside not in Q.*

---

proverbial ('Better one die than all', Tilley, O 42), and Case, *Sphaera
Civitatis*, p. 6, argues without apparent theological overtones that sometimes a single innocent man must perish for the common good.

  105.] a very common proverb (Whiting, N 151, and Tilley, N 285).
  108. *your first curse*] alluding to Matthew, xxvii.25, where the Jews
accepted responsibility for the death of Christ: 'Then answered all the
people, and said, His blood be on vs, and on our children'. Geneva adds
the gloss 'and as they wished, so this cursse taketh place to this day'.
Brooke ii argues that 'your' refers to the Jews in general, 'thy' to Barabas
himself. *Cf.* also the quotations from Philip de Mornay and Fynes
Moryson in Kocher, p. 128, and Hunter, p. 216.
  111.] Possibly alluding to the proverb, 'The Devil can cite scripture for
his purpose' (Tilley, D 230).
  113. as . . . are] I have marked this as an aside because I cannot believe
that Barabas could risk being openly as rude as this.
  115. *cast away*] rejected by God, damned.
  117.] Bennett compares Proverbs, x.2, 'The treasures of wickednes
profite nothing: but righteousnes deliuereth from death', and xii.28, 'Life
is in the way of righteousnes, and in that pathway there is no death'.
Hunter argues, pp. 237–8, that a Christian audience, believing that
righteousness could come only through Christ, would necessarily reject
Barabas's self-defence, as Ferneze does.

And which of you can charge me otherwise?
Fern. Out, wretched Barabas!
    Shamest thou not thus to justify thyself,   120
    As if we knew not thy profession?
    If thou rely upon thy righteousness,
    Be patient, and thy riches will increase.
    Excess of wealth is cause of covetousness:
    And covetousness, O, 'tis a monstrous sin!   125
Bar. Ay; but theft is worse: tush, take not from me then,
    For that is theft; and if you rob me thus,
    I must be forced to steal, and compass more.
First Knight. Grave governor, list not to his exclaims:
    Convert his mansion to a nunnery;   130
    His house will harbour many holy nuns.

Enter Officers.

Fern. It shall be so. Now, officers, have you done?
First Officer. Ay, my lord, we have seized upon the goods
    And wares of Barabas, which being valued
    Amount to more than all the wealth in Malta,   135
    And of the other we have seizèd half;
    Then we'll take order for the residue.

131.1. *Enter* Officers.] *Broughton; in margin opposite l. 130 in Q.*   133.
First Officer.] *Dyce; Offic. Q.*   137. Then] *Q; Gov. Then Robinson.*

118.] possibly echoing the phraseology of Christ's rebuke to the Jews, John, viii.46, 'Which of you can rebuke me of sinne?'
   charge] accuse.
   119. *Out*] an exclamation expressing abhorrence or reproach.
   121. *profession*] The main allusion is to Barabas's profession of faith as a Jew, but there may also be a hint that Ferneze despises Barabas's activities as merchant and usurer.
   128. *compass*] *Cf.* l. 47 n. above; possibly used here with an added implication of *O.E.D.*'s sense 2, 'machinate, contrive an evil purpose'.
   129. *exclaims*] exclamations, outcries.
   136. *the other*] the property of the other Jews.
   137.] The meaning of this line is obscure, but it is not automatically clarified by being re-attributed to Ferneze. *O.E.D.* gives 'for the residue' as a stock phrase meaning 'for the rest, as to the remainder' (*s.v.* 'residue', 1d), so it can hardly refer to the half which has been confiscated. Possibly

Bar. Well then, my lord, say, are you satisfied ?
    You have my goods, my money, and my wealth,
    My ships, my store, and all that I enjoyed,   140
    And having all, you can request no more—
    Unless your unrelenting flinty hearts
    Suppress all pity in your stony breasts,
    And now shall move you to bereave my life.
Fern. No, Barabas, to stain our hands with blood   145
    Is far from us and our profession.
Bar. Why, I esteem the injury far less,
    To take the lives of miserable men,
    Than be the causers of their misery.
    You have my wealth, the labour of my life,   150
    The comfort of mine age, my children's hope;
    And therefore ne'er distinguish of the wrong.
Fern. Content thee, Barabas, thou hast naught but right.
Bar. Your extreme right does me exceeding wrong:
    But take it to you i' the devil's name !   155
Fern. Come, let us in, and gather of these goods
    The money for this tribute of the Turk.

---

the officers have seized all the Jewish property, have taken half of the
goods belonging to Jews other than Barabas, and must now see about
giving back the remainder to its various owners.
    take order] make arrangements.

    145–6.] Hunter, p. 236, sees here an echo of Pilate's washing his hands,
Matthew, xxvii.24.
    146. *our profession*] a complacent echo of l. 121.
    147–9.] possibly inspired by ch. 17 of *The Prince*, where Machiavelli
argues that the worst offence a prince can commit is to confiscate his
subjects' property, since 'men sooner forget the death of their father than
the loss of their patrimony'.
    152. *distinguish of the wrong*] make subtle distinctions intended to mini-
mise the wrong you have done me.
    153.] *Cf.* Kyd's *The Spanish Tragedy*, I.ii.173, 'Content thee Marshal,
thou shalt have no wrong'.
    154.] proverbial (Tilley, R 122), deriving from a Latin proverb common
in Cicero's time (*De Officiis*, I.x.33), 'summum ius, summa iniuria', which
might be paraphrased as 'the more rigorously law is applied the greater the
injustice done'.

First Knight. 'Tis necessary that be looked unto:
    For if we break our day, we break the league,
    And that will prove but simple policy.   160
                    Exeunt [FERNEZE, Knights, *and* Officers].
Bar. Ay, policy, that's their profession,
    And not simplicity as they suggest.   [*Kneels.*]
    The plagues of Egypt, and the curse of heaven,
    Earth's barrenness, and all men's hatred,
    Inflict upon them, thou great Primus Motor!   165
    And here upon my knees, striking the earth,
    I ban their souls to everlasting pains
    And extreme tortures of the fiery deep
    That thus have dealt with me in my distress.
First Jew. O yet be patient, gentle Barabas.   170
Bar. O silly brethren, born to see this day!
    Why stand you thus unmoved with my laments?
    Why weep you not to think upon my wrongs?
    Why pine not I, and die in this distrcss?
First Jew. Why, Barabas, as hardly can we brook   175
    The cruel handling of ourselves in this:
    Thou seest they have taken half our goods.

160.1. *Ferneze . . .* Officers] *Broughton.*   162. *Kneels.*] *Kirschbaum*
(*opposite l. 166*).   165. Primus] *Reed; Primas Q.*

---

160. *simple policy*] a foolish trick.
161. *policy*] trickery, duplicity.
162. *simplicity*] honesty, lack of guile, 'the simplicitie that is in Christ'
(II Corinthians, xi.3). Barabas exposes the Christians' hypocrisy, though
he does not particularly admire 'simplicity' (see l. 216 below).
    Kneels] Barabas clearly kneels down (see l. 166), and presumably does
so before making the prayer in ll. 163–5. 'Why stand you thus' at l. 172
seems to be a reproach to the other Jews for not doing the same.
163. *The plagues of Egypt*] See Exodus, vii–xii.
165. *Primus Motor*] Cf. *1 Tamburlaine*, IV.ii.8–9, 'The chiefest God, first
mover of that sphere / Enchas'd with thousands ever shining lamps . . .'. In
her edition Una Ellis-Fermor comments, 'This is the Aristotelian conception of God as the "primus motor" (The "First Unmoved Mover" of
Metaphysics, XII.6 ff.), the power which turned the "primum mobile", that
in its motion gave movement to the other spheres of the Ptolemaic system'.
167. *ban*] curse.
175–6.] 'We find it as difficult as you to endure our harsh treatment'.

Bar. Why did you yield to their extortion?
  You were a multitude, and I but one,
  And of me only have they taken all.   180
First Jew. Yet, brother Barabas, remember Job.
Bar. What tell you me of Job? I wot his wealth
  Was written thus: he had seven thousand sheep,
  Three thousand camels, and two hundred yoke
  Of labouring oxen, and five hundred   185
  She-asses; but for every one of those,
  Had they been valued at indifferent rate,
  I had at home, and in mine argosy
  And other ships that came from Egypt last,
  As much as would have bought his beasts and him,   190
  And yet have kept enough to live upon;
  So that not he, but I, may curse the day,
  Thy fatal birthday, forlorn Barabas,
  And henceforth wish for an eternal night,
  That clouds of darkness may enclose my flesh,   195
  And hide these extreme sorrows from mine eyes:
  For only I have toiled to inherit here
  The months of vanity and loss of time,
  And painful nights have been appointed me.
Sec. Jew. Good Barabas, be patient.

---

184. two] *Q;* five *conj. Koeppel.*

182–6.] from Job, i.3: 'His substance also was seuen thousand shepe,
and thre thousand camels, and fyue hundreth yoke of oxen, and fyue
hundreth she asses'. Q's 'two' in l. 184 may be a compositorial misreading of 'five'.

187. *indifferent*] impartial.

189. *last*] probably meaning, 'lately, just recently'.

192–6.] from Job, iii.1–10: 'Afterward Iob opened his mouthe, and
cursed his day. And Iob cryed out, and said, Let the daye perish, wherein
I was borne, and the night when it was said, There is a manchilde con-
ceiued. Let that day be darkenes, let not God regarde it from aboue,
nether let the light shine vpon it, But let darkenes, & the shadowe of
death staine it: let the cloude remaine vpon it, & let them make it feareful
as a bitter day . . . Because it shut not vp the dores of my mothers wombe:
nor hid sorowe from mine eyes'.

197–9.] from Job, vii.3: 'So haue I had as an inheritance the moneths
of vanitie, and peineful nights haue bene appointed vnto me'.

Bar.   Ay, ay;   200
          Pray leave me in my patience. You that
          Were ne'er possessed of wealth are pleased with want.
          But give him liberty at least to mourn
          That in a field amidst his enemies
          Doth see his soldiers slain, himself disarmed,   205
          And knows no means of his recovery.
          Ay, let me sorrow for this sudden chance,
          'Tis in the trouble of my spirit I speak:
          Great injuries are not so soon forgot.

First Jew. Come, let us leave him in his ireful mood,   210
          Our words will but increase his ecstasy.

Sec. Jew. On, then: but trust me 'tis a misery
          To see a man in such affliction.
          Farewell, Barabas.   *Exeunt* [*three* Jews].

Bar. Ay, fare you well.   [*Rises.*] 215
          See the simplicity of these base slaves,
          Who for the villains have no wit themselves
          Think me to be a senseless lump of clay
          That will with every water wash to dirt!
          No, Barabas is born to better chance   220
          And framed of finer mould than common men,

200. Ay, ay;] *conj. Brennan;* I, I *Q;* Aye, I *Reed.*   210. him] *Q;* him; *Dyce.*
214. *three* Jews] *Broughton.*   215. *Rises.*] *This ed.*

---

206. *of*] for.
208.] from Job, vii.11: 'Therefore I wil not spare my mouthe, but wil speake in the trouble of my spirit, & muse in the bitternes of my minde'.
209.] possibly an echo of a dictum at the end of ch. 7 of Machiavelli's *The Prince*: 'He deceives himself who believes that with great men new benefits can make old injuries be forgotten'. The idea also occurs in *Discourses*, III, 4, and in Gentillet, III, 6 (pp. 176–8), and *cf.* II.iii.19. Tilley gives 'Injuries are written in brass' as proverbial (I 71).
211. *ecstasy*] frenzy.
215. Rises] *Cf.* l. 162 n. above. Q has no S.D., but this seems the right point for it; after the departure of the Three Jews Barabas abruptly drops his role as injured Old Testament prophet and reverts to a Machiavellian.
217. *villains*] used here to imply 'ignoble, low-minded' rather than 'evil, cunning'.
219. *with every water wash to dirt*] break apart at the first shock or crisis.

That measure naught but by the present time.
A reaching thought will search his deepest wits,
And cast with cunning for the time to come,
For evils are apt to happen every day.   225

Enter ABIGAIL, *the Jew's daughter.*

But whither wends my beauteous Abigail?
O what has made my lovely daughter sad?
What, woman, moan not for a little loss!
Thy father has enough in store for thee.
Abig. Not for myself, but agèd Barabas,   230
Father, for thee lamenteth Abigail.
But I will learn to leave these fruitless tears,
And urged thereto with my afflictions,
With fierce exclaims run to the senate-house,
And in the senate reprehend them all,   235
And rent their hearts with tearing of my hair,
Till they reduce the wrongs done to my father.
Bar. No, Abigail, things past recovery

225.1. *Enter . . . daughter.*] Dyce; after l. 226 in Q.   237. reduce] *Q;*
redress *conj.* Dyce ii.

223. *reaching*] far-reaching, foreseeing. *Cf.* the evil counsellor Hermon
in Sackville and Norton's *Gorboduc,* II.i.126–9: 'Wise men do not so hang
on passing state / Of present Princes, chiefly in their age, / But they will
further cast their reaching eye, / To viewe and weye the times and reignes
to come.'

224. *cast*] forecast, make arrangements in advance.

225.1. Abigail] See I Samuel, xxv; wife of the churlish Nabal, she made
peace between him and David, and after his death became one of David's
wives. In the table of proper names at the end of the Geneva Bible
Abigail is translated as 'the fathers ioye'; Hunter notes, p. 225, that some
biblical commentators saw her as a type of the Jew who is converted to
Christianity.

236. *rent*] a variant form in Elizabethan English of 'rend', i.e. tear.

237. *reduce*] *O.E.D.* (*vb,* 9c) glosses this as 'redress, repair', giving
Marlowe's line as the only example. But it may simply mean 'diminish'
(sense 26).

238–9.] proverbial; classified by Tilley under the heading 'Past cure,
past care' (C 921). For close parallels, *cf. R2* II.iii.171, *Mac.,* III.ii.11–12,
and *Thomas, Lord Cromwell* (1602), IV.ii.94–5, 'thinges past redresse / Tis
bootelesse to complaine'.

Are hardly cured with exclamations.
Be silent, daughter; sufferance breeds ease,   240
And time may yield us an occasion,
Which on the sudden cannot serve the turn.
Besides, my girl, think me not all so fond
As negligently to forgo so much
Without provision for thyself and me.   245
Ten thousand portagues, besides great pearls,
Rich costly jewels, and stones infinite,
Fearing the worst of this before it fell,
I closely hid.

Abig.   Where, father?
Bar.   In my house, my girl.
Abig. Then shall they ne'er be seen of Barabas: 250
For they have seized upon thy house and wares.
Bar. But they will give me leave once more, I trow,
To go into my house?
Abig.   That may they not:
For there I left the governor placing nuns,
Displacing me; and of thy house they mean   255
To make a nunnery, where none but their own sect
Must enter in; men generally barred.
Bar. My gold, my gold, and all my wealth is gone!
You partial heavens, have I deserved this plague?
What, will you thus oppose me, luckless stars,   260
To make me desperate in my poverty?
And knowing me impatient in distress,

260. What,] *Penley;* What *Q*.

---

240. *sufferance*] patient endurance. 'Sufferance breeds ease' is proverbial (Whiting, S 859, Tilley, S 955).
241–2.] 'And time, which cannot help us in this sudden crisis, may give us an opportunity to do something later on'.
246. *portagues*] large Portuguese gold coins worth at the time three or four pounds.
249. *closely*] secretly.
252. *trow*] trust.
256. *sect*] sex.
257. *generally*] completely, with no exceptions.

Think me so mad as I will hang myself,
That I may vanish o'er the earth in air,
And leave no memory that e'er I was?   265
No, I will live: nor loathe I this my life;
And since you leave me in the ocean thus
To sink or swim, and put me to my shifts,
I'll rouse my senses, and awake myself.
Daughter, I have it; thou perceiv'st the plight   270
Wherein these Christians have oppressèd me:
Be ruled by me, for in extremity
We ought to make bar of no policy.

Abig. Father, whate'er it be to injure them
That have so manifestly wrongèd us,   275
What will not Abigail attempt?

Bar.   Why, so;
Then thus: thou told'st me they have turned my house
Into a nunnery, and some nuns are there.

Abig. I did.

Bar.   Then, Abigail, there must my girl
Entreat the abbess to be entertained.   280

Abig. How, as a nun!

Bar.   Ay, daughter; for religion
Hides many mischiefs from suspicion.

Abig. Ay, but father, they will suspect me there.

---

263. *so . . . as*] equals 'so . . . that'; a normal Elizabethan usage (see Abbott, § 109, and *cf.* ll. 284–5 below and v.v.119–20).

265.] *Cf. Gent.*, v.iv.10, 'And leave no memory of what it was'.

268. *sink or swim*] a common phrase, semi-proverbial (Tilley, S 485).

put . . . shifts] i.e. put me in a desperate position, where I must fend for myself. Tilley gives 'He is put to his shifts' as proverbial (S 337).

272. *ruled*] persuaded, guided. *Cf.* II.ii.39.

273.] 'We mustn't scruple to use any device that will help us'.

281–2. *religion . . . suspicion*] In *The Prince*, ch. 18, Machiavelli insisted that a prince must appear devout even if he is not genuinely so, to the great scandal of 16th c. readers (e.g. Gentillet, II, I, pp. 92–9).

282. *mischiefs*] acts of wickedness, evil-doing; *cf.* v.i.14 and v.v.95.

283.] The line would read more smoothly if emended to 'Ay, father, but . . .', but the same syntax is found at II.iii.80.

Bar. Let 'em suspect, but be thou so precise
　　As they may think it done of holiness.　　　　　　285
　　Entreat 'em fair, and give them friendly speech,
　　And seem to them as if thy sins were great,
　　Till thou hast gotten to be entertained.
Abig. Thus, father, shall I much dissemble.
Bar.　　　　　　　　　　　　　　　Tush!
　　As good dissemble that thou never mean'st　　　290
　　As first mean truth, and then dissemble it;
　　A counterfeit profession is better
　　Than unseen hypocrisy.
Abig. Well, father, say I be entertained,
　　What then shall follow?
Bar.　　　　　　　　This shall follow then:　　295
　　There have I hid, close underneath the plank
　　That runs along the upper chamber floor,
　　The gold and jewels which I kept for thee.
　　But here they come; be cunning, Abigail.
Abig. Then, father, go with me.
Bar.　　　　　　　　No, Abigail, in this　　　300
　　It is not necessary I be seen,
　　For I will seem offended with thee for 't.
　　Be close, my girl, for this must fetch my gold.

---

290. mean'st] *Q;* meant'st *Cunningham.*　　293. unseen] *Q;* unforeseen
Cunningham; unseeing *conj. Brereton.*　　294. say] *Q;* say that *Bullen.*

---

284. *precise*] strict or scrupulous in religious matters; *cf. Edward II*,
II.i.46. The term was often applied, usually disparagingly, to the Puritans.

286. *Entreat . . . fair*] deal with them courteously; *cf.* II.ii.8 and v.ii.17.

290–1.] 'It is quite as good to begin with a deliberate deception as to
start out honestly and then lapse into trickery'.

292. *counterfeit profession*] the insincere vows as a nun which Abigail is
about to take.

296. *close*] concealed.

299. *here they come*] Barabas glances off-stage, and notices the friars and
nuns approaching in the distance.

301.] 'It is necessary that I should not be seen' (Bennett). The same
syntax occurs at IV.i.121.

303. *close*] secretive, cunning.

Enter Friar JACOMO, Friar BERNARDINE, Abbess, *and* Nun.

Jac. Sisters, we now

    Are almost at the new-made nunnery.   305

Abb. The better; for we love not to be seen.

    'Tis thirty winters long since some of us

    Did stray so far amongst the multitude.

Jac. But, madam, this house

    And waters of this new-made nunnery   310

    Will much delight you.

Abb. It may be so. But who comes here?

Abig. [*comes forward.*] Grave Abbess, and you, happy virgins'
      guide,

    Pity the state of a distressèd maid!

Abb. What art thou, daughter?   315

Abig. The hopeless daughter of a hapless Jew,

    The Jew of Malta, wretched Barabas,

    Sometimes the owner of a goodly house,

    Which they have now turned to a nunnery.

Abb. Well, daughter, say, what is thy suit with us?   320

Abig. Fearing the afflictions which my father feels

303.1. *Enter . . . Nun.*] *Broughton; Enter three Fryars and two Nuns.* Q.
306. *Abb.*] *Dyce; I Nun.* Q; *Nun. Penley.*   310. waters] Q; cloisters *conj.*
Bullen; quarters *A. Wagner.*   312. *Abb.*] *Dyce; Nun.* Q.   313. *comes*
forward.] *Dyce.*   you] Q; yon *Craik.*

---

305. *new-made nunnery*] The phrase is repeated at l. 310, and this,
combined with Q's odd stage direction after l. 303 and the confused
speech-prefixes at ll. 306 and 312, has made editors suspect textual
corruption. But it could equally indicate that this section of the MS behind
Q had been hastily written and not revised. *Cf.* III.iii.30.

310. *waters*] Emendation is unnecessary; as Bennett points out, a supply
of fresh water was essential for a nunnery.

316.] Several editors compare Kyd, *The Spanish Tragedy*, IV.iv.84, 'The
hopeless father of a hapless son'. But it is not certain that Marlowe
imitated Kyd; the exact dates of the two plays have not been established,
and a play of words on 'hope' and 'hap' is common in early Elizabethan
tragedy (see Thomas Hughes, *The Misfortunes of Arthur*, II.ii.98–101,
Gascoigne and Kinwelmersh, *Jocasta*, I.ii.58, II.i.165–8, and II.ii.131, and
'R.B.', *Apius and Virginia*, 1575, B2v–B3).

318. *Sometimes*] formerly.

Proceed from sin, or want of faith in us,
I'd pass away my life in penitence,
And be a novice in your nunnery,
To make atonement for my labouring soul.   325

Jac. No doubt, brother, but this proceedeth of the spirit.

Bern. Ay, and of a moving spirit too, brother; but come,
Let us entreat she may be entertained.

Abb. Well, daughter, we admit you for a nun.

Abig. First let me as a novice learn to frame   330
My solitary life to your strait laws,
And let me lodge where I was wont to lie;
I do not doubt, by your divine precepts
And mine own industry, but to profit much.

Bar. *As much, I hope, as all I hid is worth.*   *Aside.* 335

Abb. Come, daughter, follow us.

Bar. [*comes forward.*] Why, how now, Abigail, what makèst
thou
Amongst these hateful Christians ?

Jac. Hinder her not, thou man of little faith,
For she has mortified herself.

Bar.   How, mortified !   340

Jac. And is admitted to the sisterhood.

Bar. Child of perdition, and thy father's shame,
What wilt thou do among these hateful fiends ?

335.] *Italic not in* Q.   337. *comes forward.*] *Dyce.*   337. thou] *Q;* thou
thus *conj. this ed.*

---

325. *labouring*] troubled, distressed.
326. *of the spirit*] by divine influence; *cf.* John, iii.5–6.
327. *moving*] perhaps meant to insinuate that Bernardine finds Abigail
sexually exciting; *cf.* III.vi.41.
331. *strait*] strict, rigorous.
334–5.] an obvious pun on the spiritual and financial senses of 'profit'.
337. *what makèst thou*] What are you doing ?
339. *man . . . faith*] biblical; *cf.* Matthew, vi.30, viii.26, xiv.31, etc.
340. *mortified*] become dead to the world and the flesh. See Kocher,
p. 125.
342. *Child of perdition*] biblical (John, xvii.12). Hunter comments,
pp. 227–8, that the phrase is usually taken to refer to Judas.

    I charge thee on my blessing that thou leave
    These devils, and their damnèd heresy.   345
Abig. Father, give me—
Bar.   Nay, back, Abigail,
    And think upon the jewels and the gold;   *Whispers to her.*
    The board is markèd thus that covers it.   [*Makes sign of cross.*]
    Away, accursèd, from thy father's sight!
Jac. Barabas, although thou art in misbelief,   350
    And wilt not see thine own afflictions,
    Yet let thy daughter be no longer blind.
Bar. Blind, friar? I reck not thy persuasions.
    The board is markèd thus that covers it.   [*Makes sign of cross.*]
    For I had rather die than see her thus.   355
    Wilt thou forsake me too in my distress,
    Seducèd daughter? *Go, forget not—*   *Aside to her.*
    Becomes it Jews to be so credulous?
    To-morrow early I'll be at the door.   *Aside to her.*
    No, come not at me! If thou wilt be damned,   360
    Forget me, see me not, and so be gone.
    Farewell, remember to-morrow morning.   *Aside.*
    Out, out, thou wretch.

---

346. give] *Q;* forgive *Shone.*   347–8.] *Italic not in Q.*   348. *Makes . . .
cross.*] *Kirschbaum.*   353. Blind, friar?] *Shone;* Blind, Fryer, *Q;* Blind
Friar, *Reed.*   354. *Makes . . . cross.*] *Kirschbaum; Q prints* '†' *after* '*thus*'.
357. not] *Reed; net Q;* it not *conj. Dyce ii;* not, go *Bullen.*

344. *charge*] command.
346. *give*] Shone's emendation is not essential; as Spencer comments,
'probably Abigail is about to request a paternal blessing'.
Nay . . . Abigail] Robinson takes this to be part of Barabas's aside, but
it reads better as an apparent rejection of Abigail's half-formed appeal.
348. *Makes . . . cross*] Q prints an obelus or dagger after 'thus' in l. 354,
but not here. I assume that in both cases a gesture is called for, and that
by a deliberate irony Barabas uses a Christian symbol to mark where his
wealth is.
350. *misbelief*] false or mistaken belief (Barabas's Jewish faith).
353. *reck not*] do not care about, pay no attention to.
persuasions] reasonings, entreaties.
354.] Craik suggests, rather obscurely, that this may be a 'corrected
form' of l. 348 which has slipped in here by mistake. But it could also be
that Barabas repeats himself to make sure that Abigail understands the
vital piece of information.

[*Exit* BARABAS *on one side; exeunt* ABIGAIL, Abbess,
   Friars *and* Nun *on the other; as they go out,*]

Enter MATHIAS.

Math. Who's this? Fair Abigail, the rich Jew's daughter,
         Become a nun? Her father's sudden fall   365
         Has humbled her, and brought her down to this.
         Tut, she were fitter for a tale of love
         Than to be tirèd out with orisons:
         And better would she far become a bed,
         Embracèd in a friendly lover's arms,   370
         Than rise at midnight to a solemn mass.

Enter LODOWICK.

Lod. Why, how now, Don Mathias, in a dump?
Math. Believe me, noble Lodowick, I have seen
         The strangest sight, in my opinion,
         That ever I beheld.
Lod.   What was 't, I prithee?   375
Math. A fair young maid scarce fourteen years of age,
         The sweetest flower in Cytherea's field,
         Cropped from the pleasures of the fruitful earth,
         And strangely metamorphosed to a nun.
Lod. But say, what was she?
Math.   Why, the rich Jew's daughter.   380
Lod. What, Barabas, whose goods were lately seized?
         Is she so fair?
Math.   And matchless beautiful;

363.1–2. *Exit . . . out,*] *Dyce; Exeunt. Reed.*   379. to a] *Shone; not in* Q.

---

368. *orisons*] prayers.

372. *dump*] state of perplexity or depression. Tilley gives 'to be in the dumps' as proverbial (D 640).

377–8.] There may be an oblique allusion here to the legend of the rape of Proserpina; see Ovid, *Metamorphoses*, V, 385–96, and Milton, *Paradise Lost*, IV, 268–72. For 377 *cf. Rom.*, IV.v.29, 'the sweetest flower of all the field'.

377. *Cytherea*] Venus.

381. *lately*] recently.

As had you seen her 'twould have moved your heart,
Though countermured with walls of brass, to love,
Or at the least to pity.   385

Lod. And if she be so fair as you report,
'Twere time well spent to go and visit her:
How say you, shall we ?

Math. I must and will, sir, there's no remedy.

Lod. And so will I too, or it shall go hard.   390
Farewell, Mathias.

Math.   Farewell, Lodowick.   *Exeunt.*

384. countermured] *conj. Collier MS., Deighton;* countermin'd *Q.*

---

384. *countermured*] fortified with a double wall for extra defensive power.
O.E.D. points out that Q's 'countermin'd' is a misprint for 'countermured',
and gives another example from 1630 of the same error. *Cf.* v.iii.9, and
Kyd, *The Spanish Tragedy*, III.vii.16, 'countermur'd with walls of
diamond'.

walls of brass] This may simply mean 'a strong defence' (*cf. Faustus*,
i.87, and *3H6*, II.iv.4, 'Wert thou environ'd with a brazen wall'), but there
may be an allusion to the brazen tower intended to protect Danae from
Jove's attentions (see Ovid, *Amores*, II.xix.27, and *Edward II*, II.ii.53–4).

390. *or . . . hard*] See II.iii.95 n.

Act II

Enter BARABAS *with a light.*

Bar. Thus, like the sad presaging raven that tolls
    The sick man's passport in her hollow beak,
    And in the shadow of the silent night
    Doth shake contagion from her sable wings,
    Vexed and tormented runs poor Barabas   5
    With fatal curses towards these Christians.
    The incertain pleasures of swift-footed time
    Have ta'en their flight, and left me in despair;
    And of my former riches rests no more
    But bare remembrance, like a soldier's scar,   10
    That has no further comfort for his maim.
    O thou, that with a fiery pillar led'st
    The sons of Israel through the dismal shades,

Act II] *Actus Secundus.* Q.

II.i.1–2.] The raven was frequently described as a bird of ill omen (see Tilley, R 33); Broughton MS cites Peele's *David and Bethsabe*, ll. 555–6: 'Like as the fatall Raven, that in his voice / Carries the dreadful Summons of our deaths . . .'. J. P. Collier (*History of English Dramatic Poetry*, London, 1831, III, 136) notes an imitation of Marlowe in the eighth epigram of E. Guilpin's *Skialetheia* (London, 1598), A4: '*Like to the fatall ominous Raven which tolls,* / *The sicke mans dirge within his hollow beake . . .*'. The rest of the poem is printed in roman type, and is in a simpler style; possibly Guilpin was satirising what he felt to be the bombast of Marlowe's lines.

    2. *passport*] which will conduct him to the next world.

    3–4.] The association of the raven with contagion is less common; cf. *Tp.*,I.ii.321–3. See also *2H6*, IV.i.1–7.

    9. *rests*] remains.

    11. *maim*] a wound causing mutilation of the body, or loss of a limb. Complaints that soldiers were not adequately compensated for injuries were very frequent in this period.

    12–13.] biblical; see Exodus, xiii.21–2.

Light Abraham's offspring, and direct the hand
Of Abigail this night; or let the day   15
Turn to eternal darkness after this.
No sleep can fasten on my watchful eyes,
Nor quiet enter my distempered thoughts,
Till I have answer of my Abigail.

Enter ABIGAIL *above.*

Abig. Now have I happily espied a time   20
To search the plank my father did appoint;
And here behold, unseen, where I have found
The gold, the pearls, and jewels which he hid.
Bar. Now I remember those old women's words,
Who in my wealth would tell me winter's tales,   25
And speak of spirits and ghosts that glide by night
About the place where treasure hath been hid;
And now methinks that I am one of those:
For whilst I live, here lives my soul's sole hope,
And when I die, here shall my spirit walk.   30
Abig. Now that my father's fortune were so good
As but to be about this happy place!
'Tis not so happy: yet when we parted last,
He said he would attend me in the morn.
Then, gentle sleep, where'er his body rests,   35

[II.i] 25. wealth] *Q;* youth *conj.* Bullen.

---

14. *Light*] either 'comfort' (*O.E.D., v.*[1], 3) or 'enlighten' (*O.E.D., v.*[2], 3).
18. *distempered*] disordered, troubled.
20. *happily*] fortunately. Note that Barabas and Abigail are unaware of each other's presence until l. 41.
21. *appoint*] point out.
25. *wealth*] state of prosperity (contrasted with his present misery).
winter's tales] idle tales or stories suitable for a long winter evening. Cf. *Dido,* III.iii.59.
26–7.] a widely held superstition; *cf.* Jonson's *Every Man Out Of His Humour,* III.vii.63–4, and *Ham.,* I.i.136–8.
29. *soul's sole hope*] See I.i.33 n. and *cf.* Shakespeare's similar pun in *Mer. V.,* IV.i.123.
35–6.] Bennett notes that there may be an allusion here to Ovid's *Metamorphoses,* XI, 623 ff., 'where Sleep (Somnus) on receiving from Ino

> Give charge to Morpheus that he may dream
> A golden dream, and of the sudden walk,
> Come and receive the treasure I have found.

Bar. 'Bien para todos mi ganada no es'.
>   As good go on, as sit so sadly thus.   40
>   But stay, what star shines yonder in the east?
>   The loadstar of my life, if Abigail.
>   Who's there?

Abig.   Who's that?
Bar.   Peace, Abigail, 'tis I.
Abig. Then, father, here receive thy happiness.
Bar. Hast thou 't?   45
Abig. Here—(*throws down bags.*) Hast thou 't? There's more,
>   and more, and more.

---

37. walk] *Q;* wake *Broughton.*   39. Bien] *Van Fossen; Birn Q.*   es]
Brooke ii; er Q.   46. *throws . . . bags*] *Dyce; in margin opp. l. 45 in Q.*
Hast thou 't?] *Q; om. Shone.*

---

the command of Juno, bids his son Morpheus to appear in the form of a
dream before Halcyone'.

37. *walk*] Many editors emend to 'wake', and it could be argued that the
repetition of l. 30 is suspicious, and that if it simply means 'start walking'
the use of 'Come' in the next line is weak, even tautologous. But it may
mean 'sleepwalk', under the influence of the 'golden dream'; *cf. Mac.*,
v.i.3, 57. As Bennett notes, 'walk' is often used in Middle Scots to mean
'wake, watch', but Marlowe is unlikely to have known this usage.

39.] a Spanish phrase, of unknown origin, meaning 'my gain is not good
for everybody' (with the implication 'I don't want to hand over the money I
have gained to everybody'). Dr D. W. Lomax points out to me that it would
be possible to put a comma after 'Bien' ('Well, my money isn't for everyone').

40. *sit*] Presumably Barabas has sat down earlier in the scene, perhaps
at the end of his previous soliloquy; at this point he restlessly stands up,
and catches sight of Abigail's lantern. The whole line may be an inversion
of a common proverb, 'better sit still than rise and fall' (Whiting, S 355,
Tilley, S 491).

41.] Dyce suggests that this line influenced *Rom.*, II.ii.2–3. There may
be an irreverent allusion to the biblical star of Matthew, ii.9.

42. *loadstar*] guiding star; that on which one's attention or hopes are
fixed (*O.E.D.*). The phrase 'loadstar of my life' also occurs in Peele's *The
Old Wives Tale*, l. 434, and elsewhere (see *The Dramatic Works of George
Peele*, general ed. C. T. Prouty, New Haven, 1952–70, III, 432).

45–6. *Hast thou 't?*] The repetition of this phrase may be a sign of
textual corruption, but not necessarily, as Abigail repeats Barabas's words
with a slightly different meaning.

Bar. O my girl,

    My gold, my fortune, my felicity,

    Strength to my soul, death to mine enemy:

    Welcome, the first beginner of my bliss!   50

    O Abigail, that I had thee here too,

    Then my desires were fully satisfied;

    But I will practise thy enlargement thence.

    O girl, O gold, O beauty, O my bliss!   *Hugs his bags.*

Abig. Father, it draweth towards midnight now,   55

    And 'bout this time the nuns begin to wake;

    To shun suspicion, therefore, let us part.

Bar. Farewell, my joy, and by my fingers take

    A kiss from him that sends it from his soul.   [*Exit* ABIGAIL.]

    Now Phoebus ope the eye-lids of the day,   60

    And for the raven wake the morning lark,

    That I may hover with her in the air,

    Singing o'er these, as she does o'er her young,

    'Hermoso placer de los dineros'.   *Exit.*

[II.ii]

    Enter FERNEZE, MARTIN DEL BOSCO, *the* Knights,
               [*and* Officers].

Fern. Now captain, tell us whither thou art bound,

51. Abigail] *Broughton; Aigal, Abigal* Q.   59.1. *Exit Abigail.*] *Dyce.*
64. placer] *Robinson; Piarer* Q.   los dineros] *conj. Collier; les Denirch* Q.
Exit.] *Dyce; Exeunt.* Q.
[II.ii] 0.2 *and* Officers] *Penley.*

47–8.] *Cf.* l. 54 below, and Shylock's outcries in *Mer. V.*, II.viii. 15–24.

  51. *Abigail*] Possibly Marlowe made a mistake in writing the name, deleted it and wrote the name a second time, but the compositor failed to understand the deletion and put in both versions.

  53. *practise*] probably intended in *O.E.D.*'s sense 8b, 'plan, devise means for', though perhaps with a hint also of sense 9, 'use stratagem or artifice'.

  enlargement] release, liberation.

  56. *wake*] to perform the religious ceremony of matins; *cf.* I.ii.371.

  60. *Phoebus*] Apollo, the god of light, sometimes identified with the sun.

  eye-lids of the day] biblical, from Job, xli.9 ('the eye lids of the morning'). The phrase also occurs in the Geneva gloss on Job, iii.9.

  61. *for*] in place of.

  64. *'Hermoso...dineros'*] a Spanish phrase ('beautiful pleasure of money').

Whence is thy ship that anchors in our road,
And why thou camest ashore without our leave.

Bosco. Governor of Malta, hither am I bound;
    My ship, the Flying Dragon, is of Spain,   5
    And so am I: Del Bosco is my name,
    Vice-admiral unto the Catholic king.

First Knight. 'Tis true, my lord, therefore entreat him well.

Bosco. Our fraught is Grecians, Turks, and Afric Moors;
    For late upon the coast of Corsica,   10
    Because we vailed not to the Turkish fleet,
    Their creeping galleys had us in the chase:
    But suddenly the wind began to rise,
    And then we luffed, and tacked, and fought at ease.
    Some have we fired, and many have we sunk,   15
    But one amongst the rest became our prize:
    The captain's slain, the rest remain our slaves,
    Of whom we would make sale in Malta here.

Fern. Martin del Bosco, I have heard of thee;

---

2. road] *Reed;* Rhoad *Q.*   11. Turkish] *Scott; Spanish Q.*   14. luffed,
and tacked] *Dyce;* left, and tooke *Q.*

II.ii.5. *the Flying Dragon*] A ship with this name used to call at Dover
harbour in the 1560s, and Marlowe may have heard of it at Canterbury
(see A. D. Wraight and V. F. Stern, *In Search of Christopher Marlowe*,
London, 1965, pp. 26, 357).

7. *the Catholic king*] a traditional title of the kings of Spain, conferred
on them by Pope Alexander VI in 1494.

10. *late*] recently.

11. *vailed*] To 'vail' is to lower one's sails in token of respect or submission. For a more metaphorical use see v.ii.1.

Turkish] 'Turkish' and 'Spanish' are not very alike in the secretary
hand, and I suspect that the mistake is authorial rather than compositorial.

14. *luffed, and tacked*] Dyce's brilliant emendation is accepted by all
later editors. Both words are technical terms of sailing; to luff is to bring
the ship's head into the wind, and to tack is to sail against the wind in a
kind of zigzag. At first the winds were very light, and Del Bosco's sailing
ship, virtually becalmed, was successfully pursued by the Turkish galleys,
which were driven by oars and moved slowly ('creeping'). When the wind
rose (l. 13) the sailing ship became much faster and more manoeuvrable
than the galleys, and could defeat them easily.

15. *fired*] destroyed by fire.

Welcome to Malta, and to all of us;   20
But to admit a sale of these thy Turks
We may not, nay we dare not, give consent,
By reason of a tributary league.

First Knight. Del Bosco, as thou lovest and honour'st us,
Persuade our governor against the Turk;   25
This truce we have is but in hope of gold,
And with that sum he craves might we wage war.

Bosco. Will Knights of Malta be in league with Turks,
And buy it basely, too, for sums of gold?
My lord, remember that, to Europe's shame,   30
The Christian isle of Rhodes, from whence you came,
Was lately lost, and you were stated here
To be at deadly enmity with Turks.

Fern. Captain, we know it, but our force is small.

Bosco. What is the sum that Calymath requires?   35

Fern. A hundred thousand crowns.

Bosco. My lord and king hath title to this isle,
And he means quickly to expel them hence;
Therefore be ruled by me, and keep the gold.
I'll write unto his Majesty for aid,   40
And not depart until I see you free.

Fern. On this condition shall thy Turks be sold.

---

38. them] *Scott;* you *Q.*

---

23. *tributary league*] a treaty of friendship which involved the payment of tribute by the Maltese to the Turks.

27. *he*] the Turk.

31–3.] Rhodes had been the headquarters of the Knights from the early 14th c. until 1522, when the Turks conquered the island after a bitterly fought siege. In 1530 the emperor Charles V of Spain granted Malta to the Knights (see l. 37).

32. *stated*] *O.E.D.* glosses as 'placed, stationed', but gives no other example of this rare usage before 1734. But the word may be used here in *O.E.D.*'s sense 4, 'installed in a dignity, office, etc.'; the Knights of Malta had a duty, by virtue of their vows, to fight the Turks on all occasions, as l. 33 makes clear.

38. *them*] Q's 'you' is surely incorrect; the King of Spain would not wish to expel the Knights from Malta, but rather to remove the Turkish forces which are near the island.

Go, officers, and set them straight in show.

[*Exeunt* Officers.]

Bosco, thou shalt be Malta's general;
We and our warlike knights will follow thee   45
Against these barbarous misbelieving Turks.

Bosco. So shall you imitate those you succeed:
For when their hideous force environed Rhodes,
Small though the number was that kept the town,
They fought it out, and not a man survived   50
To bring the hapless news to Christendom.

Fern. So will we fight it out; come, let's away.
Proud-daring Calymath, instead of gold,
We'll send thee bullets wrapped in smoke and fire.
Claim tribute where thou wilt, we are resolved;   55
Honour is bought with blood, and not with gold.   *Exeunt.*

[II.iii]

Enter Officers *with* [ITHAMORE *and other*] Slaves.

First Off. This is the market-place, here let 'em stand:
Fear not their sale, for they'll be quickly bought.

Sec. Off. Every one's price is written on his back,
And so much must they yield or not be sold.

Enter BARABAS.

First Off. Here comes the Jew; had not his goods been seized,   5

43.1. *Exeunt* Officers.] *Dyce.*   54. thee] *Reed;* the *Q.*
[II.iii] 0.1. *Ithamore and other*] *Dyce.*   4.1. *Enter Barabas.*] *Van Fossen;*
Q has '*Ent. Bar.*' in margin opp. *l.* 4 and '*Enter Barabas.*' centred after *l. 6.*

---

43. *in show*] on display.
46. *misbelieving*] holding the wrong faith, non-Christians.
48–51.] historically quite inaccurate; see Introduction, p. 5.
53. *Proud-daring*] hyphenated in *Q;* a compounded adjective of a type common in Shakespeare (Abbott, § 2).
54.] Bullen compares Shakespeare's *John,* II.i.227, 'And now, instead of bullets wrapp'd in fire', but Bennett sees the line as a reminiscence of *1 Tamburlaine,* II.iii.19–20: 'And bullets like Jove's dreadful thunderbolts / Enrolled in flames and fiery smouldering mists'.
II.iii.4–7.] For comment on *Q*'s double entry for Barabas see Introduction, pp. 47 and 57 (n. 133).

He'd give us present money for them all.

Bar. In spite of these swine-eating Christians
          (Unchosen nation, never circumcised,
          Such as, poor villains, were ne'er thought upon
          Till Titus and Vespasian conquered us),   10
          Am I become as wealthy as I was.
          They hoped my daughter would ha' been a nun;
          But she's at home, and I have bought a house
          As great and fair as is the governor's;
          And there in spite of Malta will I dwell,   15
          Having Ferneze's hand, whose heart I'll have—
          Ay, and his son's too, or it shall go hard.
          I am not of the tribe of Levi, I,

9. Such . . . were] *Bullen;* Such as poore villaines were *Q;* Such poor
villains as were *Reed;* Such as poor villains were, *Shone;* Poor villains,
such as were *Dyce.*

---

6. *present money*] ready money, cash.

8. *Unchosen nation*] biblical; *cf.* Psalm xxxiii.12: 'Blessed is that nacion,
whose God is the Lord: euen the people, that he hathe chosen for his
inheritance'.

9. *ne'er . . . upon*] disregarded, held in poor esteem. For a similar use of
'think upon' *cf. Cor.*, II.iii.55, 185.

10. *Titus and Vespasian*] The Jews of Palestine revolted against their
Roman masters in A.D. 66, but were gradually suppressed by the Roman
commander Vespasian. He became emperor in A.D. 69, leaving his son
Titus to complete operations by the siege and capture of Jerusalem in
A.D. 70. The most famous account of these events is in the *History of the
Jewish Wars* by the 1st c. Jewish historian Flavius Josephus (see also
below, l. 303 n.). Elizabethan moralists often used the story to illustrate
the punishment that fell on the Jews for their rejection of Christ (see
E. D. Mackerness, '*Christs Teares* and the literature of warning', *English
Studies*, XXXIII (1952), 251–4).

16. *Having . . . hand*] 'This may mean that Barabas has a guarantee of
safety written by the Governor, or perhaps that Barabas has the Governor's
formal friendship (pretending to shake hands and forget old injuries): the
latter sense would make a better ironic contrast with Barabas's next words'
(Craik).

18. *tribe of Levi*] 'There seems to be nothing to show that the priestly
caste were so forgiving. The injury to the Levite in Judges, xix, etc., was
terribly avenged' (Bennett). Possibly Marlowe had in mind something
like the passage in John of Salisbury's *Policraticus*, IV, 6, where he refers
to Deuteronomy, xvii.18, and says that we should imitate the priests of the
tribe of Levi: 'But who are priests of the tribe of Levi? Those, namely,

That can so soon forget an injury.
We Jews can fawn like spaniels when we please,   20
And when we grin, we bite; yet are our looks
As innocent and harmless as a lamb's.
I learned in Florence how to kiss my hand,
Heave up my shoulders when they call me dog,
And duck as low as any bare-foot friar,   25
Hoping to see them starve upon a stall,
Or else be gathered for in our synagogue,
That when the offering-basin comes to me,
Even for charity I may spit into 't.
Here comes Don Lodowick, the governor's son,   30
One that I love for his good father's sake.

Enter LODOWICK.

Lod. I hear the wealthy Jew walked this way;
I'll seek him out, and so insinuate

---

who without the incentive of avarice, without the motive of ambition, without affectation of flesh and blood have been introduced into the Church by the law. And not the law of the letter, which mortifieth, but the law of the spirit, which in holiness of mind, cleanness of body, purity of faith and works of charity, giveth life' (*The Statesman's Book of John of Salisbury*, trans. J. Dickinson, New York, 1927, p. 25). Van Fossen also points out that the Levites held jurisdiction over the cities of refuge, where slayers who had killed accidentally were free from blood vengeance (Joshua, xx–xxi).

19.] See I.ii.209 n.

20. *fawn like spaniels*] proverbial (Whiting, S 549, Tilley, S 704).

21.] *Cf. R3*, I.iii.289–90, 'O Buckingham, take heed of yonder dog! / Look when he fawns, he bites . . .'

22.] a proverbial comparison (*cf.* Whiting, L 28–33, and Tilley, L 34).

23. *Florence*] the home of Machiavelli and hence a place where deception would be taught.

25. *duck*] make a jerking bow. *Cf.* III.iii.54.

26. *stall*] a bench or table, placed outside a shop and used to display goods while the shop was open. At night it might be used as a bed by street-wanderers; Barnes, *The Devil's Charter*, 1607, F2v, refers to drunkards who 'driueling sleepe on euery stall and bench'.

27. *gathered for*] have a charitable collection made for them.

31.] Bennett notes a similar irony in *Edward II*, I.i.128.

33. *insinuate*] introduce himself into Barabas's favour by cunning or devious means.

That I may have a sight of Abigail,
For Don Mathias tells me she is fair.   35

Bar. *Now will I show myself to have more of the serpent than*
    the dove; that is, more knave than fool.   [*Aside.*]

Lod. Yond walks the Jew, now for fair Abigail.

Bar. *Ay, ay, no doubt but she's at your command.*   [*Aside.*]

Lod. Barabas, thou know'st I am the governor's son.   40

Bar. I would you were his father too, sir, that's all the harm
    I wish you; *the slave looks like a hog's cheek new-*   [*Aside.*]
    singed.   [*Turns away.*]

Lod. Whither walk'st thou, Barabas?

Bar. No further: 'tis a custom held with us,   45
    That when we speak with Gentiles like to you,
    We turn into the air to purge ourselves;
    For unto us the promise doth belong.

Lod. Well, Barabas, canst help me to a diamond?

Bar. O, sir, your father had my diamonds.   50
    Yet I have one left that will serve your turn.
    I mean my daughter—but e'er he shall have her,   *Aside.*

36–7.] *Dyce; aside not in* Q.   39.] *Penley; aside not in* Q.   42-3.]
Shone; aside not in Q.   43. *Turns away.*] *Broughton.*   52. *Aside.*]
Broughton; opp. l. 53 in Q, *which has no italic.*

36–7. more . . . dove] ultimately biblical; *cf.* Matthew, x.16, 'be ye
therefore wise as serpentes, and innocent as doues'. (Geneva glosses
'innocent' as 'Not reuenging wrong, much lesse doing wrong'.) But 'to
have more of the serpent than the dove' became proverbial (Tilley, M
1162). See also Whiting, A 44.

37. more knave than fool] proverbial (Tilley, K 129); Barabas has reduced
Christ's subtle paradox to a simple alternative, 'cheat or be cheated'.

42–3.] Lodowick is a dandy whose cheeks are pink and shiny through
careful shaving; Barabas contemptuously compares him to a pig's head
that has just had its bristles singed off.

45. *custom*] I do not know the exact allusion here. Wilbur Sanders
suggests (*The Dramatist and the Received Idea*, Cambridge, 1968, p. 42)
that Barabas is putting forward a parody-inversion of the 'foetor judaicus',
an offensive smell often attributed to Jews (see Thomas Browne, *Vulgar
Errors*, Book IV, ch. 10); it is the Christian Lodowick (possibly heavily
perfumed) who is offensive.

48.] See I.i.104–5 n.

52.] It is not clear from Q whether 'I mean my daughter' is an aside or
not; I assume that it is an aside to the audience to make the situation fully

    I'll sacrifice her on a pile of wood.
    I ha' the poison of the city for him,
    And the white leprosy.   55

Lod. What sparkle does it give without a foil ?

Bar. The diamond that I talk of ne'er was foiled.
    But when he touches it, it will be foiled.   [*Aside.*]
    Lord Lodowick, it sparkles bright and fair.

Lod. Is it square or pointed ? Pray let me know.   60

Bar. Pointed it is, good sir—*but not for you.*   *Aside.*

Lod. I like it much the better.

Bar.   So do I too.

Lod. How shows it by night ?

Bar.   Outshines Cynthia's rays;
    You'll like it better far o' nights than days.

---

54. *city*] *Q; cicuta Koeppel; Styx Holthausen.*   58.] *Broughton; aside not in Q.*   61.] *Italic not in Q.*   64.] *Craik; Q has 'aside' in r.h. margin.*

---

clear. It is, after all, Lodowick who starts off the use of the double meaning, and possibly there was some kind of gesture or stage business at l. 49 by which Lodowick made it clear that he was really referring to Abigail.

53.] possibly an allusion to Abraham's sacrifice of Isaac, Genesis, xxii.

54. poison of the city] This has never been convincingly explained or emended. Bennett suggests that it may refer to the 'precious powder' bought in Ancona (III.iv.68–9), but the audience would not know about that. Craik thinks it may refer to a disease, such as the plague.

55. white leprosy] 'the most unpleasant stage of the disease, when shining white scales form on the skin' (Van Fossen). *Cf.* II Kings, v.27, 'a lepre white as snowe'.

56. *foil*] 'A thin leaf of some metal placed under a precious stone to increase its brilliancy' (*O.E.D.*). Lodowick implies that Abigail needs a husband to set her off to best advantage.

57–8. *foiled*] a play on words: 1. set with a foil (as in l. 56); 2. defiled, dishonoured (*O.E.D.*, 'foil', *v.*[1], senses 6 and 7).

60. *square or pointed*] cut in the shape of a cube or in a point. These terms were commonly applied to diamonds; *cf.* Mandeville as quoted by *O.E.D.*, *s.v.* 'pointed', 'Thei [diamonds] ben square or poynted of here owne kynde', and Harrison as quoted by Bennett. In l. 61 Barabas plays on an alternative meaning of 'pointed', 'appointed, assigned, destined'.

63. *Cynthia*] the Moon.

64.] I agree with Craik that this line is more effective as direct speech. Craik also suggests that Q's '*aside*' may have been intended in the MS to go with l. 66.

Lod. And what's the price?   65

Bar. Your life and if you have it.—O, my lord,   [*Aside.*]
    We will not jar about the price; come to my house,
    And I will give 't your honour—*with a vengeance.*   *Aside.*

Lod. No, Barabas, I will deserve it first.

Bar. Good sir,   70
    Your father has deserved it at my hands,
    Who of mere charity and Christian ruth,
    To bring me to religious purity,
    And as it were in catechizing sort,
    To make me mindful of my mortal sins,   75
    Against my will, and whether I would or no,
    Seized all I had, and thrust me out o' doors,
    And made my house a place for nuns most chaste.

Lod. No doubt your soul shall reap the fruit of it.

Bar. Ay, but my lord, the harvest is far off.   80
    And yet I know the prayers of those nuns
    And holy friars, having money for their pains,
    Are wondrous, *and indeed do no man good*;   *Aside.*
    And seeing they are not idle, but still doing,
    'Tis likely they in time may reap some fruit—   85
    I mean in fullness of perfection.

66.] *Shone; aside not in Q.*   68.] *Italic not in Q.*   82. having . . . pains]
Q; aside in Kirschbaum.

---

67. *jar*] dispute, quarrel.
72. *mere*] complete, perfect.
ruth] compassion, pity.
74. *in catechizing sort*] as if giving him oral lessons in spiritual matters.
79. *reap the fruit*] see l. 85 n. below.
82. *having . . . pains*] Kirschbaum marks this as an aside, and it is
certainly intended as a gibe. Perhaps Barabas speaks quietly so that the
insult is not obvious.
84. *still*] continually.
doing] with a play of words on 'do' as meaning, 1. be active, energetic,
2. copulate.
85. *reap some fruit*] Barabas picks up the metaphor used by Lodowick
in a spiritual sense at l. 79 (*cf.* 1.i.115 n.), but clearly intends 'fruit' in the
sense of 'children', a common biblical usage (e.g. Psalm cxxvii.3).
86. *fullness of perfection*] As Van Fossen suggests, Marlowe may be
playing on the theological sense ('a state of complete or perfect holiness')

Lod. Good Barabas, glance not at our holy nuns.

Bar. No, but I do it through a burning zeal;

  Hoping ere long to set the house afire: *Aside.*

  For though they do awhile increase and multiply,   90

  I'll have a saying to that nunnery.

  As for the diamond, sir, I told you of,

  Come home, and there's no price shall make us part,

  Even for your honourable father's sake—

  It shall go hard but I will see your death.   *Aside.*   95

  But now I must be gone to buy a slave.

Lod. And, Barabas, I'll bear thee company.

Bar. Come then; here's the market-place. What's the price

  of this slave? Two hundred crowns! Do the Turks

  weigh so much?   100

First Officer. Sir, that's his price.

Bar. What, can he steal that you demand so much?

  Belike he has some new trick for a purse;

---

89. *Aside.*] *opp. l. 90 in Q.* 99. Turks] *Reed; Turke Q.* 101. *First Officer.*] *Dyce; Off. Q (and at l. 112); 2 Off. Kirschbaum.*

---

and the sexual: 'full' can mean 'pregnant', and 'perfection' is often used to refer to the pseudo-Aristotelian doctrine that a woman's nature is completed by her union with a man (see Tilley, W 718). The phrase is used with a sexual meaning in Shakespeare's *John*, II.i.440.

 87. *glance*] make sarcastic innuendoes.

 88. *burning zeal*] Van Fossen notes that Barabas is playing on the metaphorical and literal senses of 'burning'. *Cf. Edward II*, I.iv.256.

 90. increase and multiply] The nuns, who should be chaste, are obeying God's instruction to Noah, Genesis, ix.7, 'But bring ye forthe frute and multiplie: grow plentifully in the earth, and increase therein'.

 91. have a saying] 'have something to say to'; Barabas will do something about the nunnery later on. Dyce ii notes the phrase in Barnes's *The Devil's Charter*, 1607, K3 (and *cf.* K3*v*), and see also Peele, *The Old Wives Tale*, ll. 882–3.

 93–5.] The syntax is ambiguous; Lodowick connects l. 94 with l. 93, but Barabas intends it to connect with l. 95.

 95. go hard but] According to *O.E.D.* this phrase introduces 'a statement of what will happen unless prevented by overpowering circumstances' ('hard', *adv.*, 2c). *Cf. Ham.*, III.iv.207–8.

 103–8.] Bennett glosses the passage thus: 'If he has a new way of purse-stealing, he is worth three hundred plates, provided that a perpetual

          And if he has, he is worth three hundred plates,
          So that, being bought, the town seal might be got   105
          To keep him for his lifetime from the gallows.
          The sessions day is critical to thieves,
          And few or none 'scape but by being purged.
Lod. Ratest thou this Moor but at two hundred plates?
First Off. No more, my lord.   110
Bar. Why should this Turk be dearer than that Moor?
First Off. Because he is young, and has more qualities.
Bar. What, hast the philosopher's stone? And thou hast,
          break my head with it; I'll forgive thee.
Slave. No, sir, I can cut and shave.   115
Bar. Let me see, sirrah; are you not an old shaver?
Slave. Alas, sir, I am a very youth.

104. plates] *Reed;* plats *Q* (*and at l. 109*).   115. *Slave.*] *Reed; Itha. Q.*
(*and* '*Ith.*' *at ll. 117, 120 and 124*).

---

pardon or charter with the town-seal upon it can be got to keep him from
the gallows, since the Sessions-days are crucial to thieves, and few or none
escape except they are purged for their offences'.

    104. *plates*] Spanish silver coins.
    107. *critical*] crucial, decisive; Craik points out that the word is used in
its contemporary medical sense (the 'critical day' was that on which the
patient either began to recover or got worse) and that the metaphor is
continued in 'purged'.
    108. *purged*] Craik sees this as a euphemism for 'hanged', but *O.E.D.*
gives the verb a legal meaning, derived from the medical, 'to atone for an
offence by expiation and submission'. Van Fossen thinks that both meanings are present.
    112. *qualities*] abilities, accomplishments.
    113. *the philosopher's stone*] 'A reputed solid substance or preparation
supposed by the alchemists to possess the property of changing other
metals into gold or silver, the discovery of which was the supreme object
of alchemy' (*O.E.D.*). Barabas is obviously sceptical of its existence.
    And] if.
    115–24.] Q attributes the anonymous slave's remarks to Ithamore,
whose name has not yet been mentioned in the play. This seems more
likely to be a confusion or anticipation on Marlowe's part than a compositorial misreading.
    116. *shaver*] *O.E.D.* quotes this line to illustrate sense 3 of 'shaver',
i.e. 'fellow, chap', but it may have a more powerful meaning in sense 2a,
'extortioner, swindler'.
    117–18. *youth*] Barabas treats the slave as though he has claimed to be a
character from a morality play such as *Youth* or *Lusty Juventus*.

Bar. A youth? I'll buy you, and marry you to Lady Vanity
    if you do well.

Slave. I will serve you, sir—   120

Bar. Some wicked trick or other. It may be, under colour of
    shaving, thou'lt cut my throat for my goods. Tell me,
    hast thou thy health well?

Slave. Ay, passing well.

Bar. So much the worse; I must have one that's sickly, and't 125
    be but for sparing victuals: 'tis not a stone of beef a day
    will maintain you in these chops. Let me see one that's
    somewhat leaner.

First Off. Here's a leaner; how like you him?

Bar. Where wast thou born?   130

Ithamore. In Thrace; brought up in Arabia.

Bar. So much the better; thou art for my turn.

    An hundred crowns? I'll have him; there's the coin.

                                   [Gives money.]

---

120. sir—] *Broughton;* Sir. *Q.*   125. and't] *Oxberry;* And *Q.*   130.
wast] *Reed;* was *Q.*   131. Thrace] *Reed; Trace Q.*   133.1. *Gives
money.] Dyce.*

---

118. *Lady Vanity*] another character from the morality plays, mentioned
by Nashe, *Piers Penniless* (*Works*, ed. McKerrow, I, 241) and Ben Jonson
(*Volpone*, II.v.21, *The Devil is an Ass*, I.i.42). She appears in the interlude
put on by the visiting players in IV.i of *Sir Thomas More*, but does not
seem to be found in any extant interlude (there is a masculine 'Vanity' in
The Contention between Liberality and Prodigality, 1602). 'Barabas is play-
fully perverse; of course, a Youth who "did well" would *forsake* Vanity,
and embrace Virtue or Good Counsel' (Craik).
   120–1.] I have followed Broughton in making Barabas interrupt the
slave. This turns 'serve' into a pun: 1. act as servant, 2. play a trick on his
master. For 'serve a trick' *cf. Gent.*, IV.iv.31.
   121. *colour*] pretence, appearance.
   124. *passing*] surpassingly, extremely.
   125–7.] Bennett compares Shylock's reluctance to feed his servants,
Mer. V., II.v.45.
   125–6. *and't . . . for*] if only for the sake of (Craik).
   127. *chops*] chaps, jaws.
   131. *Thrace*] It may be relevant that the Thracians were noted for
cruelty; see *Hero and Leander*, I. 81, and MacLure's note.
   132. *for my turn*] suitable for my purposes.

First Off. Then mark him, sir, and take him hence.

Bar. Ay, *mark him, you were best; for this is he*   [*Aside.*] 135
    That by my help shall do much villainy.
    My lord, farewell. [*to Ith.*] Come, sirrah, you are mine.
    [*To Lod.*] As for the diamond, it shall be yours:
    I pray, sir, be no stranger at my house;
    All that I have shall be at your command.   140
                       [*Exit* LODOWICK.]

          Enter MATHIAS *and* KATHERINE.

Math. What makes the Jew and Lodowick so private ?   [*Aside.*]
    I fear me 'tis about fair Abigail.

Bar. [*to Ith.*] Yonder comes Don Mathias; let us stay.
    He loves my daughter, and she holds him dear: [*Aside.*]
    But I have sworn to frustrate both their hopes,   145

135-6.] Shone; aside not in Q.   140.1 Exit Lodowick.] Broughton; not
in Q; after l. 143, Bullen; after l. 145, Kirschbaum; after l. 146, Dyce.
140.2. Mathias and Katherine] Dyce; Mathias, Mater Q.   141-2.] Dyce;
aside not in Q. 144-6.] This ed.; aside not in Q.

    134–5. *mark*] a pun: 1. brand, set a sign of ownership on him, 2. note
carefully.

    137. *Come . . . mine*] spoken to Ithamore ('sirrah' is slightly con-
temptuous; see I.i.70 n.). At l. 138 he turns back to Lodowick.

    140.1. Exit Lodowick.] Lines 140–6 contain three related problems:
1. where should the exit for Lodowick, omitted in Q, be placed ? (He re-
enters at l. 219.) 2. who are the 'us' of l. 143 (i.e. to whom is this speech
addressed) ? 3. does Q's 'the—Gouernor' at l. 146 represent another of
Barabas's sudden shifts of meaning at the end of a line ? Most editors
assume that ll. 143–6 are addressed to Lodowick, and Bullen glosses 'let
us stay' as 'let us stop our conversation'. But I cannot believe that l. 144 is
spoken to Lodowick, who is not supposed to know that Abigail loves
Mathias (see ll. 287–91 below). Lines 137–40 read very much like a farewell to Lodowick, and I have put his exit after l. 140, with of course the
proviso that Mathias enters in time to witness the parting. Line 143 is
spoken to Ithamore; Barabas is about to depart with him, but decides to
stay on in order to speak to Mathias. Lines 144–6 *could* be spoken to
Ithamore, but it is unlikely that Barabas would be so frank at this stage,
and I believe that they are an aside to the audience. This interpretation
assumes that Q's 'the—Gouernor' at l. 146 is a mistake, but gives, I think,
the best sense to the passage as a whole.

> *And be revenged upon the Governor.*

Kath. This Moor is comeliest, is he not? Speak, son.

Math. No, this is the better, mother; view this well.

Bar. *Seem not to know me here before your mother,*

> [*Aside to Math.*]

> *Lest she mistrust the match that is in hand.*   150
> *When you have brought her home, come to my house;*
> *Think of me as thy father; son, farewell.*

Math. *But wherefore talked Don Lodowick with you?*

Bar. *Tush, man, we talked of diamonds, not of Abigail.*

Kath. Tell me, Mathias, is not that the Jew?   155

Bar. As for the comment on the Maccabees,
     I have it, sir, and 'tis at your command.

Math. Yes, madam, and my talk with him was but
     About the borrowing of a book or two.

Kath. Converse not with him; he is cast off from heaven.   160
     [*To Off.*] Thou hast thy crowns, fellow. [*to Math.*] Come,
          let's away.

Math. Sirrah Jew, remember the book.

Bar. Marry will I, sir.

> *Exeunt* [MATHIAS, KATHERINE, *and* Slave.]

First Off. Come, I have made a reasonable market; let's away.

> [*Exeunt* Officers *with* Slaves.]

Bar. Now, let me know thy name, and therewithal   165
     Thy birth, condition, and profession.

---

146. *the Governor*] Scott; the—Gouernor *Q.*   149-54.] Shone; aside not
in *Q.*   158. was but] *conj. Dyce;* was *Q.*   163.1 *Exeunt*] Dyce; cxeunt
Q (opp. l. 161).   Mathias . . . Slave] *Dyce.*   164. First Off.] Dyce; Off.
Q.   164.1 *Exeunt . . . Slaves.*] *Broughton.*

---

146. And] Perhaps this word should receive a heavy stress; Barabas is
boasting that he will achieve several intentions simultaneously.

150. mistrust] suspect.

156. *comment on the Maccabees*] The two apocryphal books of Maccabees
were much admired in the Renaissance, but there does not seem to have
been any large-scale commentary on them. They were often reprinted as
an appendix to Latin versions of the works of Flavius Josephus (see
II.iii.10 n. above). Barabas would admire them because they show the
Jews heroically resisting oppression.

166. condition] social status, position.

Ith. Faith, sir, my birth is but mean, my name's Ithamore,
 my profession what you please.
Bar. Hast thou no trade? Then listen to my words,
 And I will teach thee that shall stick by thee: 170
 First, be thou void of these affections,
 Compassion, love, vain hope, and heartless fear;
 Be moved at nothing, see thou pity none,
 But to thyself smile when the Christians moan.
Ith. O brave, master, I worship your nose for this! 175
Bar. As for myself, I walk abroad o' nights,
 And kill sick people groaning under walls;
 Sometimes I go about and poison wells;
 And now and then, to cherish Christian thieves,
 I am content to lose some of my crowns,   180
 That I may, walking in my gallery,
 See 'em go pinioned along by my door.
 Being young, I studied physic, and began
 To practise first upon the Italian;

170. teach thee that] *Reed;* teach that *Q;* teach that that *Brooke ii.*

---

167. *Ithamore*] probably a version of Ithamar, one of Aaron's sons, first mentioned in Exodus, vi.23.

170. *stick by thee*] remain fixed in your memory.

171. *affections*] feelings, emotions.

172. *heartless*] disheartened, cowardly.

175. *brave*] an interjection: splendid! wonderful!

nose] an allusion to Barabas's large nose; see Introduction, p. 2, and *cf.* III.iii.10 n. and IV.i.23. In Chapman's *The Blind Beggar of Alexandria* Leon the Usurer has a 'great nose'.

176 ff.] Broughton MS points out the resemblance to Aaron's catalogue of villainies in *Tit.*, v.i.125 ff.

178. *poison wells*] a common late medieval accusation against the Jews (see, for example, Sebastian Munster's *Cosmographia*, Basle, 1550, pp. 133, 457–8). It seems to have originated as an attempt to explain the spread of plagues, such as the Black Death of the 14th c.

179–82.] Presumably Barabas is willing to use some of his money as a bait for thieves, so that he can have the pleasure of seeing them led off to execution.

181. *gallery*] balcony (*cf.* v.v.33, 53).

182. *pinioned*] with their arms tied together or shackled.

183. *physic*] medicine.

There I enriched the priests with burials,   185
And always kept the sexton's arms in ure
With digging graves and ringing dead men's knells;
And after that was I an engineer,
And in the wars 'twixt France and Germany,
Under pretence of helping Charles the Fifth,   190
Slew friend and enemy with my stratagems.
Then after that was I an usurer,
And with extorting, cozening, forfeiting,
And tricks belonging unto brokery,
I filled the jails with bankrupts in a year,   195
And with young orphans planted hospitals,
And every moon made some or other mad,
And now and then one hang himself for grief,
Pinning upon his breast a long great scroll
How I with interest tormented him.   200
But mark how I am blest for plaguing them:
I have as much coin as will buy the town!
But tell me now, how hast thou spent thy time?
Ith. Faith, master,
In setting Christian villages on fire,   205

185. enriched] *Reed;* enric'd *Q.*

---

186. *ure*] use, practice.
188. *engineer*] constructor of military works and devices; *cf. Ham.,*
III.iv.206.
189–90.] The struggle between Francis I, King of France, and the
Habsburg emperor Charles V, ruler of Spain and Germany, continued
intermittently from 1519 onwards, and the two sides did not reach a peace
settlement until 1559, with the treaty of Cateau-Cambrésis.
192. *usurer*] a moneylender charging a high rate of interest. See also
IV.i.52–4.
193. *cozening*] cheating.
forfeiting] exacting a fine or forfeit because a borrower of money has
been unable to fulfil his obligations.
194. *brokery*] quoted by *O.E.D.* under sense 1, 'the business or action
of a broker', but surely implying also sense 3, 'rascally dealing or trafficking'.
196. *hospitals*] charitable institutions, orphanages.
197. *some*] someone. 'Some or other' is a stock phrase (*O.E.D.*, 'some',
sense 1).

　　　Chaining of eunuchs, binding galley-slaves.
　　　One time I was an ostler in an inn,
　　　And in the night-time secretly would I steal
　　　To travellers' chambers, and there cut their throats;
　　　Once at Jerusalem, where the pilgrims kneeled,　　　210
　　　I strowèd powder on the marble stones,
　　　And therewithal their knees would rankle so,
　　　That I have laughed a-good to see the cripples
　　　Go limping home to Christendom on stilts.
Bar. Why, this is something! Make account of me　　　215
　　　As of thy fellow; we are villains both:
　　　Both circumcizèd, we hate Christians both.
　　　Be true and secret, thou shalt want no gold.
　　　But stand aside; here comes Don Lodowick.

　　　　　　　Enter LODOWICK.

Lod. O, Barabas, well met;　　　　　　　　　220
　　　Where is the diamond you told me of ?
Bar. I have it for you, sir; please you walk in with me.
　　　What ho, Abigail; open the door, I say.

　　　　　　Enter ABIGAIL [*with letters*].

Abig. In good time, father; here are letters come
　　　From Ormus, and the post stays here within.　　　225
Bar. Give me the letters. Daughter, do you hear ?

208. would I] *Q;* would *Broughton.*　　212. rankle so,] *Reed;* ranckle, so *Q.*
223.1. *with letters*] *Dyce.*　　226. letters.] *Dyce;* letters, *Q.*　　226-32.
Daughter . . . *Abraham.*] *Q;* all aside in Dyce.

---

　207. *ostler*] stable-man who looked after travellers' horses; these men
were often notorious for their tricks and deceits.
　212. *rankle*] become diseased, fester.
　213. *a-good*] heartily.
　214. *stilts*] crutches.
　215. *Make account of*] value, esteem.
　224. *In good time*] 'You arrived at the right time'.
　225. *Ormus*] a town in the Persian gulf, famous during the Renaissance
as a market for jewels; see Milton's *Paradise Lost*, II, 2.
　post] messenger.
　226-32.] The aside here follows Q exactly, but Dyce and later editors
prefer to begin the aside at 'Daughter'. It is hard to tell whether l. 229 is

Entertain Lodowick, the governor's son,
With all the courtesy you can afford,
Provided that you keep your maidenhead.
Use him as if he were a—*Philistine*:   *Aside [to Abig.]*   230
Dissemble, swear, protest, vow to love him;
He is not of the seed of Abraham.
I am a little busy, sir, pray pardon me.
Abigail, bid him welcome for my sake.

Abig. For your sake and his own he's welcome hither.   235

Bar. Daughter, a word more; *kiss him, speak him fair,*

                           [Aside to Abig.]

And like a cunning Jew so cast about
That ye be both made sure ere you come out.

Abig. O father, Don Mathias is my love!

Bar. I know it: yet I say make love to him;   240
Do, it is requisite it should be so.
Nay, on my life it is my factor's hand.
But go you in; I'll think upon the account.

                          [Exeunt LODOWICK *and* ABIGAIL.]

231. *to love him]* Q; love to him *Dyce.*   236–41.] *Dyce; aside not in* Q.
243.1. *Exeunt . . . Abigail.] Reed.*

---

an instruction to Abigail to go as far as she can without going too far, or a
rather coarse joke which Lodowick is meant to overhear. If l. 233 is an
apology to Lodowick for turning away to talk to Abigail, we might expect
his aside to be longer than in Q; Craik, however, argues that it 'refers not
to Barabas's past aside, but to his proposed withdrawal from their company to attend to business'. Line 234 may seem repetitive if ll. 226–30
are not aside, but possibly Barabas repeats himself because he is anxious
for Abigail to obey him (*cf.* 1.ii.354 n.). The problem is finely balanced,
but as a reasonable sense can be made of Q I have let it stand.

230. Philistine] The Philistines were a biblical tribe, enemies of the
Jews; Goliath, slain by David, was a Philistine (I Samuel, xvii).

231. protest] make protestations of affection.

232. seed of Abraham] biblical; *cf.* Psalm cv.6, 'Ye sede of Abraham his
seruant, ye children of Iaakob, which are his elect'.

236. speak him fair] talk to him courteously; *cf.* iv.i.27 and iv.ii.68.

237. cast about] contrive affairs.

238. made sure] betrothed. Cf. *Edward II*, 1.iv.377.

242. hand] handwriting; Barabas pretends that they have been discussing the letters Abigail gave him.

243–4. account] Barabas plays on the financial sense of the term,

The account is made, for Lodowick dies.
My factor sends me word a merchant's fled   245
That owes me for a hundred tun of wine.
I weigh it thus much: I have wealth enough.
For now by this has he kissed Abigail,
And she vows love to him, and he to her.
As sure as heaven rained manna for the Jews,   250
So sure shall he and Don Mathias die:
His father was my chiefest enemy.

Enter MATHIAS.

Whither goes Don Mathias? Stay a while.
Math. Whither but to my fair love Abigail?
Bar. Thou know'st, and heaven can witness it is true,   255
    That I intend my daughter shall be thine.
Math. Ay, Barabas, or else thou wrong'st me much.
Bar. O, heaven forbid I should have such a thought!
    Pardon me though I weep; the governor's son
    Will, whether I will or no, have Abigail: 260
    He sends her letters, bracelets, jewels, rings.
Math. Does she receive them?
Bar. She? No, Mathias, no, but sends them back,
    And when he comes, she locks herself up fast;
    Yet through the keyhole will he talk to her,   265
    While she runs to the window, looking out
    When you should come and hale him from the door.

---

244. Lodowick] *Q;* Lodovico *Dyce;* Lodowick he *Cunningham.*   252.1.
Enter Mathias.] *Dyce; after l. 253 in Q.*

---

prompted by the letters he has just received from his agent, and the metaphorical usage found in such phrases as 'to settle someone's account'; he
has decided what to do about Lodowick.

247. *thus much*] Barabas makes a derisive gesture, or snaps his fingers.
    I have . . . enough] Craik argues that this 'refers both backward (to the
slight loss) and forward (to the anticipated revenge)'.
248. *by this*] by this time. *Cf.* v.v.103.
250. *manna for the Jews*] biblical; see Exodus, xvi.13–15.
252.] i.e. during the seizure of his money, in I.ii.
264. *fast*] securely.
267. *hale*] pull violently, drag.

Math. O treacherous Lodowick!

Bar. Even now as I came home, he slipped me in,
    And I am sure he is with Abigail.   270

Math. I'll rouse him thence. [*Draws his sword.*]

Bar. Not for all Malta, therefore sheath your sword.
    If you love me, no quarrels in my house,
    But steal you in, and seem to see him not;
    I'll give him such a warning ere he goes   275
    As he shall have small hopes of Abigail.
    Away, for here they come.

Enter LODOWICK [*and*] ABIGAIL.

Math. What, hand in hand? I cannot suffer this.

Bar. Mathias, as thou lovest me, not a word.

Math. Well, let it pass, another time shall serve.   *Exit.* 280

Lod. Barabas, is not that the widow's son?

Bar. Ay, and take heed, for he hath sworn your death.

Lod. My death? What, is the base-born peasant mad?

Bar. No, no; but happily he stands in fear
    Of that which you, I think, ne'er dream upon,   285
    My daughter here, a paltry silly girl.

Lod. Why, loves she Don Mathias?

Bar. Does she not with her smiling answer you?

Abig. *He has my heart; I smile against my will.*   [*Aside.*]

271. *Draws his sword.*] Penley.   287. Why,] *Reed;* Why *Q.*   289.]
Penley; aside not in *Q*.

---

269. *slipped me in*] slipped in; 'me' is the so-called 'ethic dative' found
e.g. in *Oth.*,I.i.49.

271. *rouse*] a hunting term: to make the game or quarry come out of
hiding.

278. *suffer*] endure.

284–6.] The syntax of these lines is somewhat clumsy. Presumably
'that' is in apposition to 'daughter', though Craik takes it to refer to a
marriage between Lodowick and Abigail. Barabas's assumption in l. 285
that Lodowick is not particularly interested in Abigail must surely be
ironical, and is perhaps intended to provoke him into a declaration of
affection.

284. *happily*] perhaps; *cf.* v.iv.6.

286. *silly*] simple, unsophisticated.

Lod. Barabas, thou know'st I have loved thy daughter long.   290
Bar. And so has she done you, even from a child.
Lod. And now I can no longer hold my mind.
Bar. Nor I the affection that I bear to you.
Lod. This is thy diamond; tell me, shall I have it?
Bar. Win it, and wear it; it is yet unsoiled.   295
    O, but I know your lordship would disdain
    To marry with the daughter of a Jew:
    And yet I'll give her many a golden cross,
    With Christian posies round about the ring.
Lod. 'Tis not thy wealth, but her that I esteem;   300
    Yet crave I thy consent.
Bar. And mine you have, yet let me talk to her;
    This offspring of Cain, this Jebusite,   *Aside [to Abig.]*

295. unsoiled] *Q; unfoiled conj. Collier.*   298. yet] *Reed;* yer *Q.*   303.
Aside] Scott; opp. l. 306 in Q, which has no italic.

290.] This protestation rings hollow if this is the first time Lodowick
has seen Abigail (see ll. 33–5 above).

292. *hold my mind*] refrain from expressing my feelings.

295. *Win it, and wear it*] proverbial (Tilley, W 408).

unsoiled] *O.E.D.* quotes this line to illustrate its definition, 'not soiled
or dirtied'. Collier's conjectural emendation to 'unfoiled' is plausible, and
could have a double meaning: 1. not backed with a foil (*cf.* l. 56 n. above),
2. not damaged, unimpaired. But as Q makes reasonable sense it seems
best to leave it.

298. *cross*] coin; coins at this time frequently had crosses stamped on
them.

299. *Christian posies*] In Elizabethan times wedding rings commonly
had a 'posy' or motto engraved on them (see Middleton, *A Chaste Maid in
Cheapside*, I.i.188–91), but the main reference is to the pious Latin mottos
sometimes inscribed on coins during the 16th c. Lines 298–9 are heavily
sarcastic; Abigail, the Jewess, lacks the symbols ('cross') and doctrines
('posies') of Christianity, but her Christian lover will gladly accept a cash
equivalent.

303. offspring of Cain] possibly alluding to the Jewish tradition that the
descendants of Cain were all wicked; see Flavius Josephus, *Antiquities of
the Jews*, I.ii.2: 'even while Adam was alive, it came to pass that the
posterity of Cain became exceedingly wicked, every one successively
dying one after another, more wicked than the former. They were intolerable in war, and vehement in robberies; and if any one were slow to
murder people, yet was he bold in his profligate behaviour, in acting unjustly, and in doing injuries for gain' (*Works of Josephus*, trans. W. Whiston,
London, 1847, p. 32).

> That never tasted of the Passover,
> Nor e'er shall see the land of Canaan,   305
> Nor our Messias that is yet to come,
> This gentle maggot, Lodowick, I mean,
> Must be deluded: let him have thy hand,
> But keep thy heart till Don Mathias comes.
>
> Abig. What, shall I be betrothed to Lodowick?   310
> Bar. It's no sin to deceive a Christian,
> For they themselves hold it a principle,
> Faith is not to be held with heretics:
> But all are heretics that are not Jews:
> This follows well, and therefore, daughter, fear not.   315
> I have entreated her, and she will grant.
>
> Lod. Then, gentle Abigail, plight thy faith to me.

Jebusite] the original inhabitants of Jerusalem before its capture by King David (II Samuel, v.6–10); the word here means 'them that professed not the true God' (Geneva gloss on Judges, xix.11–12).

304. the Passover] a Jewish religious ritual (see Exodus, xii), in which non-Jews could not participate unless they were circumcised.

305. land of Canaan] promised to the Jews as part of God's covenant in Genesis, xvii.8; later conquered by Joshua.

306.] The Jews refused to believe that Christ was truly the Messiah fulfilling Old Testament prophecy. Marlowe's form 'Messias' is found in all 16th c. English translations of John, i.41 and iv.25.

307. gentle] a triple pun, as Bennett notes: 1. of good birth, 2. a maggot (the larva of the bluebottle), 3. a gentile, non-Jew.

313. Faith . . . heretics] Cf. 2 Tamburlaine, II.i.33–41. Protestant controversialists argued that this doctrine originated at the Council of Constance in 1415 to justify the burning of John Huss despite the safe-conduct he had been given, and asserted that this kind of treachery was still condoned by the Catholic Church. Tilley gives the phrase as proverbial (F 33), but quotes no example earlier than Marlowe; see, however, F. P. Wilson, Shakespearian and Other Studies (Oxford, 1969), p. 162, and Kocher, p. 123, and cf. Thomas Lupton, A Persuasion from Papistrie (London, 1581), p. 47: 'For it is a maxime and a rule with the Pope and his partakers that Fides non est seruanda haereticis, Faith (or promise) is not to be kept with Heretickes'. The Jesuit Molanus tried to defend the way Huss had been treated in his De Fide Haereticis Servanda (Cologne, 1584), which contains an attack on Machiavelli.

315. follows well] is logically argued. A term used in academic disputation; cf. Faustus, ii.4–11.

317. plight thy faith] become betrothed.

Abig. I cannot choose, seeing my father bids—　　　[*Aside.*]
　　Nothing but death shall part my love and me.
Lod. Now have I that for which my soul hath longed.　　320
Bar. So have not I, but yet I hope I shall.　　　　*Aside.*
Abig. O wretched Abigail, what hast thou done?　　[*Aside.*]
Lod. Why on the sudden is your colour changed?
Abig. I know not, but farewell: I must be gone.
Bar. Stay her, but let her not speak one word more.　　325
　　　　　　　　　　　　　　　　　　[*Aside to Ith.*]
Lod. Mute o' the sudden; here's a sudden change.
Bar. O, muse not at it, 'tis the Hebrews' guise
　　That maidens new-betrothed should weep a while.
　　Trouble her not; sweet Lodowick, depart:
　　She is thy wife, and thou shalt be mine heir.　　330
Lod. O, is 't the custom? Then I am resolved;
　　But rather let the brightsome heavens be dim,
　　And nature's beauty choke with stifling clouds,
　　Than my fair Abigail should frown on me.

Enter MATHIAS.

　　There comes the villain; now I'll be revenged.　　335
Bar. Be quiet, Lodowick; it is enough
　　That I have made thee sure to Abigail.
Lod. Well, let him go.　　　　　　　　　　*Exit.*
Bar. Well, but for me, as you went in at doors

318.] *Bowers; aside not in Q.*　319.] *Q; aside in Cunningham.*　321.]
Italic not in Q.　322.] *Penley; aside not in Q.　thou*] *Shone, Scott;* thee
Q.　325.] *This ed.; aside not in Q.*　334.1. *Enter Mathias.*] *This ed.;
after l. 335 in Q.*

318–19.] Line 318 is spoken in despair; there seems to be no escape for
her. But in l. 319 she tries an equivocation; 'my love' refers to Mathias,
but Lodowick assumes it refers to him.

325. Stay] stop; the line is addressed to Ithamore, who is to hold her
still and keep her quiet (*cf.* ll. 364–5 below).

327. guise] habit, custom. The allusion is not clear; possibly Barabas
has invented the idea to get himself out of difficulty.

331. resolved] answered, satisfied.

332. brightsome] exhibiting brightness (so *O.E.D.*, which comments,
'a vaguer word than *bright*, leaving more to the imagination').

339.] Barabas now turns to address Mathias.

You had been stabbed, but not a word on 't now;   340
Here must no speeches pass, nor swords be drawn.

Math. Suffer me, Barabas, but to follow him.

Bar. No; so shall I, if any hurt be done,
Be made an accessary of your deeds.
Revenge it on him when you meet him next.   345

Math. For this I'll have his heart.

Bar. Do so. Lo, here I give thee Abigail.

Math. What greater gift can poor Mathias have?
Shall Lodowick rob me of so fair a love?
My life is not so dear as Abigail.   350

Bar. My heart misgives me that, to cross your love,
He's with your mother; therefore after him.

Math. What, is he gone unto my mother?

Bar. Nay, if you will, stay till she comes herself.

Math. I cannot stay; for if my mother come   355
She'll die with grief.   *Exit.*

Abig. I cannot take my leave of him for tears:
Father, why have you thus incensed them both?

Bar. What's that to thee?

Abig.   I'll make 'em friends again.

Bar. You'll make 'em friends?   360
Are there not Jews enow in Malta,
But thou must dote upon a Christian?

Abig. I will have Don Mathias; he is my love.

Bar. Yes, you shall have him. [*to Ith.*] Go put her in.

Ith. Ay, I'll put her in.   [*Puts* ABIGAIL *in.*]   365

Bar. Now tell me, Ithamore, how likest thou this?

365. *Puts . . . in.*] Dyce.

---

342. *Suffer*] allow.

344. *accessary*] O.E.D. quotes Blackstone's legal definition: 'He who is not the chief actor in the offence, nor present at its performance, but in some way concerned therein, either before or after the fact committed'.

351. *misgives me*] makes me fear.

cross] thwart, hinder.

361. *enow*] Until the 18th c. this was the standard plural form of 'enough'.

364. *put . . . in*] force her into the house.

Ith. Faith, master, I think by this you purchase both their
    lives; is it not so?

Bar. True; and it shall be cunningly performed.

Ith. O master, that I might have a hand in this!   370

Bar. Ay, so thou shalt, 'tis thou must do the deed:
    Take this, and bear it to Mathias straight,

                              [Gives him a letter.]

    And tell him that it comes from Lodowick.

Ith. 'Tis poisoned, is it not?

Bar. No, no; and yet it might be done that way.   375
    It is a challenge feigned from Lodowick.

Ith. Fear not; I'll so set his heart afire that he shall verily
    think it comes from him.

Bar. I cannot choose but like thy readiness;
    Yet be not rash, but do it cunningly.   380

Ith. As I behave myself in this, employ me hereafter.

Bar. Away then.   *Exit* [ITHAMORE].
    So; now will I go in to Lodowick,
    And like a cunning spirit feign some lie,
    Till I have set 'em both at enmity.   *Exit.*   385

372.1. *Gives . . . letter.*] *Dyce.*   382. *Ithamore*] *Shone.*   383. in to] *Q;*
unto *Dyce (but not Dyce ii).*

367–8. *purchase . . . lives*] are making cunning plots to bring about their
deaths. As Bennett points out, 'purchase' here has no financial implications.

372.] As Bennett comments, Barabas has had no opportunity to write a
letter during this scene, and we must assume that the letter was prepared
in advance, to be used at a favourable moment. The incident may illustrate Marlowe's indifference to certain kinds of realistic plausibility.

379. *readiness*] promptness, eagerness.

384. *spirit*] devil; *cf. Faustus,* i.68.1, and Jump's note.

Act III

Enter [BELLAMIRA] *a Courtezan.*

Bella. Since this town was besieged, my gain grows cold:
    The time has been, that but for one bare night
    A hundred ducats have been freely given;
    But now against my will I must be chaste,
    And yet I know my beauty doth not fail.   5
    From Venice merchants, and from Padua
    Were wont to come rare-witted gentlemen,
    Scholars, I mean, learnèd and liberal;
    And now, save Pilia-Borza, comes there none,
    And he is very seldom from my house;   10
    And here he comes.

Enter PILIA-BORZA.

Act III] *Actus Tertius. Q.*   [III.i] 0.1. *Bellamira*] *Penley.*   1. *Bella.*]
Penley; not in Q.

III.i.1. *besieged*] Bennett and others note that strictly speaking the siege does not begin until after III.v, and suggest that some textual rearrangement has taken place here. But the discrepancy seems minor, and perhaps we should assume that the presence of the Turkish fleet near Malta (see I.ii.29–31) has had the effect of a blockade.

my . . . cold] my profits have fallen off.

2. *bare*] an obscene pun: 1. mere ('only one night'), 2. naked.

3. *ducats*] a gold coin current in various European countries. Bellamira may allude to the Venetian ducat, first coined in 1284, and worth about five shillings of Elizabethan money.

6. *Padua*] Bennett quotes Greene's *Mamillia* (London, 1583), A4, 'The Cittie of Padua, renowned . . . for the antiquitie of the famous Uniuersitie'.

8. *liberal*] generous.

9. *Pilia-Borza* i.e. cutpurse or pickpocket; from Italian, though the normal Italian form is 'tagliaborza'.

Pilia. Hold thee, wench; there's something for thee to spend.

                                [*Gives her money from a bag.*]

Bella. 'Tis silver; I disdain it.

Pilia. Ay, but the Jew has gold,

    And I will have it, or it shall go hard.   15

Bella. Tell me, how camest thou by this?

Pilia. Faith, walking the back lanes through the gardens I
    chanced to cast mine eye up to the Jew's counting-house,
    where I saw some bags of money, and in the night I
    clambered up with my hooks, and as I was taking my   20
    choice I heard a rumbling in the house; so I took only
    this, and run my way: but here's the Jew's man.

                       Enter ITHAMORE.

Bella. Hide the bag.

Pilia. Look not towards him; let's away. Zounds, what a
    looking thou keep'st, thou'lt betray 's anon.   25

                [*Exeunt* BELLAMIRA *and* PILIA-BORZA.]

Ith. O, the sweetest face that ever I beheld! I know she is a

12.1. *Gives ... bag.*] *This ed.; Shewing a bag of silver. Dyce.*   25.1. *Exeunt
... Pilia-Boraz.*] *Broughton.*

---

    12. *Hold thee*] 'Take what I offer'; *cf.* v.v.42 and *The Massacre at Paris*,
xix.13.

    17–20.] Pilia-Borza has some affinity with a type of petty thief described
by Thomas Harman (*A Caveat for Common Cursetors*, London, 1567,
B4*v*–C1) as 'A Hooker, or Angler': 'as they walke a day times from house
to house to demaund charite thei vigelantly marke where or in what place
they may attayne to there praye, casting there eyes vp to euery wyndow
wel noting what they se their, whether apparell, or linnen, hanginge nere
vnto the sayde windowes ... they customably carry with them a staffe of
v. or vi. foote long, in which within one ynch of the tope thereof is a little
hole bored through in which hole they putte an yron hoke and with the
same they wyll plucke vnto them quicly any thing that they may reche
ther with'. This account was plagiarised by Dekker, *The Belman of
London* (London, 1608), C4. Bennett cites from Broughton MS a number
of contemporary allusions to thieves' hooks, but suggests unconvincingly
that Ithamore used his hooks to climb up to the window.

    24. *Zounds*] i.e. 'By God's wounds'; a very common oath.

    24–5. *what ... keep'st*] Bellamira keeps gazing nervously at Ithamore.

    25. *anon*] immediately.

    26–7.] It is not clear what 'attire' Marlowe had in mind for Bellamira.
An Elizabethan prostitute commonly wore a red taffeta petticoat (see

courtezan by her attire: now would I give a hundred of
the Jew's crowns that I had such a concubine.
Well, I have delivered the challenge in such sort
As meet they will, and fighting die; brave sport!   30

                                                    Exit.

[III.ii]

Enter MATHIAS.

Math. This is the place; now Abigail shall see
    Whether Mathias holds her dear or no.

Enter LODOWICK *reading.*

Lod. What, dares the villain write in such base terms?

[III.ii] 2.1. *Enter . . . reading.*] *Q; Enter Lodowick. Dyce.*   3. *Lod.*] *Scott;*
Math. Q, Dyce (who adds S.D. 'looking at a letter').

Shakespeare's *1H4*, I.ii.10, and A. R. Humphreys's note in his Arden
edition, and *cf.* Jonson, *Cynthia's Revels*, II.ii.101–2). But she may have
been a Venetian: Bullen compares a stage direction from Brome's *The
Covent-Garden Weeded*, I.i: '*Enter Dorcas aboue . . . habited like a Curtizan
of Venice*'. Venetian prostitutes were notorious throughout Europe: see
William Thomas, *The Historie of Italie*, London, 1549, ff. 84*v*–85, and
Thomas Coryate, *Coryate's Crudities*, London, 1611, pp. 263–71. An
engraving of an 'aulicum scortum Venetum' (a courtly Venetian whore)
can be found in J. J. Boissard's *Habitus variarum orbis gentium* (1581; reproduced in Max von Boehn, *Modes and Manners, Vol. II: The Sixteenth
Century*, trans. Joan Joshua, London, 1932, p. 211). She wears a richly
embroidered gown with long sleeves and a full skirt, and has an elaborate,
horn-shaped, hair-style, but does not seem noticeably different from the
'noble Venetian matron' who is portrayed standing beside her.

III.ii.3 ff.] Editors have had difficulty in sorting out the arrangements
for the duel between Mathias and Lodowick. At II.iii.372 ff. Barabas
orders Ithamore to deliver to Mathias a written challenge 'feigned from
Lodowick', and at ll. 383–5 says that he himself will go to Lodowick and
'feign some lie' to stir up enmity between the rivals. In the present scene
the duel takes place, but ll. 3–4 hardly make sense as they stand in Q. A
further complication is that at III.iii.20–2 Ithamore claims to have carried
the written challenge 'first to Lodowick and imprimis to Mathias'. This
directly contradicts what is said at the end of II.iii, and there seems to be
no way of reconciling the two versions. At 3–4 I have adopted Scott's
emendation, which simply transposes the two speech-prefixes. I assume,
like Cunningham, that Lodowick enters reading Mathias's *reply* to the
forged challenge, and is surprised and angered at the violence of the
language used by his social inferior (compare the tone of l. 3 to that of

Math. I did it, and revenge it if thou darest.   [*They*] *fight.*

Enter BARABAS *above.*

Bar. O bravely fought; and yet they thrust not home.   5
      Now, Lodowick; now, Mathias; so.   [*Both fall dead.*]
      So; now they have showed themselves to be tall fellows.
[*Voices*] *within.* Part 'em, part 'em!
Bar. Ay, part 'em now they are dead: farewell, farewell.

                                                  Exit [*above*].

Enter FERNEZE, KATHERINE[, *and* Citizens *of Malta*].

Fern. What sight is this? My Lodowick slain!   10
      These arms of mine shall be thy sepulchre.
Kath. Who is this? My son Mathias slain!
Fern. O Lodowick, hadst thou perished by the Turk,
      Wretched Ferneze might have venged thy death.
Kath. Thy son slew mine, and I'll revenge his death.   15
Fern. Look, Katherine, look, thy son gave mine these wounds.
Kath. O leave to grieve me, I am grieved enough.
Fern. O that my sighs could turn to lively breath,
      And these my tears to blood, that he might live.
Kath. Who made them enemies?   20
Fern. I know not, and that grieves me most of all.

4. *Math.*] *Scott; Lod. Q.   They*] *Robinson.   6. Both . . . dead.*] *Scott.*
8. *Voices*] *Broughton.   9.1. above*] *Dyce.   9.2. and . . . Malta*] *Craik;
and Attendants Dyce.*

II.iii.283, 'What, is the base-born peasant mad?'). Mathias of course is
prepared to stand by his letter. This interpretation would harmonise with
II.iii.372 ff. but not with III.iii.20–2. It is possible, as Bennett suggests,
that Q's double speech-prefix for Mathias indicates that a speech for
Lodowick has dropped out from the text, and Craik makes an unconvincing attempt to supply it.

    5. *home*] deeply, to the heart.
    7. *tall*] brave; *cf.* IV.ii.10.
    10. *What sight*] Dyce points out that this equals 'what a sight'; the 'a'
in this position was often omitted in Elizabethan English (Abbott, § 86).
    11.] Dyce compares *3H6*, II.v.114–15: 'These arms of mine shall be
thy winding-sheet; / My heart, sweet boy, shall be thy sepulchre'.
    17. *leave*] cease.
    18. *lively*] necessary to life, vital.

Kath. My son loved thine.

Fern.   And so did Lodowick him.

Kath. Lend me that weapon that did kill my son,
  And it shall murder me.

Fern. Nay, madam, stay; that weapon was my son's,   25
  And on that rather should Ferneze die.

Kath. Hold; let's enquire the causers of their deaths,
  That we may venge their blood upon their heads.

Fern. Then take them up, and let them be interred
  Within one sacred monument of stone;   30
  Upon which altar I will offer up
  My daily sacrifice of sighs and tears,
  And with my prayers pierce impartial heavens,
  Till they reveal the causers of our smarts,
  Which forced their hands divide united hearts.   35
  Come, Katherine, our losses equal are,
  Then of true grief let us take equal share.

                                        Exeunt [*with the bodies*].

[III.iii]

Enter ITHAMORE.

Ith. Why, was there ever seen such villainy,
  So neatly plotted and so well performed:

---

33. impartial] *Q;* the impartial *Broughton.*   34. reveal] *Dyce; not in Q;*
disclose *conj. Collier.*   37.1. *with the bodies*] *Dyce.*

31–2.] Bullen compares *Gent.*, III.ii.73–4: 'Say that upon the altar of her
beauty / You sacrifice your tears, your sighs, your heart'.

33. *impartial*] *O.E.D.* points out that 'impartial' is sometimes mistakenly
used for 'partial', and quotes from the 'bad quarto' of *Romeo and Juliet*,
l. 1856, 'Cruel, vniust, impartiall destinies'.

34. *reveal*] Most later editors agree with Dyce that a verb has been
omitted from Q. Craik prefers Collier's conjecture because it 'suits the
alliterative style (disclose, causers; *cf.* prayers, pierce; hands, hearts)',
but the logic of this is not compelling, and any reading must be largely
guesswork.

  smarts] pains, sorrows.

35. *Which*] here equivalent to 'Who'; a common usage (Abbott, § 265).

Both held in hand, and flatly both beguiled!

Enter ABIGAIL.

Abig. Why, how now, Ithamore, why laugh'st thou so?
Ith. O mistress, ha, ha, ha!   5
Abig. Why, what ail'st thou?
Ith. O, my master!
Abig. Ha!
Ith. O, mistress, I have the bravest, gravest, secret, subtle,
    bottle-nosed knave to my master that ever gentleman   10
    had.
Abig. Say, knave, why rail'st upon my father thus?
Ith. O, my master has the bravest policy.
Abig. Wherein?
Ith. Why, know you not?   15
Abig. Why, no.
Ith. Know you not of Mathias' and Don Lodowick's
    disaster?
Abig. No, what was it?
Ith. Why, the devil invented a challenge, my master writ it,   20
    and I carried it, first to Lodowick and imprimis to
    Mathias.

[III.iii] 17. Mathias'] *Reed; Mathia Q.*   Lodowick's] *Reed; Lodowick Q.*

III.iii.3. *held in hand*] kept in suspense or expectation (*O.E.D.*, 'hand', *sb.*,
sense 29e).

   flatly] completely, decisively.

   6. *What . . . thou?*] What's the matter with you?

   9. *bravest*] finest, best.

   10. *bottle-nosed*] with a bottle-shaped, swollen nose. T. W. Craik points
out (*The Tudor Interlude*, Leicester, 1958, p. 51) that the phrase is applied
to the Devil in such interludes as Lupton's *All For Money* and Fulwell's
Like Will to Like. It is also used of the usurer Leon in Chapman's *The
Blind Beggar of Alexandria*.

   12. *rail'st upon*] abuse, mock.

   17–18.] This is the bottom line of sig. F2 of Q; if the copy was cast-off
(see Introduction, p. 39) the compositor may have slightly overestimated
the required amount of copy, and abbreviated the names to squeeze the
line on to the page.

   21. *imprimis*] 'in the first place'; obviously Ithamore does not understand the word, and thinks it means 'next'. Elsewhere in the play he tries
to use refined speech with ludicrous results (e.g. at IV.ii.103).

And then they met, and as the story says,

In doleful wise they ended both their days.

Abig. And was my father furtherer of their deaths ?   25

Ith. Am I Ithamore ?

Abig. Yes.

Ith. So sure did your father write and I carry the challenge.

Abig. Well, Ithamore, let me request thee this:

Go to the new-made nunnery, and inquire   30

For any of the friars of Saint Jacques,

And say, I pray them come and speak with me.

Ith. I pray, mistress, will you answer me to one question ?

Abig. Well, sirrah, what is 't ?

Ith. A very feeling one: have not the nuns fine sport with the   35

friars now and then ?

Abig. Go to, sirrah sauce, is this your question ? Get ye gone.

Ith. I will forsooth, mistress.   *Exit.*

Abig. Hard-hearted father, unkind Barabas,

Was this the pursuit of thy policy,   40

To make me show them favour severally,

---

23. and as] *Shone;* as *Q.*   40. policy,] *Shone;* policie ? *Q.*

23–4.] This pseudo-archaic diction is intended to mock the pathos of the lovers' deaths. 'As the story says' is a stock phrase of medieval narrative; *cf.* Chaucer, *The House of Fame*, l. 406, 'as the story telleth us', and *The Squire's Tale*, F 655.

25. *furtherer*] a helper, agent.

31. *friars of St. Jacques*] i.e. black friars, or Dominicans, so called because in 1218 they were given the hospital of St Jacques in Paris, which became the headquarters of their order. *Cf.* IV.i.104.

35. *feeling*] deeply felt (but undoubtedly used here with an indecent implication).

37. *sirrah sauce*] impudent fellow; see *O.E.D.*, 'sauce', sense 6a, and *cf.* I.i.70 n.

39. *Hard-hearted*] A term often used against the Jews, who were regarded as having hardened their hearts against the truth of Christianity (John, xii.40). *Cf.* IV.i.52 and *Mer. V.*, IV.i.78–80.

unkind] used here with a range of meanings common at the time: harsh, cruel, unnatural, devoid of the affection that should exist between parents and children. *Cf.* III.iv.2.

40. *pursuit*] purpose, intention.

41. *severally*] separately, individually.

That by my favour they should both be slain?
Admit thou lovedst not Lodowick for his sire,
Yet Don Mathias ne'er offended thee.
But thou wert set upon extreme revenge,   45
Because the prior dispossessed thee once,
And couldst not venge it, but upon his son,
Nor on his son, but by Mathias' means,
Nor on Mathias, but by murdering me.
But I perceive there is no love on earth,   50
Pity in Jews, nor piety in Turks.
But here comes cursed Ithamore with the friar.

> *Enter* ITHAMORE [*and*] *Friar* [JACOMO].

Jac. Virgo, salve.
Ith. When, duck you?
Abig. Welcome, grave friar; Ithamore, be gone.   55
                                        Exit [ITHAMORE].
      Know, holy sir, I am bold to solicit thee.
Jac. Wherein?

43. sire] *Dyce;* sinne *Q.*   46. prior] *Q;* Governor *Cunningham;* sire
Brooke.   52.1. *Jacomo*] *Dyce.*   54. When,] *Bullen;* When *Q.*   55.1
Ithamore] *Shone.*

---

46. *prior*] Most recent editors agree that emendation is needed here,
and Cunningham comments, 'I cannot find that the Grand Master of the
Order was ever called a Prior'. But the word was commonly applied to the
commanders of the different nationalities within the order, and Marlowe
may simply have transferred it rather loosely to the Grand Master. *O.E.D.*
gives 'grand prior' as meaning 'the commander of a priory of the Knights
of . . . Malta', but has no example earlier than 1703, though one occurs in
The Return of Pasquill (1589), an anti-Marprelate pamphlet sometimes
attributed to Nashe, where the author speaks of 'the graund Prior of
France', glossed by McKerrow as 'the chief of the French section or
"language" of the Knights of Malta' (Nashe, *Works*, ed. McKerrow, II,
81 and IV, 54). According to Louis Le Roy, *Aristotle's Politiques, or Discourses of Gouernment* (London, 1598), p. 170, 'The great Maister of Malta
is elected out of the principal Priors of his religion', and *cf.* W. Fulbecke,
A Parallel or Conference . . . (London, 1601), pp. 1v–2.
   53. *Virgo, salve*] A Latin phrase: 'Greetings, maiden' (so Craik).
   54.] The Friars were given to bobs and curtsies (see II.iii.25 n.). 'When'
is an exclamation of impatience.

Abig. To get me be admitted for a nun.

Jac. Why, Abigail, it is not yet long since
  That I did labour thy admission,   60
  And then thou didst not like that holy life.

Abig. Then were my thoughts so frail and unconfirmed,
  And I was chained to follies of the world;
  But now experience, purchasèd with grief,
  Has made me see the difference of things.   65
  My sinful soul, alas, hath paced too long
  The fatal labyrinth of misbelief,
  Far from the Son that gives eternal life.

Jac. Who taught thee this?

Abig.   The abbess of the house,
  Whose zealous admonition I embrace;   70
  O therefore, Jacomo, let me be one,
  Although unworthy, of that sisterhood.

Jac. Abigail, I will, but see thou change no more,
  For that will be most heavy to thy soul.

Abig. That was my father's fault.

Jac.   Thy father's? How? 75

Abig. Nay, you shall pardon me. *O, Barabas,*   [*Aside.*]
  Though thou deservest hardly at my hands,
  Yet never shall these lips bewray thy life.

Jac. Come, shall we go?

Abig.   My duty waits on you.   *Exeunt.*

---

63. And] *Q;* As *Dyce ii;* That *Shone.* 68. Son] *Reed;* Sonne *Q;* sun
Shone. 72. unworthy,] *Reed;* unworthy *Q.* 76-8.] *Broughton; aside
not in Q.*

---

 60. *labour*] work hard for, urge strenuously.
 62. *unconfirmed*] not yet made firm or sure.
 68. *Son*] Q's pun on 'son' and 'sun' cannot be reproduced in a modern-spelling edition.
 eternal life] A common New Testament phrase e.g. Matthew, xix.16.
 70. *admonition*] serious advice, warning.
 embrace] accept eagerly.
 74. *heavy*] dangerous, distressing.
 77. *hardly*] to be treated severely.
 78. *bewray*] to expose someone to danger by revealing his secrets.

[III.iv]

Enter BARABAS *reading a letter.*

Bar. What, Abigail become a nun again ?
    False and unkind! What, hast thou lost thy father,
    And all unknown and unconstrained of me,
    Art thou again got to the nunnery ?
    Now here she writes, and wills me to repent.   5
    Repentance! Spurca! What pretendeth this ?
    I fear she knows ('tis so) of my device
    In Don Mathias' and Lodovico's deaths:
    If so, 'tis time that it be seen into,
    For she that varies from me in belief   10
    Gives great presumption that she loves me not,
    Or loving, doth dislike of something done.

              [*Enter* ITHAMORE.]

    But who comes here ? O Ithamore, come near;
    Come near, my love, come near, thy master's life,
    My trusty servant, nay, my second self!   15
    For I have now no hope but even in thee,
    And on that hope my happiness is built.
    When saw'st thou Abigail ?

[III.iv] 2. What,] *Scott;* What *Q.*   8. Lodovico's] *Q;* Lodowick's *Reed.*
12.1. *Enter Ithamore.*] *Reed.*   15. self] *Penley;* life *Q.*

III.iv.2. *lost*] apparently in the sense 'cut yourself off from'.

  5. *wills*] wishes.

  6. *Spurca*] from Italian *sporco*, 'dirty, filthy'; as it is in the feminine
form, it may be an insult directed at Abigail herself (*cf.* IV.i.20 n.).

  pretendeth] portends. Dyce compares Marlowe's translation of *Lucan's
First Book*, l. 625, 'And which (aye me) ever pretendeth ill'.

  9. *seen into*] looked into, dealt with.

  11. *presumption*] in *O.E.D.*'s sense 4, 'ground or reason for presuming
or believing'.

  15. *second self*] Q's 'second life' would make sense (*cf. 2 Tamburlaine*,
II.iv.68), but the repetition of 'life' suggests that it was caught up by
eye-skip from the line above. 'Second self' is proverbial (Tilley, F 696),
and is part of the standard Renaissance phraseology of passionate friendship (see L. J. Mills, *M.P.*, XXXII (1934–35), 18–19).

Ith. Today.

Bar. With whom?   20

Ith. A friar.

Bar. A friar? False villain, he hath done the deed.

Ith. How, sir?

Bar. Why, made mine Abigail a nun.

Ith. That's no lie, for she sent me for him.   25

Bar. O unhappy day!
    False, credulous, inconstant Abigail!
    But let 'em go: and Ithamore, from hence
    Ne'er shall she grieve me more with her disgrace;
    Ne'er shall she live to inherit aught of mine,   30
    Be blessed of me, nor come within my gates,
    But perish underneath my bitter curse,
    Like Cain by Adam, for his brother's death.

Ith. O master!

Bar. Ithamore, entreat not for her; I am moved,   35
    And she is hateful to my soul and me:
    And 'less thou yield to this that I entreat,
    I cannot think but that thou hatest my life.

Ith. Who, I, master? Why, I'll run to some rock, and throw
    myself headlong into the sea; why, I'll do anything for   40
    your sweet sake.

Bar. O trusty Ithamore, no servant, but my friend!
    I here adopt thee for mine only heir,

37. 'less] *conj. Collier;* least *Q.*

---

31. *within my gates*] a biblical phrase, used frequently in Deuteronomy, usually in the form 'within thy gates'.

32–3.] not strictly accurate (see Genesis, iv.9–16); Cain was cursed by God, not by Adam.

35. *moved*] provoked, angered (*cf.* iv.iii.42).

37. *'less*] unless. Q's 'least' does not make sense in the context, and most editors accept Collier's conjecture; for other examples of the form see *O.E.D.*, 'less', *conj.*

39–40.] The phraseology may echo that used in the biblical story of the Gadarene swine, as in Mark, v.11–13: 'Now there was there in the mountaines a great herd of swine, feeding . . . and the herd ran headling [*sic*] from the high banke into the sea'. For 'ran headling' Geneva gives an alternative marginal rendering, 'ran with violence headlong'.

All that I have is thine when I am dead,
And whilst I live use half; spend as myself;   45
Here, take my keys—I'll give 'em thee anon.
Go buy thee garments—but thou shalt not want;
Only know this, that thus thou art to do.
But first go fetch me in the pot of rice
That for our supper stands upon the fire.   50

Ith. [*aside.*] *I hold my head my master's hungry*; I go, sir.   *Exit.*

Bar. Thus every villain ambles after wealth,
Although he ne'er be richer than in hope.
But husht.

Enter ITHAMORE *with the pot.*

Ith. Here 'tis, master.   55
Bar. Well said, Ithamore.
What, hast thou brought the ladle with thee too ?
Ith. Yes, sir; the proverb says, he that eats with the devil
had need of a long spoon: I have brought you a ladle.
Bar. Very well, Ithamore, then now be secret;   60
And for thy sake, whom I so dearly love,
Now shalt thou see the death of Abigail,
That thou mayst freely live to be my heir.
Ith. Why, master, will you poison her with a mess of rice—

45. half] *Reed;* helfe *Q.*   46. keys—] *Penley;* keyes, *Q.*
47. garments—] *Penley;* garments: *Q.*   51.] *Dyce; aside not in Q.*

46–7.] I have followed Penley's use of dashes in these lines because
Barabas is clearly luring Ithamore with promises which are then with-
drawn. (Possibly 'when I am dead' in l. 44 should be marked off in the
same way.)

48. *thus . . . do*] this is what you can expect to do, can look forward to.

51. *hold*] bet, wager.

56. *Well said*] frequently used in Shakespeare (see Onions, *Shakespeare
Glossary*) with the sense 'well done' rather than 'well spoken'.

58–9. *proverb . . . spoon*] an old and very widely used proverb (Whiting,
S 639, Tilley, S 771).

64. *mess*] commonly used at the time for a rather liquid kind of food,
such as broth, porridge, etc. This may echo the 'messe of potage' for which
Esau sold his birthright, Genesis, xxv; in the Geneva Bible the phrase
occurs in the chapter-heading, but not in the actual text (see *O.E.D.*'s note
on 'mess', *sb.* 2).

porridge, that will preserve life, make her round and   65
plump, and batten more than you are aware?

Bar. Ay, but Ithamore, seest thou this?   [*Brings out poison.*]
It is a precious powder that I bought
Of an Italian in Ancona once,
Whose operation is to bind, infect,   70
And poison deeply: yet not appear
In forty hours after it is ta'en.

Ith. How, master?

Bar. Thus, Ithamore:
This even, they use in Malta here ('tis called   75
Saint Jacques' Even), and then I say they use
To send their alms unto the nunneries:
Among the rest bear this, and set it there.
There's a dark entry where they take it in,
Where they must neither see the messenger,   80
Nor make enquiry who hath sent it them.

Ith. How so?

Bar. Belike there is some ceremony in 't.
There, Ithamore, must thou go place this pot:

---

67. *Brings out poison.*] *This ed.*   76. Jacques'] *Scott;* Iagues *Q;* Jacques's
Broughton.   84. pot] *Reed;* plot *Q.*

---

66. *batten*] fatten, nourish.

67 ff.] Both Jews and Machiavellians had an evil reputation as poisoners: Malevole, in Marston's *The Malcontent*, v.iv.33, claims that he can poison skilfully, 'no Jew, 'pothecary, or politician better'. The kind of delayed-action poison mentioned below is referred to in an anonymous pamphlet attacking the Earl of Leicester; the author claims to have heard one of the Earl's doctors 'maintein, that poyson might be so tempered and giuen as it should not apeare presentlie, and yet should kill the partie afterward at what time should be appointed' (*The Copy of a Letter . . .*, n.p., 1584, p. 29). See also Mario Praz, *The Flaming Heart*, New York, 1958, p. 128, and *cf.* Webster, *The Duchess of Malfi*, v.ii.265–6.

69. *Ancona*] an Italian port on the Adriatic. In the early 16th c. it had been unusually tolerant towards Jews, and a thriving Jewish community developed there. But in 1555 Cardinal Caraffa became Pope Paul IV, and in 1556 on his instructions all the Jews in Ancona were forcibly converted, burnt as heretics, or expelled. See Cecil Roth, *A History of the Marranos* (New York, 1959), pp. 205–8.

75. *This even, they use*] tonight they have a custom.

Stay, let me spice it first.   85

Ith. Pray do, and let me help you, master. Pray let me taste
    first.

Bar. Prithee do. [*Ithamore tastes.*] What say'st thou now?

Ith. Troth, master, I'm loath such a pot of pottage should be
    spoiled.   90

Bar. [*puts in poison.*] Peace, Ithamore, 'tis better so than
    spared.

    Assure thyself thou shalt have broth by the eye:
    My purse, my coffer, and myself is thine.

Ith. Well, master, I go.

Bar. Stay, first let me stir it, Ithamore.   95
    As fatal be it to her as the draught
    Of which great Alexander drunk and died:
    And with her let it work like Borgia's wine,
    Whereof his sire, the Pope, was poisonèd;
    In few, the blood of Hydra, Lerna's bane,   100
    The juice of hebon, and Cocytus' breath,

---

88. *Ithamore tastes.*] *Dyce.*   91. *puts in poison.*] *Dyce.*

---

92. *by the eye*] as much as you like, in unlimited quantities (*O.E.D.*,
'eye', *sb.*, 4b). Tilley gives the phrase as proverbial (E 249).

96–7.] Alexander the Great died of fever at Babylon in 323 B.C., but one
version of his death was that he was given poisoned wine by his follower
Antipater (see Plutarch's *Life of Alexander*). The story is also found in the
context of a curse in Ovid's *Ibis*, ll. 297–8, a poem Marlowe probably
knew (see Prologue, l. 25 n.).

98–9.] It was widely, though erroneously, believed in the 16th c. that
Pope Alexander VI (Rodrigo Borgia) died accidentally through drinking
poisoned wine that his son, Cesare Borgia, had prepared for other victims.
There were numerous versions of the story, differing slightly in detail;
Marlowe may have found it in Fenton's translation of Guicciardini's
History of Italy, 1579, pp. 307–8. Neither Machiavelli nor Gentillet men-
tions the story.

100. *In few*] in few words, in short.

Hydra, Lerna's bane] The Hydra, a poisonous water-snake, lived in the
marshes of Lerna, near Argos. One of the labours of Hercules was to kill
it; he then dipped his arrows in the Hydra's blood, which made their
wounds incurable. *Cf. 1 Tamburlaine*, IV.iv.21–2.

101. *juice of hebon*] *Cf. Hamlet*, I.v.62, 'with juice of cursed hebona
(*quartos*), hebenon (*folio*) in a vial'. In both plays obviously a poison, but
its exact nature has been much debated (see articles by Nicholson and

And all the poisons of the Stygian pool,
Break from the fiery kingdom, and in this
Vomit your venom, and envenom her
That like a fiend hath left her father thus.   105

Ith. *What a blessing has he given't ! Was ever pot of rice-*   [*Aside.*]
porridge so sauced ? What shall I do with it ?

Bar. O my sweet Ithamore, go set it down,
And come again so soon as thou hast done,
For I have other business for thee.   110

Ith. Here's a drench to poison a whole stable of Flanders
mares: I'll carry it to the nuns with a powder.

Bar. And the horse-pestilence to boot; away!

106-7.] Dyce; aside not in Q.

W. A. Harrison in *Trans. New Shakespeare Soc.* (1880–86), 21–31, 295–
321, by Bradley and Montgomery, *M.L.R.*, xv (1920), 85–7, 305–7, and
T. P. Harrison, *M.L.R.*, XL (1945), 310–11). The word seems to derive
ultimately from Latin *hebenus*, 'ebony', mistakenly assumed to be
soporific, and associated with such genuine poisons as yew, henbane, and
hemlock (see Spenser, *Faerie Queene*, II.vii.51–2).

   Cocytus' breath] Cocytus was one of the four rivers of the classical
underworld, with particular associations of darkness and lamentation (*cf.*
Spenser, *Faerie Queene*, II.vii.56, and Milton, *Paradise Lost*, II, 579).

   102. *Stygian pool*] Styx was the principal river of the underworld. The
name was also applied to a small river in Arcadia which was regarded as
poisonous: Sidney refers in his *Arcadia* to 'poisonous *Stygian* water'
(*Works*, ed. Feuillerat, 1912, I, 63). *Cf.* also *1 Tamburlaine*, V.ii.193–5.

   111. *drench*] a dose of medicine given to an animal.

   111–12. *Flanders mares*] a breed of horse, apparently difficult to control
(*O.E.D.* cites William Browne's *Britannia's Pastorals*, 1613, I.v.504–5, 'a
stubborn nag of Galloway, / Or unback'd jennet, or a Flanders mare').
But the term could refer to violently lascivious women (i.e. the nuns), as
in Ford's *Love's Sacrifice*, III.i (1633, F4*v*), where Ferentes says of his
three mistresses, 'oh for three Barbary stone horses to top three Flanders
Mares'. *Cf.* also Beaumont and Fletcher, *The Scornful Lady*, I.ii.86 and
IV.i.157, and the epilogue to Wycherley's *The Country Wife*, l. 22.

   112. *with a powder*] Some editors have been unnecessarily puzzled by
this phrase, clearly explained by Hazelton Spencer, *M.L.N.*, XLVII (1932),
35, who notes that *O.E.D.* records it as meaning 'impetuously, violently,
in haste' (and see Tilley, P 533). Ithamore uses the phrase with a double
meaning, alluding also to the poison, the 'precious powder' (l. 68 above),
that Barabas has put in the pot.

   113. *horse-pestilence*] This compound, not in *O.E.D.*, seems to refer to
some disease of horses which Barabas would also like to inflict on the nuns.
   to boot] in addition.

Ith. I am gone;
        Pay me my wages, for my work is done.   115

                                        Exit [with the pot].

Bar. I'll pay thee with a vengeance, Ithamore.   *Exit.*

[III.v]

                Enter FERNEZE, [MARTIN DEL] BOSCO, Knights
                             [*and*] Bashaw.

Fern. Welcome, great bashaw; how fares Calymath?
         What wind drives you thus into Malta road?
Bash. The wind that bloweth all the world besides,
         Desire of gold.
Fern.   Desire of gold, great sir?
         That's to be gotten in the Western Ind: 5
         In Malta are no golden minerals.
Bash. To you of Malta thus saith Calymath:
         The time you took for respite is at hand
         For the performance of your promise passed,
         And for the tribute-money I am sent.   10

115.1. *with the pot*] *Dyce.*

[III.v] 1. bashaw] *Reed;* Bashaws *Q.*   2. road] *Reed;* rhode *Q.*
9. passed] *Dyce ii;* past *Q.*

---

116. *with a vengeance*] another of Barabas's sudden shifts of meaning,
possibly spoken aside or after Ithamore has gone out.

III.v.1. *bashaw*] 'Great sir' (l. 4) and 'Bashaw' (l. 11) suggest that the
singular is needed, and Q's 'Bashaws' may be a compositorial misreading
of the MS; see I.ii.0.1 n.
2. *What . . . thus*] A semi-proverbial phrase (Whiting, W 343, Tilley,
W 441).
5. *Western Ind*] At this time 'Indies' could refer to the mainland of
America as well as to the small islands; Marlowe is thinking of the gold
and silver mines of South America. *Cf.* Kyd, *The Spanish Tragedy*,
III.xiv.6–7, and Arthur Freeman's comment on the lines, *Thomas Kyd:
Facts and Problems* (Oxford, 1967), pp. 53–4.
9. *passed*] As Bennett notes, Q's 'past' is ambiguous: 1. in the past, 2.
made or given. The latter seems more likely.

Fern. Bashaw, in brief, shalt have no tribute here,
    Nor shall the heathens live upon our spoil:
    First will we raze the city-walls ourselves,
    Lay waste the island, hew the temples down,
    And shipping off our goods to Sicily,   15
    Open an entrance for the wasteful sea,
    Whose billows, beating the resistless banks,
    Shall overflow it with their refluence.
Bash. Well, governor, since thou hast broke the league
    By flat denial of the promised tribute,   20
    Talk not of razing down your city-walls;
    You shall not need trouble yourselves so far,
    For Selim-Calymath shall come himself,
    And with brass bullets batter down your towers,
    And turn proud Malta to a wilderness   25
    For these intolerable wrongs of yours;
    And so farewell.
Fern. Farewell.   [*Exit* Bashaw.]
    And now, you men of Malta, look about,
    And let's provide to welcome Calymath: 30
    Close your portcullis, charge your basilisks,
    And as you profitably take up arms,
    So now courageously encounter them;
    For by this answer, broken is the league,
    And naught is to be looked for now but wars,   35
    And naught to us more welcome is than wars.   *Exeunt.*

---

13. raze] *Reed;* race *Q.*   15. off] *Reed;* of *Q.*   21. razing] *Reed;*
racing *Q.*   28. *Exit* Bashaw.] *Reed.*

---

16. *wasteful*] causing devastation and ruin.
17. *resistless*] unresisting.
18. *refluence*] flowing back, reflux.
31. *portcullis*] a heavy wooden grid which could be lowered in a gateway
to form a defensive barrier.
    basilisks] large cannons, generally made of brass.
32. *profitably*] Presumably Ferneze intends the meaning 'for a good
cause, beneficially', though the other sense, 'with a good financial profit'
is obviously present.

[III.vi]

Enter Friar JACOMO *and* Friar BERNARDINE.

Jac. O brother, brother, all the nuns are sick,
    And physic will not help them; they must die.
Bern. The abbess sent for me to be confessed:
    O, what a sad confession will there be!
Jac. And so did fair Maria send for me.   5
    I'll to her lodging; hereabouts she lies.   *Exit.*

Enter ABIGAIL.

Bern. What, all dead save only Abigail?
Abig. And I shall die too, for I feel death coming.
    Where is the friar that conversed with me?
Bern. O, he is gone to see the other nuns.   10
Abig. I sent for him, but seeing you are come,
    Be you my ghostly father; and first know
    That in this house I lived religiously,
    Chaste, and devout, much sorrowing for my sins;
    But ere I came—   15
Bern. What then?
Abig. I did offend high heaven so grievously
    As I am almost desperate for my sins:
    And one offence torments me more than all.
    You knew Mathias and Don Lodowick?   20
Bern. Yes, what of them?
Abig. My father did contract me to 'em both:

[III.vi] 0.1. *Enter . . . Bernardine.*] Dyce; *Enter two Fryars and Abigall.* Q.

III.vi.0.1.] Q gives a double entry for Abigail, here and after l. 6 (see
Introduction, p. 47).
    4. *sad*] sorrowful, lamentable. Another anti-Catholic joke; the Abbess
will have a great deal to confess (and so, presumably, will 'fair Maria').
This helps to prepare us for the coarseness of l. 41 below.
    9.] a reference to her conversation with Jacomo at III.iii.53–79.
    12. *ghostly father*] spiritual father, confessor.
    18. *desperate*] in the theological sense, 'without hope of salvation'.
    22. *contract*] betroth.

First to Don Lodowick—him I never loved;
Mathias was the man that I held dear,
And for his sake did I become a nun.   25
Bern. So; say how was their end?
Abig. Both, jealous of my love, envied each other:
And by my father's practice, which is there
Set down at large, the gallants were both slain.
                                    [*Gives a paper.*]
Bern. O monstrous villainy!   30
Abig. To work my peace, this I confess to thee;
Reveal it not, for then my father dies.
Bern. Know that confession must not be revealed;
The canon law forbids it, and the priest
That makes it known, being degraded first,   35
Shall be condemned, and then sent to the fire.
Abig. So I have heard; pray therefore keep it close.
Death seizeth on my heart; ah, gentle friar,
Convert my father that he may be saved,
And witness that I die a Christian.   [*Dies.*]   40
Bern. Ay, and a virgin, too, that grieves me most.
But I must to the Jew and exclaim on him,
And make him stand in fear of me.

Enter Friar JACOMO.

29.1. *Gives a paper.*] *Broughton.*   40. *Dies.*] *Reed.*

---

27. *envied*] showed ill-will or malice towards. The word should be stressed on its second syllable.

28. *practice*] scheming, trickery.

29. *at large*] at length, in full.

31. *work my peace*] gain absolution.

33–6.] According to canon law a priest who broke the seal of confession could be 'degraded' (deprived of orders), and possibly excommunicated, but he would certainly not be burnt alive, as 'sent to the fire' suggests (and *cf.* l. 51 below). Probably Marlowe deliberately exaggerated the heinous nature of the offence to emphasise the ironic contrast between Bernardine's theory and practice, as he immediately goes off to make use of the knowledge he has gained.

42. *exclaim on*] accuse, cry out against.

Jac. O brother, all the nuns are dead; let's bury them.

Bern. First help to bury this; then go with me,   45
    And help me to exclaim against the Jew.

Jac. Why, what has he done?

Bern. A thing that makes me tremble to unfold.

Jac. What, has he crucified a child?

Bern. No, but a worse thing: 'twas told me in shrift;   50
    Thou know'st 'tis death and if it be revealed.
    Come, let's away.   *Exeunt [with the body].*

---

52. *with the body*] Van Fossen.

---

46. *exclaim against*] Bennett notes that this is less emphatic than 'exclaim on', and means 'rail at, complain of'.

49.] One of the commonest atrocity stories told against the Jews was that they kidnapped young Christian children and crucified them in mockery of Christ's crucifixion. It can be found at least as early as Socrates Scholasticus, a church historian of the early 5th c., who wrote in Greek (see *The Ecclesiasticall Historie of Socrates Scholasticus*, VII, 16, trans. Meredith Hanmer, London, 1585, pp. 384–5); there are innumerable later references.

50. *shrift*] confession.

Act IV

Enter BARABAS [*and*] ITHAMORE. *Bells within.*

Bar. There is no music to a Christian's knell:
How sweet the bells ring, now the nuns are dead,
That sound at other times like tinkers' pans!
I was afraid the poison had not wrought;
Or though it wrought, it would have done no good,   5
For every year they swell, and yet they live;
Now all are dead, not one remains alive.
Ith. That's brave, master, but think you it will not be known?
Bar. How can it if we two be secret?
Ith. For my part fear you not.   10
Bar. I'd cut thy throat if I did.
Ith. And reason too.
But here's a royal monastery hard by;
Good master, let me poison all the monks.
Bar. Thou shalt not need, for now the nuns are dead,   15
They'll die with grief.
Ith. Do you not sorrow for your daughter's death?
Bar. No, but I grieve because she lived so long;
An Hebrew born, and would become a Christian!

Act IV] *Actus Quartus Q.*   [IV.i] 18. long;] *Oxberry;* long *Q.*   19.
Christian!] *Shone;* Christian. *Q.*

IV.i.1. *to*] compared to.
4. *wrought*] worked, taken effect.
6. *swell*] become pregnant.
12. *reason*] with reason, rightly. *Cf.* v.ii.116 and *3H6*, II.ii.93.
13. *royal*] in the colloquial sense (*O.E.D.*, 8d), 'splendid, first-rate'.
18–19.] Q has no punctuation after 'long', and it would be possible to read these two lines as a continuous sentence. But l. 18 is more effective in isolation: Barabas is not grieved that Abigail died so young, but that she lived as long as she did.

Cazzo, diavola!   20

Enter Friar JACOMO *and* Friar BERNARDINE.

Ith. Look, look, master, here come two religious caterpillars.
Bar. I smelt 'em ere they came.
Ith. [*aside.*] *God-a-mercy, nose;* come, let's be gone.
Bern. Stay, wicked Jew; repent, I say, and stay.
Jac. Thou hast offended, therefore must be damned.   25
Bar. [*aside to Ith.*] *I fear they know we sent the poisoned broth.*
Ith. *And so do I, master, therefore speak 'em fair.*
Bern. Barabas, thou hast—
Jac. Ay, that thou hast—
Bar. True, I have money; what though I have?   30
Bern. Thou art a—
Jac. Ay, that thou art, a—
Bar. What needs all this? I know I am a Jew.
Bern. Thy daughter—
Jac. Ay, thy daughter—   35
Bar. O speak not of her, then I die with grief.
Bern. Remember that—
Jac. Ay, remember that—
Bar. I must needs say that I have been a great usurer.
Bern. Thou hast committed—
Bar.   Fornication?   40

20. Cazzo,] *Dyce; Catho Q.*   diavola] *Q (diabola);* diabolo *Collier.*
20.1. *Enter ... B∘rnardine.*] *Dyce; Enter the two Fryars. Q.*   23.] *This ed.;*
aside not in Q.   26-7.] *Shone; aside not in Q.*

20. *Cazzo*] an Italian obscenity, glossed by Florio, *A World of Words*,
1598, *s.v.*, as 'a mans priuie member'. In Elizabethan English it was used
either as a vague expression of contempt and disgust (as in Marston's
Malcontent, I.iii.104 and v.iv.26), or to mean 'rogue, rascal' (Jonson, *Every
Man Out of his Humour*, II.i.20).
   diavola] 'she-devil'; there is no need to make the word masculine if we
regard it as directed at Abigail.
21. *caterpillars*] probably used here with a double meaning: I. to refer
contemptuously to the black robes of the friars, 2. to imply *O.E.D.*'s sense
2, 'an extortioner, one who preys upon society' (*cf. 2H6*, IV.iv.37).
23. God-a-mercy] 'Thank you!' (a stock phrase; *cf.* IV.iii.32).
28-40.] For comment on this passage see Introduction, p. 32.

But that was in another country:
And besides, the wench is dead.
Bern. Ay, but Barabas, remember Mathias and Don Lodowick.
Bar. Why, what of them?
Bern. I will not say that by a forged challenge they met.   45
Bar. She has confessed, and we are both undone.   [*Aside.*]
My bosom inmates!—*but I must dissemble.*   Aside.
O, holy friars, the burden of my sins
Lie heavy on my soul; then pray you tell me,
Is 't not too late now to turn Christian?   50
I have been zealous in the Jewish faith,
Hard-hearted to the poor, a covetous wretch,
That would for lucre's sake have sold my soul.
A hundred for a hundred I have ta'en;
And now for store of wealth may I compare   55
With all the Jews in Malta; but what is wealth?
I am a Jew, and therefore am I lost.
Would penance serve for this my sin,
I could afford to whip myself to death—

46.] *Broughton; aside not in Q.*   47. inmates] *Q;* inmate *Broughton;*
intimates *Brooke i (but not Brooke ii).*   49. Lie] *Q;* Lies *Shone.*   58.
serve] *Q;* serve t'atone *Broughton.*   59. death—] *Broughton;* death. *Q.*

46–7.] Editors who follow Broughton assume that both these lines are
addressed to Ithamore. It seems preferable to leave l. 47 as it stands in Q
and assume that 'My bosom inmates' is addressed to the friars ('You now
know all my secrets'), but that 'but I must dissemble' is directed to Ithamore, who may be puzzled by this abrupt change of front.

49. *Lie*] As Dyce points out, no emendation is needed; 'examples of
similar phraseology—of a nominative singular followed by a plural verb
when a plural genitive intervenes,—are common in our early writers'.

54. *A hundred for a hundred*] interest of 100 per cent on a loan. This may
derive from Gentillet, Avi, 'the Italians do often returne their money with
the gaine of fiftie, yea often of an hundreth, for an hundreth'. But *cf.* also
Harrison's *Description of England* (1577), ed. F. J. Furnivall (London,
1877), p. 242, where he wants to 'hang vp such as take *centum pro cento*,
for they are no better worthie as I doo iudge in conscience'.

57. *lost*] used here in its theological sense, 'damned'.

58.] Something may have dropped out from this short line, but it could
be filled up in various ways, all of which would be sheer guesswork.

Ith. And so could I; but penance will not serve—   60
Bar. To fast, to pray, and wear a shirt of hair,
         And on my knees creep to Jerusalem.
         Cellars of wine, and sollars full of wheat,
         Warehouses stuffed with spices and with drugs,
         Whole chests of gold, in bullion and in coin,   65
         Besides I know not how much weight in pearl,
         Orient and round, have I within my house;
         At Alexandria, merchandise unsold:
         But yesterday two ships went from this town,
         Their voyage will be worth ten thousand crowns;   70
         In Florence, Venice, Antwerp, London, Seville,
         Frankfurt, Lubeck, Moscow, and where not,
         Have I debts owing; and in most of these,
         Great sums of money lying in the banco;
         All this I'll give to some religious house,   75

---

60. serve—] *Broughton;* serue. *Q.*   65. bullion] *Reed; Bulloine Q.*   68.
unsold] *Q;* untold *Dyce.*   71. Seville] *Reed; Ciuill Q.*

60.] I follow Broughton in assuming that this is a hasty interjection by
Ithamore which interrupts the continuity of Barabas's speech. Alarmed
at the direction in which Barabas's argument seems to be going, Ithamore
makes it clear that he himself will not submit to severe penitential punishment.

62.] Bennett suggests that Marlowe may be remembering 'the medieval
custom of creeping to the Cross on Good Friday'. But Barabas characteris-
tically exaggerates: he would travel to Jerusalem in this way. *Cf.* II.iii.
210–14.

63. *sollars*] lofts or attics, used as store rooms.

65. *bullion*] Bennett notes that the compositor evidently misread this
word as the place-name 'Boulogne'. Both words had various spellings
which could easily be confused.

68. *unsold*] i.e. he has not yet made his profit on it. Dyce's emendation
is unnecessary.

71–2.] This list seems reasonably accurate; in the introduction to his
edition of Thomas Wilson's *A Discourse Upon Usury* (London, 1925), p.
63, R. H. Tawney gives a list of important financial centres in the 16th c.
including Antwerp, Lyons, Frankfurt and Venice, 'and, in the second
rank, Rouen, Paris, Strasburg, Seville, and London'. *Cf.* the cities listed
by Wilson himself (*ibid.*, pp. 311–12).

74. *banco*] *O.E.D.* quotes this line *s.v.* 'bank', sense 7. Marlowe seems
to be using the Italian form of the word.

  So I may be baptized and live therein.
Jac. O good Barabas, come to our house!
Bern. O no, good Barabas, come to our house!
  And Barabas, you know—
Bar. [*to Bern.*] I know that I have highly sinned.   80
  You shall convert me, you shall have all my wealth.
Jac. O Barabas, their laws are strict.
Bar. [*to Jac.*] I know they are, and I will be with you.
Bern. They wear no shirts, and they go barefoot too.
Bar. [*to Bern.*] Then 'tis not for me; and I am resolved   85
  You shall confess me, and have all my goods.
Jac. Good Barabas, come to me.
Bar. [*to Bern.*] You see I answer him, and yet he stays;
  Rid him away, and go you home with me.
Bern. I'll be with you to-night!   90
Bar. [*to Jac.*] Come to my house at one o' clock this night.
Jac. [*to Bern.*] You hear your answer, and you may be gone.
Bern. Why, go get you away.

84. Bern.] Reed; 1. Q (*i.e. Jacomo*).   90. Bern.] Q. (*2*); Jac. Dyce.

---

  77 ff.] The attribution of speeches in the quarrel between Jacomo and
Bernardine has been a problem for editors. Q assigns l. 84 to Jacomo and
l. 90 to Bernardine; Reed and Dyce reversed these attributions, and most
subsequent editors have followed them. J. C. Maxwell, however, has
proposed a more complicated rearrangement in which l. 84 remains with
Jacomo but all the speech-prefixes of the two friars in ll. 87–96 are
reversed and re-assigned to each other ('The assignment of speeches in
The Jew of Malta', *M.L.R.*, XLIII (1948), 510–12). But as Craik cogently
observes, 'this view overlooks Barabas's lines 103–5, which make it plain
that Bernardine has abused Jacomo's house too; it also misses the farcical
stage-effect of Barabas consciously playing the weathercock between the
two friars'. Certainly l. 84 could be read as following on from l. 82, but
ll. 85–6 read like a sudden change of mind by Barabas, and it seems best
to regard l. 84 as a counter-attack by Bernardine. I have not emended
l. 90, which in my opinion reads better as an expression of naive delight
by Bernardine than as further pestering by Jacomo. Some details in the
passage will remain slightly obscure however it is arranged, but the
ludicrous speed with which the alliance of the two friars collapses at the
mention of money suggests that the incident should not be viewed too
realistically.
  89. *Rid . . . away*] get rid of, remove him.

Jac. I will not go for thee.

Bern. Not? Then I'll make thee, rogue.   95

Jac. How, dost call me rogue?   [*They*] *fight.*

Ith. Part 'em, master, part 'em.

Bar. This is mere frailty; brethren, be content.

Friar Bernardine, go you with Ithamore:

You know my mind; let me alone with him.   100

Jac. Why does he go to thy house? Let him be gone.

Bar. I'll give him something, and so stop his mouth.

>   *Exeunt* ITHAMORE *and* Friar BERNARDINE.

I never heard of any man but he

Maligned the order of the Jacobins:

But do you think that I believe his words?   105

Why, brother, you converted Abigail,

And I am bound in charity to requite it;

And so I will—O Jacomo, fail not but come!

Jac. But Barabas, who shall be your godfathers?

For presently you shall be shrived.   110

Bar. Marry, the Turk shall be one of my godfathers,

---

95. thee, rogue.] *conj. Collier MS.;* thee goe. *Q.*   96. They] *Shone.*
100. You] *Dyce; Ith.* You *Q.*   101. *Jac.* Why] *Broughton;* Why *Q.*
102.1. *Exeunt . . . Bernardine.*] *Reed; Exit. Q.*

---

94. *for thee*] at your order.

95. *rogue*] Van Fossen, who retains Q's 'go', argues that Jacomo mishears the word and misunderstands it as 'rogue'. But it seems more probable that a compositorial misreading is involved.

100–1.] Q assigns both lines to Ithamore. All recent editors assume that l. 100 is meant to reassure Bernardine that Barabas will get rid of Jacomo, but it is just possible that 'You know my mind' is an aside to Ithamore and 'let me alone with him' is Ithamore's reply.

let . . . him] leave me to deal with him. *Cf.* IV.ii.68, 86, IV.iv.78.

104. *Jacobins*] See III.iii.31 n., and *cf. The Massacre at Paris,* xxiii.24.

110. *presently*] usually meaning 'immediately' in Elizabethan English (*cf.* IV.iii.64), though here, as in a few other cases, it may have the more modern meaning, 'in a short while'.

shrived] confessed, given absolution.

111. *the Turk*] presumably a reference to Ithamore (*cf.* l. 127 below), though earlier he describes himself as a Thracian brought up in Arabia (II.iii.131). But obviously he is anti-Christian, and to make him a godfather is a crashing insult which Jacomo willingly swallows in his greed for money.

But not a word to any of your convent.
Jac. I warrant thee, Barabas.   *Exit.*
Bar. So, now the fear is past, and I am safe,
    For he that shrived her is within my house.   115
    What if I murdered him ere Jacomo comes?
    Now I have such a plot for both their lives
    As never Jew nor Christian knew the like.
    One turned my daughter, therefore he shall die;
    The other knows enough to have my life,   120
    Therefore 'tis not requisite he should live.
    But are not both these wise men to suppose
    That I will leave my house, my goods, and all,
    To fast and be well whipped? I'll none of that.
    Now, Friar Bernardine, I come to you: 125
    I'll feast you, lodge you, give you fair words,
    And after that, I and my trusty Turk—
    No more but so: it must and shall be done.

Enter ITHAMORE.

Ithamore, tell me, is the friar asleep?
Ith. Yes; and I know not what the reason is,   130
    Do what I can he will not strip himself,
    Nor go to bed, but sleeps in his own clothes;

128.1. *Enter Ithamore.*] Dyce; *after l. 129 in* Q.

---

113. *warrant*] assure; 'I warrant you' was commonly used to express
strong affirmation (*O.E.D.*, sense 5).

117–18.] As Craik notes, this reads as though Barabas has suddenly
thought of the plan for dealing with the two friars on the spur of the
moment, but on his return (ll. 130–40) Ithamore speaks as though he
knows the plan, and it is Ithamore who suggests that Bernardine should
be propped up on a stick. *Cf.* ll. 137–8 n.

119. *turned*] converted; possibly with a pejorative implication, 'per-
verted'.

121.] See I.ii.301 n.

127.] Presumably at the end of this line Barabas makes a gesture (such
as slitting the throat) to indicate his intention.

128. *No . . . so*] i.e. without more ado; Barabas will carry out his plan
immediately. *Cf.* IV.ii.81–2.

130–2.] 'The Friars were not allowed by the rules of their Orders to
undress completely at night, but lay down in their robes' (Bennett).

I fear me he mistrusts what we intend.

Bar. No, 'tis an order which the friars use:

Yet if he knew our meanings, could he 'scape?   135

Ith. No, none can hear him, cry he ne'er so loud.

Bar. Why, true, therefore did I place him there:

The other chambers open towards the street.

Ith. You loiter, master; wherefore stay we thus?

O how I long to see him shake his heels!   140

             [*Draws curtains, revealing* BERNARDINE *asleep.*]

Bar. Come on, sirrah:

Off with your girdle, make a handsome noose;

Friar, awake!   [*Puts the noose round his neck.*]

Bern. What, do you mean to strangle me?

Ith. Yes, 'cause you use to confess.   145

Bar. Blame not us but the proverb, 'confess and be hanged'.

Pull hard.

---

135. meanings] *Q; meaning Shone.*   140.1. *Draws . . . asleep.*] *Brooke ii (after l. 143).*   143. *Puts . . . neck.*] *Dyce.*   144. What,] *Shone; What Q.*

---

134. *order*] regular custom.

135. *meanings*] Shone's emendation to 'meaning' is attractive, since Q has false plurals elsewhere (see I.ii.0.1 n.), and the singular is often used when the word means 'purpose, intention'. *Cf.* IV.iv.78–9.

137–8.] Broughton conjectured that these lines should be spoken by Ithamore. This is very unlikely, but it does draw attention to a slight inconsistency in Q; Barabas has been on stage throughout the scene and has had no chance to assign a bedroom to Bernardine. Robinson and other editors avoid this difficulty by giving an exit for Barabas at l. 128 and starting a new scene at l. 129. This break in the action would also give Bernardine time for a meal (see l. 126), and Barabas time to explain his plans to Ithamore. But as Craik sensibly comments, 'Marlowe does not trouble about verisimilitude in these matters.'

139. *stay*] linger, delay.

140. *shake his heels*] shake about in the throes of death; a common phrase normally used in connection with hanging.

140.1.] See Appendix C for discussion of the staging of this incident.

142. *Off . . . girdle*] Dyce and most later editors assume that this is addressed to Ithamore, but surely Bernardine is strangled with his own girdle, taken from him before he is fully awake?

144. *strangle*] Bullen compares the strangling of the Cardinal in scene xxii of *The Massacre at Paris.*

145. *use to confess*] 'make a practice of hearing confession' (Craik).

146. *confess . . . hanged*] a very common proverb (Tilley, C 587).

Bern. What, will you have my life?

Bar. Pull hard, I say! You would have had my goods.

Ith. Ay, and our lives too, therefore pull amain.   150

                                    [*They strangle him.*]

    'Tis neatly done, sir, here's no print at all.

Bar. Then is it as it should be. Take him up.

Ith. Nay, master, be ruled by me a little. [*Stands up the body.*]

    So, let him lean upon his staff; excellent, he stands as if

    he were begging of bacon.   155

Bar. Who would not think but that this friar lived?

    What time o' night is 't now, sweet Ithamore?

Ith. Towards one.

Bar. Then will not Jacomo be long from hence.   [*Exeunt.*]

Enter [Friar] JACOMO.

Jac. This is the hour wherein I shall proceed;   160

    O happy hour,

    Wherein I shall convert an infidel,

    And bring his gold into our treasury!

    But soft, is not this Bernardine? It is;

    And understanding I should come this way,   165

    Stands here o' purpose, meaning me some wrong,

---

148. have] *Shone;* saue *Q.*   150.1. *They . . . him.*] *Broughton.*   153.
Stands . . . body.] *Cunningham.*   159. *Exeunt.*] *Reed.*   159.1. *Enter . . .*
Jacomo.] *Reed; Enter Iocoma. Q (after l. 158).*

---

148. *have*] As Ellis notes, the emendation is justified by Barabas's jeering
retort in the next line, 'You would have had my goods'.

150. *amain*] violently, with all one's might.

151. *print*] mark from the noose.

153–5.] Bennett compares *Tit.*, v.i.135–6: 'Oft have I digg'd up dead
men from their graves, / And set them upright at their dear friends' door'.

155. *begging*] 'Abbott, § 178, explains this apparent participle as a
verbal noun, before which a prepositional 'a', 'in', etc., should be inserted'
(Bennett).

160. *proceed*] make progress, prosper.

160–3.] The repetition of 'wherein I shall' suggests that Marlowe wrote
two versions of these lines but did not clearly indicate which was the final
one. What we have here may thus be the compositor's muddled conflation
of the two versions.

And intercepts my going to the Jew.
Bernardine!
Wilt thou not speak? Thou think'st I see thee not.
Away, I'd wish thee, and let me go by.   170
No, wilt thou not? Nay then, I'll force my way;
And see, a staff stands ready for the purpose.
As thou likest that, stop me another time.

Strikes him, he falls.

Enter BARABAS [*and* ITHAMORE].

Bar. Why, how now, Jacomo, what hast thou done?
Jac. Why, stricken him that would have struck at me.   175
Bar. Who is it? Bernardine? Now out, alas, he is slain!
Ith. Ay, master, he's slain; look how his brains drop out on's
     nose.
Jac. Good sirs, I have done 't, but nobody knows it but you
     two, I may escape.   180
Bar. So might my man and I hang with you for company.
Ith. No, let us bear him to the magistrates.
Jac. Good Barabas, let me go.
Bar. No, pardon me, the law must have his course.
     I must be forced to give in evidence   185

---

167. And intercepts] *This ed.;* And intercept *Q;* To intercept *Shone;* And
t' intercept *conj. Bennett.*   173.1. *Strikes*] *Reed; Strike Q.*   173.2. *and
Ithamore*] *Reed.*   175. struck] *Reed;* stroke *Q.*   176. it?] *Reed;* it *Q.*
184. his] *Q;* its *Oxberry.*

172.] Craik argues that this cannot be the staff mentioned at l. 154
above; Jacomo 'could hardly say that it stood ready for his purpose, nor
take it without dislodging the body. This is evidently another staff, left
conveniently on stage by Barabas'. But it seems rather clumsy for two
staffs to be needed, and it would surely be possible on the stage for
Jacomo to snatch up the staff on which Bernardine is propped and strike
him with it before he slumps to the ground. Craik seems to demand a
verisimilitude here that he does not expect elsewhere in the scene (see
ll. 137–8 n. above).

177. *on's*] i.e. of his; a common usage (Abbott, § 182).

184. *his*] Oxberry's emendation is unnecessary, though it has been
adopted by several later editors; 'his' was the usual genitive form of 'it'
at this time (Abbott, § 228).

That being importuned by this Bernardine
To be a Christian, I shut him out,
And there he sat: now I, to keep my word,
And give my goods and substance to your house,
Was up thus early, with intent to go   190
Unto your friary, because you stayed.

Ith. Fie upon 'em, master, will you turn Christian, when
holy friars turn devils and murder one another?

Bar. No; for this example I'll remain a Jew.
Heaven bless me; what, a friar a murderer!   195
When shall you see a Jew commit the like?

Ith. Why, a Turk could ha' done no more.

Bar. To-morrow is the sessions; you shall to it.
Come, Ithamore, let's help to take him hence.

Jac. Villains, I am a sacred person; touch me not.   200

Bar. The law shall touch you, we'll but lead you, we.
'Las, I could weep at your calamity.
Take in the staff too, for that must be shown:
Law wills that each particular be known.   *Exeunt.*

[IV.ii]

Enter BELLAMIRA *and* PILIA-BORZA.

Bella. Pilia-Borza, didst thou meet with Ithamore?

Pilia. I did.

Bella. And didst thou deliver my letter?

Pilia. I did.

Bella. And what think'st thou, will he come?   5

Pilia. I think so, and yet I cannot tell, for at the reading of
the letter he looked like a man of another world.

Bella. Why so?

---

191. *stayed*] See l. 139 n. above.
204. *wills*] requires, orders.
    particular] item of information or evidence.

IV.ii.7. *man . . . world*] ghost or spirit; *cf.* Shelton's translation of Part I
of Cervantes' *Don Quixote*, III.ii (1612, p. 125), 'he seemed unto them a
man of the other world', and III.iv (p. 142), 'spirits, or people of another
world'.

Pilia. That such a base slave as he should be saluted by such
    a tall man as I am, from such a beautiful dame as   10
    you.

Bella. And what said he?

Pilia. Not a wise word; only gave me a nod, as who should
    say, 'Is it even so?'; and so I left him, being driven to
    a non-plus at the critical aspect of my terrible counte-   15
    nance.

Bella. And where didst meet him?

Pilia. Upon mine own freehold, within forty foot of the
    gallows, conning his neck-verse, I take it, looking of
    a friar's execution, whom I saluted with an old hempen   20
    proverb, 'hodie tibi, cras mihi', and so I left him to the

[IV.ii] 21. hodie] *Q (corrected); Hidie Q (uncorrected).*

---

9. *saluted*] greeted.

10. *tall*] see III.ii.7 n. Tilley gives 'he is a tall man of his hands' as proverbial (M 163).

15. *non-plus*] state of bewilderment, in which no action is possible.
Tilley gives 'he is put to a non-plus' as proverbial (N 206).

critical] Bennett glosses this as 'censorious, fault-finding' but Craik
takes 'critical aspect' to be an astrological phrase meaning 'sinister
influence'. Certainly 'aspect' can have an astrological sense (*O.E.D.*, sense
4), but 'critical' here seems rather to mean 'having the power to control
events' and hence 'awe-inspiring'. *Cf.* II.iii.107 n.

18. *mine own freehold*] private estate. Possibly pilia-Borza can pick
pockets easily in the crowds watching executions, or else he may be
making a wry joke, that the gallows is the only territory he has any right to.

18–19. *within . . . gallows*] *Cf. Faustus,* ii.18–19, 'within forty foot of the
place of execution'. Tilley gives as proverbial (F 581), 'He will not come
within forty foot of him', meaning 'He will keep away from someone
dangerous', so the implication here seems to be that Pilia-Borza's way of
life brings him perilously close to the gallows.

19. *conning his neck-verse*] The 'neck-verse' is 'the verse (generally the
beginning of the 51st Psalm, *Miserere mei,* &c.) read by a criminal to en-
title him to benefit of clergy' (Dyce). Ithamore is 'conning' it (i.e. learning
it by heart) because he will inevitably be in danger of hanging one day,
and will need to know it.

looking of] looking on, at (see *O.E.D.*, 'look', *v.*, sense 17).

20–1. *hempen proverb*] 'Perhaps a proverb said at the foot of the gallows,
since *hempen* is frequently used in phrases and locutions referring to the
hangman's halter. See below, l. 27' (Bennett).

21. *hodie tibi, cras mihi*] 'Your turn today, mine tomorrow'. A common
proverb in Latin and English (Whiting, T 349, Tilley, T 371).

mercy of the hangman; but the exercise being done, see
where he comes.

Enter ITHAMORE.

Ith. I never knew a man take his death so patiently as this
friar; he was ready to leap off ere the halter was about   25
his neck, and when the hangman had put on his hempen
tippet, he made such haste to his prayers, as if he had
had another cure to serve. Well, go whither he will,
I'll be none of his followers in haste. And now I
think on 't, going to the execution, a fellow met me   30
with a muschatoes like a raven's wing, and a dagger
with a hilt like a warming-pan, and he gave me a letter
from one Madam Bellamira, saluting me in such sort as
if he had meant to make clean my boots with his lips;
the effect was, that I should come to her house. I   35
wonder what the reason is; it may be she sees more in
me than I can find in myself, for she writes further that
she loves me ever since she saw me, and who would not
requite such love? Here's her house, and here she
comes, and now would I were gone, I am not worthy to   40
look upon her.

Pilia. This is the gentleman you writ to.

Ith. 'Gentleman'! He flouts me, what gentry can be in a   [*Aside.*]
poor Turk of tenpence? I'll be gone.

---

31. muschatoes] *Q;* mustachios *Reed.*   38. loves] *Q;* loved *Shone.*
43-4.] *Dyce; aside not in Q.*

---

22. *exercise*] act of worship. 'Marlowe humorously uses the word to
describe the ceremonial of an execution' (Bennett).

26–7. *hempen tippet*] a mocking allusion to the noose round the friar's
neck; a tippet is part of a priest's clothing, 'a band of silk or other material
round the neck, with the two ends pendant from the shoulders in front'
(*O.E.D.*).

28. *cure*] cure of souls, parish.

31. *muschatoes*] pair of moustaches. The word existed in many forms in
the 16th and 17th c.; Dyce compares Dekker's *The Noble Spanish Soldier*,
II.i.12, 'Tuskes more stiffe than are a Cats muschatoes'.

35. *effect*] purport, meaning (of the letter).

43. *flouts*] mocks.

44. Turk of tenpence] worthless fellow. Marlowe seems to have

Bella. Is 't not a sweet-faced youth, Pilia?   45

Ith. [*aside*.] *Again, 'sweet youth'! Did not you, sir, bring the*
            sweet youth a letter?

Pilia. I did, sir, and from this gentlewoman, who, as myself
            and the rest of the family, stand or fall at your service.

Bella. Though woman's modesty should hale me back,   50
            I can withhold no longer; welcome, sweet love.

Ith. *Now am I clean, or rather foully, out of the way.*   [*Aside*.]

Bella. Whither so soon?

Ith. *I'll go steal some money from my master to make me*   [*Aside*.]
            handsome.—Pray pardon me, I must go see a ship dis-   55
            charged.

Bella. Canst thou be so unkind to leave me thus?

Pilia. And ye did but know how she loves you, sir!

Ith. Nay, I care not how much she loves me. Sweet Bella-
            mira, would I had my master's wealth for thy sake.   60

Pilia. And you can have it, sir, and if you please.

Ith. If 'twere above ground I could and would have it, but
            he hides and buries it up as partridges do their eggs,
            under the earth.

46.] *Dyce; aside not in Q.*   52.] *Dyce; aside not in Q.*   54-5.] *Shone;
aside not in Q.*   59-60. Bellamira] *Reed; Allamira Q.*   63. partridges]
Q; ostriches *conj. Seaton ii.*

invented the phrase, which was popular with later writers; Dyce compares
Middleton and Rowley, *A Fair Quarrel*, III.i.73, and John Taylor's *Works*
(1630), p. 82, and Bullen compares Dekker's *Satiromastix*, IV.ii.32.

49. *family*] members of the household (with the implication that they
are Ithamore's servants).

stand or fall] used here with obscene implications.

52. clean . . . foully] Ithamore plays on two senses of 'clean': 1. completely (*cf.* I.i.178), 2. not dirty.

out of the way] going in the wrong direction, following the wrong course
of action. Ithamore feels that he is not smart enough to encounter Bellamira.

58. *And*] If only . . .

59–60. *Bellamira*] Some editors argue that Q's *Allamira* is deliberately
intended, and that Ithamore gets the name wrong. But Q is full of
misprints of names (see Introduction, p. 42), and Ithamore gets it right
at l. 33 above.

63. *partridges*] Miss Seaton's emendation to 'ostriches', supported by a
reference to Job, xxxix.14, is ingenious but unnecessary. Pliny records the
secretive habits of partridges: 'they cover their egges with a soft carpet or

Pilia. And is 't not possible to find it out ?   65
Ith. By no means possible.
Bella. [*aside to Pilia.*] *What shall we do with this base villain,*
    then ?
Pilia. [*to Bella.*] *Let me alone, do but you speak him fair.*
    But you know some secrets of the Jew,
    Which if they were revealed would do him harm.   70
Ith. Ay, and such as—Go to, no more, I'll make him send
    me half he has, and glad he 'scapes so too. Pen and ink!
    I'll write unto him, we'll have money straight.
Pilia. Send for a hundred crowns at least.
Ith. Ten hundred thousand crowns. (*He writes.*) 'Master   75
    Barabas—'
Pilia. Write not so submissively, but threatening him.
Ith. 'Sirrah Barabas, send me a hundred crowns.'
Pilia. Put in two hundred at least.
Ith. 'I charge thee send me three hundred by this bearer,   80
    and this shall be your warrant; if you do not, no more
    but so.'
Pilia. Tell him you will confess.
Ith. 'Otherwise I'll confess all.' Vanish, and return in a
    twinkle.   85

67-8.] *Robinson; asides not in Q.*   72. Pen and ink!] *Q; omitted Dyce; as*
S. D. Cunningham.   75. He writes.] *Dyce; on separate line in Q under l. 74.*

---

hilling as it were of fine dust: neither doe they sit where they laid them
first, nor yet in a place which they suspect to bee much frequented with
resort of passengers, but convey them to some other place' (*Natural
History*, Book x, trans. Philemon Holland, London, 1601, p. 289). These
ideas were carried over into medieval bestiary lore, where the partridge is
described as cunning and deceitful, and is even regarded as a type of the
devil (e.g. T. H. White, *The Book of Beasts*, London, 1954, pp. 136–7).

72. *Pen and ink*] Dyce argued that this was a stage direction that had
crept into the text, but the phrase makes perfect sense as a request by
Ithamore for writing materials. *Cf. The Massacre at Paris*, xv.1.

78. *Sirrah*] This form of address is an impertinence on the part of
Ithamore; *cf.* I.i.70 n. and III.iii.37 n.

84–5. *return . . . twinkle*] Bennett glosses this as a conjuring phrase, but
O.E.D. gives no support for this interpretation. Bennett may be thinking
of *Faustus*, xviii.98, but here again the phrase may simply mean 'instantly,
without delay'.

Pilia. Let me alone, I'll use him in his kind.   [*Exit.*]
Ith. Hang him, Jew!
Bella. Now, gentle Ithamore, lie in my lap.
    Where are my maids ? Provide a running banquet;
    Send to the merchant, bid him bring me silks;   90
    Shall Ithamore my love go in such rags ?
Ith. And bid the jeweller come hither too.
Bella. I have no husband, sweet, I'll marry thee.
Ith. Content, but we will leave this paltry land,
    And sail from hence to Greece, to lovely Greece: 95
    I'll be thy Jason, thou my golden fleece;
    Where painted carpets o'er the meads are hurled,
    And Bacchus' vineyards overspread the world,
    Where woods and forests go in goodly green,
    I'll be Adonis, thou shalt be Love's Queen.   100
    The meads, the orchards, and the primrose lanes,
    Instead of sedge and reed, bear sugar-canes:
    Thou in those groves, by Dis above,

86. *Exit.*] *Scott, Shone.*   98. overspread] *Reed;* ore-spread *Q.*

---

86. *use*] treat.

in his kind] As Van Fossen notes, with a double meaning: 1. according to his unpleasant nature, 2. as a Jew; 'to use someone like a Jew' is proverbial for harsh ill-treatment (Tilley, J 52).

88. *lie . . . lap*] Used, as Van Fossen notes, with a sexual implication; *cf.* IV.iv.26 and *Ham.*, III.ii.108.

89.] Penley gives an entrance and exit for the maids, but as Dyce points out, 'it is evident that the maids do not enter; they are supposed to hear their mistress' order *within*'. The banquet is to take place off-stage; see l. 140 below.

89. *running banquet*] a light meal or snack. Bullen compares *H8*, I.iv.12 and v.iv.62.

96.] According to Greek mythology, Jason and the Argonauts succeeded in gaining the golden fleece from the kingdom of Colchis after various adventures.

97. *painted carpets*] used metaphorically for an expanse of brightly coloured flowers or plants.

100.] The love of Venus for Adonis is one of the most popular of classical legends. In classical poetry (e.g. Ovid, *Metamorphoses*, Book X) Adonis usually responds to Venus' wooing, but with some Renaissance poets (e.g. Shakespeare) he does not.

103. *Dis*] The Roman god of the underworld, equivalent to the Greek Hades or Pluto. Ithamore's use of 'above' is a kind of schoolboy howler.

Shalt live with me and be my love.

Bella. Whither will I not go with gentle Ithamore?   105

Enter PILIA-BORZA.

Ith. How now? Hast thou the gold?

Pilia. Yes.

Ith. But came it freely, did the cow give down her milk
freely?

Pilia. At reading of the letter, he stared and stamped, and   110
turned aside; I took him by the beard, and looked upon
him thus, told him he were best to send it; then he
hugged and embraced me.

Ith. Rather for fear than love.

Pilia. Then like a Jew he laughed and jeered, and told me   115
he loved me for your sake, and said what a faithful
servant you had been.

Ith. The more villain he to keep me thus: here's goodly
'parel, is there not?

Pilia. To conclude, he gave me ten crowns.   120

111. beard] *Reed;* sterd *Q.*

104.] It is tempting to believe that Marlowe is here parodying his own
famous lyric beginning 'Come live with me and be my love'.

108. *give down*] 'Of a cow: to let flow (milk)', *O.E.D.* (which gives no
illustration earlier than 1699). In a letter to Dudley Carleton of 15
February 1599 John Chamberlain says that the lawyers have been asked
to make a 'benevolence', or forced loan of money, to the queen; they were
reluctant, 'but in the end they must giue downe theyre milke' (*Letters*, ed.
N. E. McClure, Philadelphia, 1939, I, 68).

111. *took . . . beard*] *O.E.D.* glosses the phrase (without citing Marlowe)
as 'to attack resolutely', with a reference to I Samuel, xvii.35, but Van
Fossen's comment that this action was 'a great insult in Elizabethan times'
seems more to the point.

112. *thus*] At this point Pilia-Borza mimes the ferocious glare he gave
to Barabas.

119. *'parel*] apparel, clothing; Ithamore points to the rags in which he
is dressed.

120. *ten crowns*] It appears from IV.iii.18–20 that Barabas handed over
the full amount of three hundred crowns, so this must be a kind of tip for
Pilia-Borza.

Ith. But ten? I'll not leave him worth a grey groat. Give me
    a ream of paper, we'll have a kingdom of gold for 't.

Pilia. Write for five hundred crowns.

Ith. [*writes.*] 'Sirrah Jew, as you love your life send me five
    hundred crowns, and give the bearer a hundred.' Tell   125
    him I must have 't.

Pilia. I warrant your worship shall have 't.

Ith. And if he ask why I demand so much, tell him I scorn
    to write a line under a hundred crowns.

Pilia. You'd make a rich poet, sir. I am gone.   *Exit.*   130

Ith. Take thou the money, spend it for my sake.

Bella. 'Tis not thy money but thyself I weigh:
    Thus Bellamira esteems of gold—   [*Throws it aside.*]
    But thus of thee.   *Kisses him.*

Ith. That kiss again! *She runs division of my lips.* [*Aside.*]   135
    What an eye she casts on me! It twinkles like a star.

Bella. Come, my dear love, let's in and sleep together.

Ith. O that ten thousand nights were put in one, that we
    might sleep seven years together afore we wake!

Bella. Come, amorous wag, first banquet and then sleep.   140
                                                  [*Exeunt.*]

---

124. *writes.*] *Penley.*   125. a hundred] *Broughton;* 100 *Q;* one hundred
Reed.   133. *Throws it aside.*] *Broughton, Oxberry.*   134. *Kisses*] *Reed;*
Kisse Q.   135-6.] *Dyce; aside not in Q.*   140.1. *Exeunt.*] *Reed.*

---

121. *grey groat*] a small silver coin worth fourpence. 'Not worth a grey
groat' is proverbial for something of slight value (Whiting, G 474 and
Tilley, G 458).

122. *ream*] Dyce quotes parallel passages which confirm that Ithamore
is punning on 'ream' (a standard quantity of paper, normally 480 sheets),
and 'realm' (kingdom), the 'l' of which was often not sounded in Elizabethan pronunciation.

135. division] a musical term, meaning the dividing of long notes into
short notes, and hence the execution of an elaborate variation or descant
on a theme. Bellamira is a virtuoso in the art of kissing.

138-9.] Since Ithamore has been showing off his classical knowledge at
ll. 94-104 above, it is just possible that he is asking for a wildly exaggerated version of the three nights in one that Jove spent with Alcmene,
when he begat Hercules.

140. *wag*] an affectionate term for a somewhat mischievous or impudent
young man; *cf. Dido,* I.i.23.

[IV.iii]

Enter BARABAS *reading a letter.*

Bar. 'Barabas, send me three hundred crowns.'
    Plain Barabas: O that wicked courtezan!
    He was not wont to call me Barabas.
    'Or else I will confess'; ay, there it goes:
    But if I get him, coupe de gorge for that!   5
    He sent a shaggy tottered staring slave,
    That when he speaks, draws out his grisly beard,
    And winds it twice or thrice about his ear;
    Whose face has been a grindstone for men's swords,
    His hands are hacked, some fingers cut quite off;   10
    Who, when he speaks, grunts like a hog, and looks
    Like one that is employed in catzerie
    And crossbiting; such a rogue
    As is the husband to a hundred whores—
    And I by him must send three hundred crowns!   15
    Well, my hope is, he will not stay there still;
    And when he comes—O that he were but here!

Enter PILIA-BORZA.

[IV.iii] 5. that!] *Oxberry;* that *Q.*

IV.iii.3. *wont*] accustomed.

    5. *coupe de gorge*] i.e. 'I'll cut his throat'. Bennett compares *H5*, II.i.69.

    6–14.] Bullen compares the description of a similar villain in the anonymous *Arden of Faversham*, ii.47–52: 'A lean-faced, writhen knave, / Hawk-nosed and very hollow-eyed, / With mighty furrows in his stormy brows, / Long hair down his shoulders curled; / His chin was bare, but on his upper lip / A mutchado, which he wound about his ear.' There may, however, have been a stock description of this kind; see M. L. Wine's note in his Revels edition, 1973, p. 41.

    6. *tottered*] tattered; both forms were common in Elizabethan English.

    12. *catzerie*] cheating, trickery; presumably formed from Italian 'cazzo' (see IV.i.20 n.). *O.E.D.* records no other example of the word.

    13. *crossbiting*] swindling (with the implication 'to cheat in return; to cheat by outwitting'). Lines 13–14 may refer to a common trick whereby a rogue pretends to be the husband of a prostitute in order to blackmail one of her clients.

    16. *still*] for ever, for good.

Pilia. Jew, I must ha' more gold.

Bar. Why, want'st thou any of thy tale?

Pilia. No; but three hundred will not serve his turn.   20

Bar. Not serve his turn, sir?

Pilia. No, sir; and therefore I must have five hundred more.

Bar. I'll rather—

Pilia. O good words, sir; and send it you were best: see,
          there's his letter.   25

Bar. Might he not as well come as send? Pray bid him
          come and fetch it; what he writes for you, ye shall have
          straight.

Pilia. Ay, and the rest too, or else—

Bar. [*aside.*] *I must make this villain away.* Please you dine   30
          with me, sir; and you shall be most heartily *poisoned.*   *Aside.*

Pilia. No, God-a-mercy; shall I have these crowns?

Bar. I cannot do it, I have lost my keys.

Pilia. O, if that be all, I can pick ope your locks.

Bar. Or climb up to my counting-house window? You   35
          know my meaning.

Pilia. I know enough, and therefore talk not to me of your
          counting-house; the gold, or know, Jew, it is in my
          power to hang thee.

Bar. *I am betrayed.*   [*Aside.*]   40
          'Tis not five hundred crowns that I esteem,

---

30. *I . . . away*] *Shone; aside not in* Q.   31. *poisoned*] *Brooke ii (italic not*
in Q); *and . . . poisoned aside in Shone.*   40.] *Shone; aside not in* Q.

---

19. *want'st . . . tale?*] Is anything missing from the total amount you
should have?

24. *good words*] a phrase used elliptically for 'do not speak so fiercely'
(*O.E.D.*, 'good', *adj.*, 7b), and in such proverbs as Tilley, W 803–11.
Cf. v.ii.61.

27. *what . . . you*] 'i.e. the hundred crowns to be given to the bearer;
see IV.ii.125' (Dyce).

30. *make . . . away*] a euphemism for kill, murder.

31. *poisoned*] Q does not indicate how much is aside; most editors follow
Shone, but it seems best to regard it as another of Barabas's last-minute
reversals of meaning.

35–6.] Evidently Barabas knows about the events described at III.i.17–
22.

I am not moved at that: this angers me,
That he who knows I love him as myself
Should write in this imperious vein. Why, sir,
You know I have no child, and unto whom   45
Should I leave all but unto Ithamore?

Pilia. Here's many words, but no crowns; the crowns!

Bar. Commend me to him, sir, most humbly,
And unto your good mistress as unknown.

Pilia. Speak, shall I have 'em, sir?   50

Bar. Sir, here they are.   [*Gives money.*]
O that I should part with so much gold!   [*Aside.*]
Here, take 'em, fellow, with as good a will—
As I would see thee hanged; O, love stops my breath:
Never loved man servant as I do Ithamore.   55

Pilia. I know it, sir.

Bar. Pray when, sir, shall I see you at my house?

Pilia. Soon enough to your cost, sir: fare you well.   *Exit.*

Bar. Nay, to thine own cost, villain, if thou comest.
Was ever Jew tormented as I am?   60
To have a shag-rag knave to come demand
Three hundred crowns, and then five hundred crowns?
Well, I must seek a means to rid 'em all,
And presently: for in his villainy
He will tell all he knows, and I shall die for 't.   65
I have it.
I will in some disguise go see the slave,
And how the villain revels with my gold.   *Exit.*

---

51. *Gives money.*] *Penley.*   52.] *Dyce; aside not in Q.*   61. demand]
Bowers; not in Q; force from me *Dyce ii;* and fetch *conj. Holthausen;*
convey *conj. Brereton ii.*

47.] possibly imitating the proverb, 'Many words, little matter'
(Whiting, W 599).
49. *as unknown*] not known to Barabas.
61. *shag-rag*] ragged, rascally.
demand] Most editors agree that something has dropped out from Q,
but we can only guess at a suitable word.

[IV.iv]

Enter BELLAMIRA, ITHAMORE, [*and*]
PILIA-BORZA.

Bella. I'll pledge thee, love, and therefore drink it off.

Ith. Say'st thou me so ? Have at it; and do you hear ?   [*Whispers.*]

Bella. Go to, it shall be so.

Ith. Of that condition I will drink it up; here's to thee.

Bella. Nay, I'll have all or none.   5

Ith. There; if thou lovest me do not leave a drop.

Bella. Love thee ? Fill me three glasses!

Ith. Three and fifty dozen I'll pledge thee.

Pilia. Knavely spoke, and like a knight at arms.

Ith. Hey, Rivo Castiliano! A man's a man.   10

[IV.iv] 2. *Whispers.*] *Scott.*   5. *Bella.*] *Broughton; Pil. Q.*   9.
Knavely] *Q;* Bravely *Broughton.*

IV.iv.2. Whispers] Presumably Ithamore is making arrangements to
sleep with Bellamira.

5.] Brereton ii unconvincingly attempts to defend Q's attribution of this
line to Pilia-Borza. At l. 4 Ithamore drinks to Bellamira ('here's to thee')
but does not finish his glass. At l. 5 Bellamira demands that he should do
so, partly because the etiquette of the toast requires it, but also because
she wants to get him drunk. At l. 6 he empties his glass ('There') and asks
Bellamira to do the same for him.

9. *Knavely*] According to Craik, Marlowe is 'playing on the sound of the
usual phrase "bravely spoke" (*cf.* l. 18, "bravely done"), and the anti-
thesis of "knave" and "knight"'. Pilia-Borza is 'applauding Ithamore's
valour in thus venturing upon the drink and the Courtesan'. But the play
on words is not very pointed; Ithamore is not insulted to his face elsewhere
in the scene, and there is something to be said for Broughton's emendation
to 'Bravely'.

10. *Rivo Castiliano*] This phrase seems to express a rather drunken
pleasure and excitement, but its origin is uncertain. If it is Italian it would
mean 'river of Castile (in Spain)', perhaps implying that the speaker was
calling for plenty of Spanish wine (Dekker refers to 'Castilian licour' in
The Shoemaker's Holiday, I.iv.103). 'Rivo' is often used by itself; *cf. 1H4*,
II.iv.105 ('"Rivo" says the drunkard'), Middleton, *Blurt, Master Constable*, I.ii.203, and Massinger, *The Renegado*, II.vi.27. Robinson compares
the anonymous comedy *Look About You* (1600), sig. L4: 'And Ryuo will
he cry, and Castile too', though the speaker is a soldier rather than a
drunkard.

A man's a man] proverbial (Tilley, M 243); perhaps abbreviated from
the longer form, 'A man's a man, though he have but a hose on his head'
(Tilley, M 244).

Bella. Now to the Jew.

Ith. Ha, to the Jew! And send me money you were best.

Pilia. What wouldst thou do if he should send thee none?

Ith. Do nothing; but I know what I know. He's a murderer.

Bella. I had not thought he had been so brave a man.   15

Ith. You knew Mathias and the governor's son; he and I
    killed 'em both, and yet never touched 'em.

Pilia. O bravely done.

Ith. I carried the broth that poisoned the nuns, and he and
    I, snickle hand too fast, strangled a friar.   20

Bella. You two alone?

Ith. We two; and 'twas never known, nor never shall be for
    me.

Pilia. [*aside to Bella.*] *This shall with me unto the governor.*

Bella. [*to Pilia.*] *And fit it should; but first let's ha' more
    gold.*   25

---

12. you] *Q;* he *Shone.*   14. Do nothing] *Q;* Do? Nothing *Kirschbaum.*
20. snickle hand too fast] *Q (subs.);* snicle hand to fist *conj. Steevens;*
snickle hard and fast *conj. Cunningham;* Snickle! hand to! fast! *Kittredge.*
24-5.] *Penley; asides not in Q.*

11.] Craik argues that Bellamira is here ironically proposing a toast to
Barabas, but it is more likely that she thinks it time for another demanding
letter to be sent to him.

12. *you*] 'There is no need to emend to *he*. It is more dramatic for the
drunken Turk to shake his fist at the absent Jew' (Spencer). We could also
argue that Ithamore has begun to compose in his mind another letter to
Barabas.

14. *I know what I know*] proverbial (Tilley, K 173); sometimes used in
a longer form, 'I know what I know though I say nothing'.

20. *snickle hand too fast*] the most puzzling crux in the play, which has
never been definitively explained or emended. 'Snickle' is a dialect word
used as noun or verb to mean 'snare, noose'. Kittredge, to my mind
unconvincingly, repunctuates Q and glosses it as 'Snare him! lay your
hand to it! firmly now! (with appropriate gestures)'. There is a verb
'handfast', meaning 'to grasp firmly with the hand', and the phrase may
mean 'making too firm a noose with our hands'. Steevens's emendation to
'hand to fist' is plausible; this is a stock phrase (*O.E.D.*, 'hand', *sb.*, 55b),
equivalent to 'hand to hand' and used to describe fighting at close quarters,
as in Butler's *Hudibras*, III.ii.257-8, 'While ev'ry Individual Brother /
Strove hand to fist against another'. If this emendation is accepted, the
whole phrase would mean something like 'struggling against each other
with our hands to pull the noose'.

22-3. *for me*] so far as I am concerned (Van Fossen).

      Come, gentle Ithamore, lie in my lap.
Ith. Love me little, love me long. Let music rumble,
      Whilst I in thy incony lap do tumble.

                Enter BARABAS *with a lute, disguised.*

Bella. A French musician! Come, let's hear your skill.
Bar. Must tuna my lute for sound, twang, twang, first.   30
Ith. Wilt drink, Frenchman? Here's to thee with a—Pox on
      this drunken hiccup!
Bar. Gramercy, monsieur.
Bella. Prithee, Pilia-Borza, bid the fiddler give me the posy
      in his hat there.   35
Pilia. Sirrah, you must give my mistress your posy.
Bar. A vôtre commandement, madame. [*Giving nosegay.*]
Bella. How sweet, my Ithamore, the flowers smell.
Ith. Like thy breath, sweetheart; no violet like 'em.
Pilia. Foh, methinks they stink like a hollyhock.   40
Bar. *So, now I am revenged upon 'em all.*   [*Aside.*]
      The scent thereof was death; I poisoned it.
Ith. Play, fiddler, or I'll cut your cat's guts into chitter-
      lings.

---

28. incony] *Reed; incoomy Q.*   37. *Giving nosegay.*] *Dyce.*   41-2.]
Shone; aside not in Q.

---

   27. *Love me little, love me long*] proverbial (Whiting, L 568, Tilley, L
559).
   27-8.] Bennett compares *The Two Italian Gentlemen* (London, 1585),
sig. G4: 'these fine Criminadoes, that can tumble in a Gentlewomans lap,
and rumble in her eare'.
   28. *incony*] fine, delicate. Craik notes a pun on 'coney' as used in
Marlowe's translation of Ovid's *Amores* I.x.21-2, 'The whore stands to be
bought for each man's money, / And seeks vile wealth by selling of her
coney'.
   33. *Gramercy*] 'May God reward you!', 'Thank you!'
   34. *posy*] nosegay, small bouquet of flowers.
   42.] Cf. *Edward II*, v.iv.31, 'I learn'd in Naples how to poison flowers'.
This device is also mentioned in papers connected with the trial of
Dr Lopez; see John Gwyer, 'The Case of Dr. Lopez', *T.J.H.S.E.*, XVI
(1945-51), 183.
   43. *cat's guts*] the lute strings.
   43-4. *chitterlings*] the smaller intestines of beasts, e.g. pigs, used as food.

Bar. Pardonnez-moi, be no in tune yet; so, now, now all be   45
     in.

Ith. Give him a crown, and fill me out more wine.

Pilia. There's two crowns for thee; play.

Bar. *How liberally the villain gives me mine own gold.*   *Aside.*

Pilia. Methinks he fingers very well.   50

Bar. *So did you when you stole my gold.*   *Aside.*

Pilia. How swift he runs!

Bar. *You run swifter when you threw my gold out of my*
     window.   *Aside.*

Bella. Musician, hast been in Malta long?   55

Bar. Two, three, four month, madame.

Ith. Dost not know a Jew, one Barabas?

Bar. Very mush, monsieur; you no be his man?

Pilia. His man!

Ith. I scorn the peasant, tell him so.   60

Bar. *He knows it already.*   [*Aside.*]

Ith. 'Tis a strange thing of that Jew, he lives upon pickled
     grasshoppers and sauced mushrooms.

Bar. *What a slave's this! The governor feeds not as I do.*   *Aside.*

Ith. He never put on clean shirt since he was circumcised.   65

Bar. *O rascal! I change myself twice a day.*   *Aside.*

Ith. The hat he wears Judas left under the elder when he
     hanged himself.

---

45. *Bar.*] *Reed; not in Q, except as catchword on foot of H4.*   Pardonnez-
moi] *Shone;* Pardona moy *Q (and at l. 71).*   49, 51, 53-4.] *Italic not in Q.*
53. *run*] *Q;* ran *Scott.*   61.] *Penley; aside not in Q.*   64, 66, 69.] *Italic
not in Q.*

---

50. *fingers*] used with a play of meaning: 1. skilfully plays with the
fingers, 2. handles money with the intention of stealing it. *Cf.* Dekker and
Middleton, *The Roaring Girl*, IV.i.176-82.

52. *runs*] plays a run or rapid sequence of notes.

62-3. *pickled . . . mushrooms*] i.e. cheap and unappetising food. For
'pickled grasshopper' *cf.* Middleton's 'pickled spyder' in a similar context
(*A Game at Chess*, III.ii.30).

67-8.] There was a medieval tradition that Judas hanged himself on an
elder tree (see *L.L.L.*, v.ii.597-600, and Jonson, *Every Man Out of his
Humour*, IV.v.60-1), but the hat seems to be Marlowe's invention.

Bar. *'Twas sent me for a present from the Great Cham.*   *Aside.*

Pilia. A musty slave he is. Whither now, fiddler ?   70

Bar. Pardonnez-moi, monsieur, me be no well.   *Exit.*

Pilia. Farewell, fiddler. One letter more to the Jew.

Bella. Prithee, sweet love, one more, and write it sharp.

Ith. No, I'll send by word of mouth now. Bid him deliver
    thee a thousand crowns, by the same token that the nuns   75
    loved rice, that Friar Bernardine slept in his own clothes
    —any of 'em will do it.

Pilia. Let me alone to urge it now I know the meaning.

Ith. The meaning has a meaning. Come, let's in:
    To undo a Jew is charity, and not sin.   *Exeunt.*   80

---

70. musty] *Bullen;* masty *Q;* nasty *Reed.*   71. me] *Reed;* we *Q.*

---

69. Great Cham] 'Cham' is 'an obsolete form of Khan formerly com-
monly applied to the rulers of the Tartars and Mongols, and to the
Emperor of China' (*O.E.D.*). *Cf. Ado*, II.i.238, and Dekker, *Old Fortunatus*,
I.ii.199 and II.i.12.

70. *musty*] *O.E.D.* gives only two possibly relevant meanings to Q's
'masty' ('Of a swine: fattened', and 'burly, big-bodied'), but neither seems
very appropriate, especially as Barabas has just been described as exces-
sively abstemious. 'Musty' would have *O.E.D.*'s sense 3, 'ill-humoured,
peevish, sullen'.

71. *me*] Q's 'we' could be defended, but 'me' for 'I' is common in the
jargon of stage-Frenchmen of the time.

Act V

Enter FERNEZE, Knights, MARTIN DEL BOSCO[,
and Officers].

Fern. Now, gentlemen, betake you to your arms,
And see that Malta be well fortified.
And it behoves you to be resolute;
For Calymath, having hovered here so long,
Will win the town, or die before the walls.   5
First Knight. And die he shall, for we will never yield.

Enter BELLAMIRA [*and*] PILIA-BORZA.

Bella. O bring us to the governor.
Fern. Away with her, she is a courtezan.
Bella. Whate'er I am, yet, governor, hear me speak;
I bring thee news by whom thy son was slain: 10
Mathias did it not, it was the Jew.
Pilia. Who, besides the slaughter of these gentlemen,
poisoned his own daughter and the nuns, strangled a
friar, and I know not what mischief beside.
Fern. Had we but proof of this!   15
Bella. Strong proof, my lord; his man's now at my lodging
That was his agent, he'll confess it all.
Fern. Go fetch him straight. [*Exeunt* Officers.] I always
feared that Jew.

Act V] *Actus Quintus. Q.*   [v.i] 0.2. *and* Officers] *Dyce.*   6. *First
Knight.*] *Broughton; Kni. Q. (and at l. 25); Knights. Reed.*   18. *Exeunt*
Officers.] *Dyce.*

v.i.4. *hovered*] 'Hover' was used in the 16th–18th c. in a semi-technical
fashion to refer to a ship or fleet waiting near a particular point; see
O.E.D., $v.^1$, sense 2.

Enter Officers *with* BARABAS *and* ITHAMORE.

Bar. I'll go alone; dogs, do not hale me thus.

Ith. Nor me neither; I cannot outrun you, constable. O my   20
    belly!

Bar. One dram of powder more had made all sure;   [*Aside.*]
    What a damned slave was I!

Fern. Make fires, heat irons, let the rack be fetched.

First Knight. Nay, stay, my lord; 't may be he will confess.   25

Bar. Confess! What mean you, lords, who should confess?

Fern. Thou and thy Turk; 'twas you that slew my son.

Ith. Guilty, my lord, I confess. Your son and Mathias were
    both contracted unto Abigail; he forged a counterfeit
    challenge.   30

Bar. Who carried that challenge?

Ith. I carried it, I confess, but who writ it? Marry, even he
    that strangled Bernardine, poisoned the nuns and his
    own daughter.

Fern. Away with him! His sight is death to me.   35

Bar. For what? You men of Malta, hear me speak;
    She is a courtezan, and he a thief,
    And he my bondman. Let me have law;
    For none of this can prejudice my life.

Fern. Once more, away with him! You shall have law.   40

Bar. Devils, do your worst; I'll live in spite of you.   [*Aside.*]

18.1. *Enter . . . Ithamore.*] *Broughton; Enter Iew, Ithimore. Q.*   22-3.]
Dyce; aside not in Q.   29. he] *Reed; not in Q.*   41.] *Dyce; aside not in
Q.   I'll*] *Dyce;* I *Q.*

---

   20. *outrun*] run faster than, run away from. Tilley gives 'To outrun the
constable' as proverbial (C 615).

   35.] *Cf.* Kyd, *The Spanish Tragedy,* I.iii.89: 'Away with him, his sight is
second hell'. Both lines are spoken by fathers about the man they consider
to be the murderer of their son.

   38. *bondman*] slave. 'In medieval England a master had great power over
his serfs or bondmen, and could stay many accusations by refusing to
plead in answer to his own bondman' (Bennett).

   39. *prejudice*] be prejudicial to (Van Fossen).

   41. *I'll*] I have accepted Dyce's emendation because Barabas is here
asserting that he will continue to survive in the future, whatever his
enemies do to him.

As these have spoke so be it to their souls.
I hope the poisoned flowers will work anon.   [*Aside.*]
    Exeunt Officers *with* BARABAS, ITHAMORE, BELLAMIRA,
                                    and PILIA-BORZA.

Enter KATHERINE.

Kath. Was my Mathias murdered by the Jew?
      Ferneze, 'twas thy son that murdered him.   45
Fern. Be patient, gentle madam; it was he,
      He forged the daring challenge made them fight.
Kath. Where is the Jew? Where is that murderer?
Fern. In prison, till the law has passed on him.

Enter [First] Officer.

First Off. My lord, the courtezan and her man are dead;   50
      So is the Turk, and Barabas the Jew.
Fern. Dead?
First Off. Dead, my lord, and here they bring his body.

[*Enter* Officers, *carrying* BARABAS *as dead.*]

Bosco. This sudden death of his is very strange.
Fern. Wonder not at it, sir, the heavens are just.   55
      Their deaths were like their lives, then think not of 'em;
      Since they are dead, let them be buried.
      For the Jew's body, throw that o'er the walls,
      To be a prey for vultures and wild beasts.
                              [BARABAS *thrown down.*]
      So; now away, and fortify the town.   60
                              Exeunt [*all but* BARABAS.]

43.] *Broughton; aside not in* Q.   43. 1-2. *Exeunt . . . Pilia-Borza.*]
Broughton; Exit. Q.   49.1. First] *Dyce.*   50. First Off.] *Dyce; Offi.* Q
(*and at l. 53*).   53.1. *Enter . . . dead.*] *Dyce* (*after l. 54*).   59.1. *Barabas
. . . down.*] *Kirschbaum* (*after l. 60*).   60.1. *all but Barabas*] *Dyce.*

──

   49. *passed*] passed sentence.
   59.1.] Q has no S.D. here; presumably Barabas is bundled to one side
of the stage to symbolise that he has been thrown over the walls. In any
case the scene is not staged realistically, since it begins inside the city
walls but after l. 60 shifts to outside the walls.

Bar. [*rising.*] What, all alone? Well fare, sleepy drink!
　　　I'll be revengèd on this accursèd town,
　　　For by my means Calymath shall enter in.
　　　I'll help to slay their children and their wives,
　　　To fire the churches, pull their houses down;　　　　　　　65
　　　Take my goods too, and seize upon my lands.
　　　I hope to see the governor a slave,
　　　And, rowing in a galley, whipped to death.

　　　　　Enter CALYMATH, Bashaws, [*and*] Turks.

Calym. Whom have we there, a spy?
Bar. Yes, my good lord, one that can spy a place　　　　　　70
　　　Where you may enter, and surprise the town.
　　　My name is Barabas; I am a Jew.
Calym. Art thou that Jew whose goods we heard were sold
　　　For tribute-money?
Bar.　　　　　　　The very same, my lord:
　　　And since that time they have hired a slave, my man,　　　75
　　　To accuse me of a thousand villainies.
　　　I was imprisoned, but escaped their hands.
Calym. Didst break prison?
Bar. No, no:
　　　I drank of poppy and cold mandrake juice,　　　　　　　80
　　　And being asleep, belike they thought me dead,

---

61. *rising*] Dyce.　　　　69. *there*] *Q;* here *Broughton.*　　　77. *escaped*] *Scott;*
scap'd *Q.*

---

　　61. *Well fare*] See I.i.8 n.
　　64-5.] Cf. *Faustus*, vi.100-1, where Faustus promises 'To burn his
scriptures, slay his ministers, / And make my spirits pull his churches
down', and *Edward II*, I.iv.100-1, where Edward vows to destroy Rome:
'I'll fire thy crazed buildings, and enforce / The papal towers to kiss the
lowly ground'. The similar passage in *The Massacre at Paris*, XXIV.62-3,
may be a memorial recollection of *Edward II*.
　　69. *a spy*] See Natalis Comes as cited in the Introduction, p. 51, n. 38.
　　71. *surprise*] capture by surprise.
　　80.] Both the opium poppy and the mandrake plant yield powerful
soporific drugs. Bullen compares *Oth.*, III.iii.334-7, and *cf.* Jonson,
Sejanus, III.598, 'The iuice of poppie, and of mandrakes'. 'To drink the
juice of mandrake' is proverbial (Tilley, J 101).

And threw me o'er the walls. So, or how else,
The Jew is here, and rests at your command.
Calym. 'Twas bravely done. But tell me, Barabas,
Canst thou, as thou reportest, make Malta ours?   85
Bar. Fear not, my lord; for here, against the sluice,
The rock is hollow, and of purpose digged
To make a passage for the running streams
And common channels of the city.
Now whilst you give assault unto the walls,   90
I'll lead five hundred soldiers through the vault,
And rise with them i' the middle of the town,
Open the gates for you to enter in,
And by this means the city is your own.
Calym. If this be true, I'll make thee governor.   95
Bar. And if it be not true, then let me die.
Calym. Thou'st doomed thyself. Assault it presently.   *Exeunt.*

[v.ii]

> *Alarms. Enter* [CALYMATH,] *Turks,* [*and*] BARABAS,
> [*with*] FERNEZE *and* Knights *prisoners.*

Calym. Now vail your pride, you captive Christians,

86. sluice] *Broughton;* Truce *Q;* trench *Dyce;* truss *Simmons (v. Appendix*
C).   89. city] *Q;* citadel *A. Wagner.*
[v.ii] 0.1. *Calymath*] *Broughton, Penley.*

---

82. *or how else*] The meaning is not clear, but the phrase suggests that
Barabas is not interested in discussing the precise detail of his devices.

85.] F. L. Lucas (*The Works of John Webster,* II, 339) points out that
Webster seems to allude to this part of the play in *The Devil's Law-Case,*
III.ii.1–16, where Romelio disguises himself as an 'Italienated Jew' and boasts
of the villainies he could perform, such as 'Betray a Towne to th' Turke'.

86. *sluice*] Van Fossen retains Q's 'truce' and glosses 'against the truce'
as 'either (1) contrary to the treaty or (2) in anticipation of the cessation of
hostilities'. But both these senses are rather forced; ll. 86–9 clearly refer to
a sewer or drainage channel, and 'sluice' (valve or barrier for controlling
the flow of water) fits the context much better. J. L. Simmons's emendation to 'truss', and his theories about the staging of this scene, are discussed
in Appendix C.

89. *channels*] gutters, sewers.

97. *doomed*] judged, sentenced.

v.ii.1. *vail*] See II.ii.11 n.

And kneel for mercy to your conquering foe.
Now where's the hope you had of haughty Spain?
Ferneze, speak: had it not been much better
To keep thy promise than be thus surprised?   5
Fern. What should I say? We are captives and must yield.
Calym. Ay, villains, you must yield, and under Turkish yokes
Shall groaning bear the burden of our ire;
And Barabas, as erst we promised thee,
For thy desert we make thee governor.   10
Use them at thy discretion.
Bar.   Thanks, my lord.
Fern. O fatal day, to fall into the hands
Of such a traitor and unhallowed Jew!
What greater misery could heaven inflict?
Calym. 'Tis our command; and, Barabas, we give   15
To guard thy person, these our Janizaries:
Entreat them well, as we have usèd thee.
And now, brave bashaws, come, we'll walk about
The ruined town, and see the wrack we made.
Farewell, brave Jew, farewell, great Barabas.   20
Bar. May all good fortune follow Calymath!

Exeunt [CALYMATH *and* Bashaws].

And now, as entrance to our safety,
To prison with the governor and these
Captains, his consorts and confederates.

---

5. To keep] *A. Wagner;* To kept *Q;* T'have kept *Shone.*   10. thee] *Reed;*
the *Q.*   21.1. *Exeunt*] *Dyce; after l. 20 in Q.*   Calymath ... Bashaws]
Shone.

3.] This seems to be a reference back to II.ii.40, though it is not
explained how Calymath came to know about it.

5. *surprised*] See v.i.71 n.

9. *erst*] just now, a short while ago.

16. *Janizaries*] a *corps d'élite* of infantry in the Turkish army, who
played an important part in the siege of Malta. They were rigorously
trained in military discipline and in the 16th c. were among the most
formidable soldiers in Europe.

19. *wrack*] devastation, destruction. *Cf.* l. 58 below.

22. *entrance ... safety*] i.e. the first step in making ourselves secure.

24. *consorts*] companions.

Fern. O villain, heaven will be revenged on thee!   25
Bar. Away, no more! Let him not trouble me.
                         Exeunt [Turks *with* FERNEZE *and* Knights].
          Thus hast thou gotten, by thy policy,
          No simple place, no small authority:
          I now am governor of Malta. True,
          But Malta hates me, and in hating me,   30
          My life's in danger; and what boots it thee,
          Poor Barabas, to be the governor,
          Whenas thy life shall be at their command?
          No, Barabas, this must be looked into;
          And since by wrong thou got'st authority,   35
          Maintain it bravely by firm policy,
          At least unprofitably lose it not:
          For he that liveth in authority
          And neither gets him friends, nor fills his bags,
          Lives like the ass that Aesop speaketh of,   40
          That labours with a load of bread and wine,
          And leaves it off to snap on thistle tops.

26.1. *Exeunt*] *Penley; after l. 25 in* Q.   Turks ... Knights] *Dyce.*

---

27 ff.] Barabas's meditation on his new position may possibly owe a
little to the beginning of ch. 7 of *The Prince*, where Machiavelli discusses
the problems of rulers who acquire power easily, by fortune or the help of
others, but have difficulty in maintaining it, and also to ch. 19, where the
ruler is advised not to make himself hated by the people he rules.

31. *boots*] avails, profits.

33. *Whenas*] seeing that.

37.] i.e. 'don't give it up without making a profit on the deal'.

40–2.] No Aesopic fable of this kind has yet been discovered, but
H. G. Rusche (*N. & Q.*, CCIX, 1964, 261) points out that in Whitney's
A Choice of Emblemes (Leiden, 1586, p. 18) a picture of a laden donkey
eating thistles symbolises a rich man who does not enjoy his riches.
Whitney's emblem is borrowed from Alciati's *Emblemata* (Antwerp, 1581,
n. 85, p. 313), and the idea derives ultimately from an epigram in the
Greek Anthology (XI, 397). Tilley gives it as proverbial (A 360), but
quotes no example earlier than *Caes.*, IV.i.21–7. It was obviously current
in various forms; *cf.* De la Primaudaye, *The French Academie* (London,
1586, p. 446), where covetous men are compared to 'Mules that carie
great burthens of golde and siluer on their backes, and yet eate but hay'.

42. *snap*] feed with quick, sudden bites (*O.E.D.*).

But Barabas will be more circumspect.
Begin betimes, Occasion's bald behind;
Slip not thine opportunity, for fear too late   45
Thou seek'st for much, but canst not compass it.
Within here!

Enter FERNEZE *with a* Guard.

Fern. My lord?
Bar. Ay, 'lord'; thus slaves will learn.   [*Aside.*]
Now, governor, stand by there.—Wait within!   50
[*Exit* Guard.]

This is the reason that I sent for thee:
Thou seest thy life, and Malta's happiness,
Are at my arbitrament, and Barabas
At his discretion may dispose of both;
Now tell me, governor, and plainly too,   55
What think'st thou shall become of it and thee?
Fern. This, Barabas: since things are in thy power,
I see no reason but of Malta's wrack,
Nor hope of thee but extreme cruelty;

---

47. here] *Q;* there *Penley.*   49.] *This ed.; aside not in Q.*   50.]
Cunningham; Now Gouernor stand by there, wait within, *Q;* Now,
Governor,—stand by there, wait within: *Reed.*   50.1. *Exit* Guard.] *Reed*

---

44. *betimes*] quickly, before it is too late.
44–5. *Occasion's . . . opportunity*] Renaissance art and literature are full
of illustrations and descriptions of the personified figure of Occasion as a
naked woman standing on a sphere or wheel, who has a long forelock of
hair but is bald at the back of her head. She is sometimes called Time or
Opportunity, and must be seized by her forelock before she passes by
(see Tilley, T 311). The origins of the figure are discussed by Erwin
Panofsky, *Studies in Iconology* (New York, 1962), p. 72. Marlowe may
have remembered one of the *Distichs of Cato,* a popular school textbook:
'Rem tibi quam noris aptam dimittere noli: / Fronte capillata, post est
Occasio calva' (Do not let go something you know to be favourable to you;
with hair in front, Occasion is bald behind).
50.] I assume with Cunningham that 'stand by there' is addressed to
Ferneze rather than to the guard. Ferneze is to wait until the guard is out
of earshot.
58.] i.e. 'I cannot see any reason why Malta should not be destroyed'.
Cf. Shr., II.i.399.

Nor fear I death, nor will I flatter thee.   60
Bar. Governor, good words! Be not so furious;
    'Tis not thy life which can avail me aught.
    Yet you do live, and live for me you shall,
    And as for Malta's ruin, think you not
    'Twere slender policy for Barabas   65
    To dispossess himself of such a place?
    For sith, as once you said, within this isle,
    In Malta here, that I have got my goods,
    And in this city still have had success,
    And now at length am grown your governor,   70
    Yourselves shall see it shall not be forgot:
    For as a friend not known but in distress,
    I'll rear up Malta, now remediless.
Fern. Will Barabas recover Malta's loss?
    Will Barabas be good to Christians?   75
Bar. What wilt thou give me, governor, to procure
    A dissolution of the slavish bands
    Wherein the Turk hath yoked your land and you?
    What will you give me if I render you
    The life of Calymath, surprise his men,   80
    And in an outhouse of the city shut
    His soldiers, till I have consumed 'em all with fire?
    What will you give him that procureth this?
Fern. Do but bring this to pass which thou pretendest,

67. within] *Q;* 'tis in *Cunningham.*

---

63. *for me*] See IV.iv.22–3 n.
67. *sith*] since. Brooke ii notes that the word should be linked with 'that' in l. 68; *cf. Edward II*, IV.iv.17, 'sith that we are by sufferance of heaven . . .'
72.] proverbial (Whiting, F 634, Tilley, F 694).
73. *rear up*] raise up, relieve from distress.
remediless] without hope of remedy, in a desperate position.
79. *render*] hand over, deliver.
81. *outhouse*] apparently used in a sense not recorded in *O.E.D.*, to refer to a building, not necessarily small, standing just outside the walls of a city. *Cf.* v.iii.36–7.
84. *pretendest*] This could be either sense 3a of *O.E.D.*, 'claim to be able to do', or sense 8, 'intend, purpose'.

    Deal truly with us as thou intimatest,   85
    And I will send amongst the citizens
    And by my letters privately procure
    Great sums of money for thy recompense—
    Nay, more; do this, and live thou governor still.

Bar. Nay, do thou this, Ferneze, and be free.   90
    Governor, I enlarge thee; live with me,
    Go walk about the city, see thy friends.
    Tush, send not letters to 'em, go thyself,
    And let me see what money thou canst make.
    Here is my hand that I'll set Malta free.   95
    And thus we cast it: to a solemn feast
    I will invite young Selim-Calymath,
    Where be thou present only to perform
    One stratagem that I'll impart to thee,
    Wherein no danger shall betide thy life,   100
    And I will warrant Malta free for ever.

Fern. Here is my hand; believe me, Barabas,
    I will be there, and do as thou desirest.
    When is the time?

Bar.   Governor, presently.
    For Calymath, when he hath viewed the town,   105
    Will take his leave and sail toward Ottoman.

Fern. Then will I, Barabas, about this coin,
    And bring it with me to thee in the evening.

Bar. Do so, but fail not; now farewell, Ferneze.

                          [*Exit* FERNEZE.]

    And thus far roundly goes the business.   110
    Thus, loving neither, will I live with both,
    Making a profit of my policy;

109.1. *Exit Ferneze*] *Reed.*

---

    91. *enlarge*] set free.
    100. *betide*] happen to.
    106. *Ottoman*] This may refer to Calymath's father, the Ottoman Emperor, or to Turkey itself; *cf.* v.iii.16 and v.v.113.
    110. *roundly*] rapidly, briskly.

And he from whom my most advantage comes
Shall be my friend.
This is the life we Jews are used to lead,   115
And reason, too, for Christians do the like.
Well, now about effecting this device:
First, to surprise great Selim's soldiers,
And then to make provision for the feast,
That at one instant all things may be done.   120
My policy detests prevention:
To what event my secret purpose drives,
I know; and they shall witness with their lives.   *Exit.*

[v.iii]

                    Enter CALYMATH [*and*] Bashaws.

Calym. Thus have we viewed the city, seen the sack,
And caused the ruins to be new repaired,
Which with our bombards' shot and basilisks'
We rent in sunder at our entry,
Two lofty turrets that command the town.   5

120. done.] *Brooke;* done, *Q.*

[v.iii] 3. basilisks'] *Broughton;* Basiliske *Q.*   5.] *Craik; after l. 10 in Q;
after l. 11 in Robinson; after l. 7, conj. Hoeniger.*

113–14.] Perhaps ultimately from ch. 18 of *The Prince*, where Machiavelli asserted that a prince should not keep faith with his promises when it
would be to his disadvantage. Gentillet was scandalised: 'doth not hee
say, That a prince, nor any other, ought to observe his faith but for his
profit?' (p. 135; *cf.* p. 69).

121. *prevention*] anticipation; 'I hate to have my cunning plots revealed
in advance'. The plotter's desire for secrecy can be paralleled in Lorenzo's
soliloquy in Kyd's *The Spanish Tragedy*, III.iv.82–8.

v.iii.1. *seen the sack*] This could mean 'watched the soldiers as they
plundered the city', or alternatively 'sack' could mean 'booty, plundered
goods', though *O.E.D.* records this as a rare usage, with no example
earlier than 1859.

3. *bombards*] The bombard was an early type of cannon, throwing a
stone ball or large shot.

basilisks] See III.v.31 n.

5.] This line is obviously misplaced in Q, and Craik's ingenious rearrangement makes better sense than Robinson's, to which Bennett makes
cogent objections. Seaton ii argues that the two turrets are the twin forts of

And now I see the situation,
And how secure this conquered island stands,
Environed with the Mediterranean sea,
Strong countermured with other petty isles,
And toward Calabria backed by Sicily,   10
Where Syracusian Dionysius reigned;
I wonder how it could be conquered thus.

Enter a Messenger.

Mess. From Barabas, Malta's governor, I bring
A message unto mighty Calymath.
Hearing his sovereign was bound for sea,   15
To sail to Turkey, to great Ottoman,
He humbly would entreat your majesty
To come and see his homely citadel,
And banquet with him ere thou leavest the isle.
Calym. To banquet with him in his citadel?   20
I fear me, messenger, to feast my train
Within a town of war so lately pillaged
Will be too costly and too troublesome.
Yet would I gladly visit Barabas,
For well has Barabas deserved of us.   25
Mess. Selim, for that, thus saith the governor:
That he hath in store a pearl so big,

6. And now] *Q;* And, now *Reed.*   9. countermured] *? conj. Collier MS.,
Deighton;* contermin'd *Q.*   11. Where] *Robinson;* When *Q.*   27. in]
Q; in his *Broughton.*

Saint Elmo and Saint Angelo, on opposite sides of the Grand Harbour of
what is now Valetta. The Turks did in fact capture Saint Elmo in June
1565, but not Saint Angelo.

6–12.] Reed's re-punctuation of 'And now' suggests that he saw these
lines as a syntactical unit: 'And, now that I see . . . I wonder . . .' But Q
makes reasonable sense as it stands.

9. *countermured*] Collier MS underlines 'countermin'd' and puts a cross
in the margin; presumably he intended it to be emended as at I.ii.384.

11. *Dionysius*] probably Dionysius the Elder, a notorious Sicilian tyrant
of the early 6th c. B.C., often mentioned in 16th c. discussions of tyranny.

12.] 'I marvel that we conquered it so easily'.

21. *train*] attendants, retinue.

So precious, and withal so orient,
As, be it valued but indifferently,
The price thereof will serve to entertain   30
Selim and all his soldiers for a month.
Therefore he humbly would entreat your highness
Not to depart till he has feasted you.

Calym. I cannot feast my men in Malta walls,
Except he place his tables in the streets.   35

Mess. Know, Selim, that there is a monastery
Which standeth as an outhouse to the town;
There will he banquet them, but thee at home,
With all thy bashaws and brave followers.

Calym. Well, tell the governor we grant his suit;   40
We'll in this summer evening feast with him.

Mess. I shall, my lord.   *Exit.*

Calym. And now, bold bashaws, let us to our tents,
And meditate how we may grace us best
To solemnize our governor's great feast.   *Exeunt.*   45

[v.iv]

Enter FERNEZE, Knights, [*and* MARTIN]
DEL BOSCO.

Fern. In this, my countrymen, be ruled by me:
Have special care that no man sally forth
Till you shall hear a culverin discharged
By him that bears the linstock, kindled thus;
Then issue out and come to rescue me,   5
For happily I shall be in distress,
Or you releasèd of this servitude.

First Knight. Rather than thus to live as Turkish thralls,
What will we not adventure?

---

v.iv.3. *culverin*] a kind of cannon with a long muzzle.
4. *linstock*] a staff about three feet long with a forked head to hold a
lighted match; used to ignite cannon.
8. *thralls*] slaves, captives.
9. *adventure*] risk, attempt.

Fern. On then, be gone.
Knights.   Farewell, grave governor. [*Exeunt.*]   10

[v.v]
            Enter [BARABAS] *with a hammer above, very busy*[,
                        and Carpenters].

Bar. How stand the cords ? How hang these hinges, fast ?
    Are all the cranes and pulleys sure ?
Carpenter.   All fast.
Bar. Leave nothing loose, all levelled to my mind.
    Why, now I see that you have art indeed.
    There, carpenters, divide that gold amongst you: 5
    Go swill in bowls of sack and muscadine;
    Down to the cellar, taste of all my wines.
Carpenters. We shall, my lord, and thank you.
                                        Exeunt [Carpenters].
Bar. And if you like them, drink your fill—and die;
    For so I live, perish may all the world.   10
    Now, Selim-Calymath, return me word
    That thou wilt come, and I am satisfied.

                    Enter Messenger.

    Now sirrah, what, will he come ?

[v.iv] 10. *Knights.*] Reed; *Kni: Q; Knight.* Robinson.   grave] *Q;* brave
Ribner.   Exeunt.] *Shone.*
[v.v] 0.1. *Barabas*] Reed.   *and* Carpenters] *Broughton.*   2. *Carpenter.*]
Broughton; Serv. Q.   8. *Carpenters.*] Reed; *Carp. Q.*   9. *fill*—] *This
ed.;* fill *Q.*   12.1. *Enter* Messenger.] *Dyce; after l. 13 in Q.*

_____

    10. *grave*] Ribner's emendation is unnecessary; *cf.* I.ii.10 and 129.
    v.v.3. *levelled*] presumably used here in a sense appropriate to a
carpenter's level: 'well made, accurately and symmetrically constructed'.
    to my mind] according to my wish or purpose.
    6. *sack*] a general name for Spanish white wines.
    muscadine] the wine now called muscatel.
    9. *and die*] another of Barabas's last-minute reversals of meaning. As
Bennett suggests, Barabas may have poisoned his wine to remove the
witnesses of his crime.
    10. *so*] provided that (Craik).

Mess. He will; and has commanded all his men
    To come ashore, and march through Malta streets,   15
    That thou mayst feast them in thy citadel.   [*Exit.*
Bar. Then now are all things as my wish would have 'em;
    There wanteth nothing but the governor's pelf—

              Enter FERNEZE.

    And see, he brings it. Now, governor, the sum?
Fern. With free consent a hundred thousand pounds.   20
Bar. Pounds, say'st thou, governor? Well, since it is no more,
    I'll satisfy myself with that; nay, keep it still,
    For if I keep not promise, trust not me.
    And, governor, now partake my policy:
    First, for his army, they are sent before,   25
    Entered the monastery, and underneath
    In several places are field-pieces pitched,
    Bombards, whole barrels full of gunpowder,
    That on the sudden shall dissever it,
    And batter all the stones about their ears,   30
    Whence none can possibly escape alive.
    Now, as for Calymath and his consorts,
    Here have I made a dainty gallery,
    The floor whereof, this cable being cut,
    Doth fall asunder, so that it doth sink   35
    Into a deep pit past recovery.
    Here, hold that knife, and when thou seest he comes,
    And with his bashaws shall be blithely set,
    A warning-piece shall be shot off from the tower
    To give thee knowledge when to cut the cord,   40
    And fire the house; say, will not this be brave?

16. *Exit.*] *Broughton.*   18.1. *Enter Ferneze.*] *Dyce; after l. 19 in Q.*

---

24. *partake*] share in, learn about.
27. *field-pieces*] light cannon for use on a battlefield (*O.E.D.*).
29. *dissever*] break up, shatter.
37.] At this point Barabas throws down a knife to Ferneze.
38. *blithely set*] cheerfully seated at table (Craik).
39. *warning-piece*] a gun fired as a signal or alarm.

Fern. O, excellent! Here, hold thee, Barabas;
      I trust thy word, take what I promised thee.
Bar. No, governor, I'll satisfy thee first:
      Thou shalt not live in doubt of anything.   45
      Stand close, for here they come.   [FERNEZE *retires.*]
                                Why, is not this
      A kingly kind of trade, to purchase towns
      By treachery, and sell 'em by deceit?
      Now tell me, worldlings, underneath the sun
      If greater falsehood ever has been done.   50

                    Enter CALYMATH *and* Bashaws.

Calym. Come, my companion bashaws, see I pray
      How busy Barabas is there above
      To entertain us in his gallery;
      Let us salute him. Save thee, Barabas!
Bar. Welcome, great Calymath.   55
Fern. *How the slave jeers at him!*   [*Aside.*]
Bar. Will 't please thee, mighty Selim-Calymath,
      To ascend our homely stairs?
Calym.   Ay, Barabas;
      Come, bashaws, attend.
Fern. [*comes forward.*]   Stay, Calymath;
      For I will show thee greater courtesy   60
      Than Barabas would have afforded thee.
Knight. [*within.*] Sound a charge there!

---

46. *Ferneze retires.*] *Penley.*   49. sun] *Reed;* summe *Q.*   56.] *Shone;
aside not in Q.   59. comes forward.*] *Penley.*   62. *Knight.*] *Broughton;
Kni. Q; Knights. Reed.   within*] *Dyce.*

42.] Ferneze offers Barabas a bag of money.

49. *worldlings*] those devoted to worldly matters, and hence indifferent
to religion, selfish, or avaricious. Barabas here addresses the audience
directly, with the bland assumption that as connoisseurs of villainy they
will admire him.

62. *charge*] signal for attack. This is a trumpet call (see l. 104 below),
but at v.iv.2–4 and ll. 39–40 above the signal is supposed to be a culverin-
shot.

A charge [sounded], the cable cut, a cauldron discovered
[into which BARABAS *has fallen].*
[Enter MARTIN DEL BOSCO *and* Knights.]

Calym. How now, what means this?

Bar. Help, help me, Christians, help!

Fern. See, Calymath, this was devised for thee.   65

Calym. Treason, treason: bashaws, fly!

Fern. No, Selim, do not fly;
　　　See his end first, and fly then if thou canst.

Bar. O help me, Selim, help me, Christians!
　　　Governor, why stand you all so pitiless?   70

Fern. Should I in pity of thy plaints or thee,
　　　Accursèd Barabas, base Jew, relent?
　　　No, thus I'll see thy treachery repaid,
　　　But wish thou hadst behaved thee otherwise.

Bar. You will not help me then?

Fern.   No, villain, no.   75

Bar. And, villains, know you cannot help me now.
　　　Then, Barabas, breathe forth thy latest fate,
　　　And in the fury of thy torments strive
　　　To end thy life with resolution.
　　　Know, governor, 'twas I that slew thy son;   80
　　　I framed the challenge that did make them meet.
　　　Know, Calymath, I aimed thy overthrow,
　　　And had I but escaped this stratagem

62.1. *A . . . discovered*] Printed by Q in right margin opp. ll. 62–3.　　*sounded*]
Broughton.　　62.2. *into . . . fallen.*] Cunningham.　　62.3. *Enter . . .*
Knights.] Dyce.　　77. fate] *Q;* hate Penley.

62.1. *discovered*] revealed. Ferneze cuts the cable securing the trapdoor
(see ll. 34–40 above), which drops down to let Barabas fall into the
cauldron. Ferneze then draws the curtains which have concealed the
cauldron.

77. *latest fate*] Penley's emendation is not needed, and Q could be
paraphrased, 'breathe out the last moments of life allotted to you by fate'.
Cf. Marlowe's translation of the *Amores*, II.ix.42, 'long shalt thou rest
when Fates expire thy breath', where the image of the last three words is
not in the Latin, 'longa quiescendi tempora fata dabunt'.

82. *aimed*] planned, intended.

I would have brought confusion on you all,
Damned Christian dogs, and Turkish infidels!   85
But now begins the extremity of heat
To pinch me with intolerable pangs:
Die, life: fly, soul; tongue, curse thy fill and die!   [*Dies.*]
Calym. Tell me, you Christians, what doth this portend?
Fern. This train he laid to have entrapped thy life.   90
　　Now, Selim, note the unhallowed deeds of Jews:
　　Thus he determined to have handled thee,
　　But I have rather chose to save thy life.
Calym. Was this the banquet he prepared for us?
　　Let's hence, lest further mischief be pretended.   95
Fern. Nay, Selim, stay, for since we have thee here,
　　We will not let thee part so suddenly.
　　Besides, if we should let thee go, all's one,
　　For with thy galleys couldst thou not get hence,
　　Without fresh men to rig and furnish them.   100
Calym. Tush, governor, take thou no care for that;
　　My men are all aboard,
　　And do attend my coming there by this.
Fern. Why, heard'st thou not the trumpet sound a charge?
Calym. Yes; what of that?
Fern.   Why, then the house was fired,   105
　　Blown up, and all thy soldiers massacred.
Calym. O monstrous treason!
Fern.   A Jew's courtesy;
　　For he that did by treason work our fall
　　By treason hath delivered thee to us.
　　Know, therefore, till thy father hath made good   110

85. Christian dogs] *Broughton;* Christians, dogges *Q.*   88. *Dies.*] *Reed.*

---

85. *Christian dogs*] Broughton's emendation makes better sense than
Q—Barabas curses both groups of enemies impartially—and Q's 'Christians' may be another false plural (see I.ii.0.1 n).
88. *curse . . . die*] Possibly echoing Job, ii.9, where Job's wife tells him
to 'Blaspheme God, and dye'.
90. *train*] trick, device.
95. *pretended*] offered, put forward.

> The ruins done to Malta and to us,
> Thou canst not part: for Malta shall be freed,
> Or Selim ne'er return to Ottoman.
> *Calym.* Nay, rather, Christians, let me go to Turkey,
> In person there to meditate your peace;   115
> To keep me here will naught advantage you.
> *Fern.* Content thee, Calymath, here thou must stay,
> And live in Malta prisoner; for come all the world
> To rescue thee, so will we guard us now,
> As sooner shall they drink the ocean dry,   120
> Than conquer Malta, or endanger us.
> So, march away, and let due praise be given
> Neither to fate nor fortune, but to heaven.   [*Exeunt.*]

FINIS.

115. meditate] *Q;* mediate *Shone.*   118. all] *Reed;* call *Q.*   123.
Exeunt.] *Robinson.*

---

115. *meditate*] Shone's 'mediate' is an attractive emendation, but in
Richard Knolles's translation of Bodin's *The Six Bookes of a Common-
weale* (London, 1606) there are four examples of such phrases as 'to send
Ambassadors to meditate a peace' and 'to meditate an agreement' (pp.
624–5, 632), and on p. 144 'meditation' is used to mean 'mediation'.
Unless these are all misprints (and on p. 624 there is a marginal note, 'It
is not safe for a neuter to mediat peace'), it looks as though 'meditate'
could mean something like 'to arrange by thought and discussion'.

118. *come all the world*] *Cf.* the concluding speech of the Bastard in
Shakespeare's *John*, v.vii.116–17, 'Come the three corners of the world in
arms, / And we shall shock them . . .'

120. *drink . . . dry*] proverbial (Tilley, O 9).

123.] Early patristic writers attacked the pagan concept of fortune, and
asserted that events are brought about by divine providence. But Machiavelli ignored providence and laid great stress on fortune (*The Prince*,
ch. 25), for which Gentillet rebuked him (pp. 139–41). Thomas Fitzherbert complained that some contemporary historians 'referre al kind of
effects and accidents to *fate* or *fortune*, more prophanely then many of the
Painyms were wont to doe, in whom a man shal find very pious and
religious obseruations of Gods infinite wisdome, prouidence, and iustice'
(*The First Part of a Treatise*, Douay, 1606, p. 109). See also R. W.
Battenhouse, *Marlowe's Tamburlaine* (Nashville, 1942), pp. 86–98.

Heywood's Dedication, Prologues, and Epilogues

[*Dedication*]

TO MY WORTHY FRIEND, MASTER THOMAS HAMMON, OF GRAY'S INN, &c.

This play, composed by so worthy an author as Master Marlowe, and the part of the Jew presented by so unimitable an
actor as Master Alleyn, being in this later age commended to
the stage, as I ushered it unto the Court, and presented it to the
Cockpit, with these prologues and epilogues here inserted, so   5
now being newly brought to the press, I was loath it should be

Dedication

Thomas Hammon] Heywood also dedicated to Hammon two of his own
plays, Part II of *The Fair Maid of the West* (1631) and Part I of *The Iron
Age* (1632). Hammon may be the Thomas Hammond listed in Venn's
Alumni Cantabrigienses, Part I (Cambridge, 1922), II, 295, who was born
c. 1592, matriculated from Christ's College, Cambridge, in December
1608, was admitted to Gray's Inn in 1611, and became a barrister in 1617.

3. *Master Alleyn*] Edward Alleyn (1566–1626) was one of the most
distinguished actors of the late 16th c. He has a particular connection with
Marlowe in that he first acted the roles of Tamburlaine, Faustus and Barabas.

4. *ushered*] announced or introduced as an usher (*O.E.D.*). There is
nothing here to indicate that Heywood has tampered with the text.

the Court] The title page claims that the play was presented before the
King and Queen 'in his Majesties Theatre at *White-Hall*'. This may
suggest that it was performed in the Cockpit-in-Court, remodelled as a
theatre in 1629–30, rather than in the banqueting house, designed by
Inigo Jones and built *c.* 1619–22. See G. E. Bentley, *The Jacobean and
Caroline Stage* (Oxford, 1941–68), VI, 259–84.

5. *the Cockpit*] 'The Phoenix, or Cockpit, in Drury Lane was one of the
two principal Caroline theatres' (Bentley, *op. cit.*, VI, 47). Bentley gives a
full account of the theatre (*ibid.*, pp. 47–77).

6. *newly*] The evidence of *O.E.D.*, and the title pages quoted by
Bennett, indicate that 'newly' could mean either 'very recently, for the
first time' or 'afresh, for the second time'. The word is therefore of no
help in deciding whether there was an edition of the play earlier than 1633.

published without the ornament of an epistle; making choice of
you unto whom to devote it, than whom (of all those gentlemen and acquaintance within the compass of my long knowledge) there is none more able to tax ignorance, or attribute   10
right to merit. Sir, you have been pleased to grace some of mine
own works with your courteous patronage; I hope this will not
be the worse accepted because commended by me, over whom
none can claim more power or privilege than yourself. I had
no better a new year's gift to present you with; receive it there-   15
fore as a continuance of that inviolable obligement by which he
rests still engaged who, as he ever hath, shall always remain,

> *Tuissimus*,
> THO. HEYWOOD.

The Prologue spoken at Court

Gracious and great, that we so boldly dare
('Mongst other plays that now in fashion are)
To present this, writ many years agone,
And in that age thought second unto none,
We humbly crave your pardon. We pursue   5
The story of a rich and famous Jew
Who lived in Malta; you shall find him still,
In all his projects, a sound Machevill,
And that's his character. He that hath passed
So many censures, is now come at last   10
To have your princely ears; grace you him, then
You crown the action and renown the pen.

10. *tax*] rebuke.
right] justice, a true valuation.
15. *new year's gift*] In Heywood's time gifts were exchanged at New
Year rather than at Christmas, and the titles of books published then
sometimes used formulae similar to Heywood's, e.g. Kathrine Chidley,
A New-Yeares Gift of a Brief Exhortation to Mr. Thomas Edwards (n.p.,
1645). *Cf.* also Thomas Middleton's manuscript dedication to William
Hammond of *A Game at Chess* (ed. R. C. Bald, Cambridge, 1929, p. 48);
and see E. H. Miller, 'New Year's Day gift books in the sixteenth century',
Studies in Bibliography, xv (1962), 233–41.
16. *obligement*] obligation, indebtedness.
18. *Tuissimus*] 'Yours most of all'.

The Prologue spoken at Court

5. *pursue*] follow, trace.
8. *sound*] genuine, thoroughgoing.
9–10. *passed . . . censures*] been frequently judged by audiences.
11. *grace*] *Cf.* Marlowe's Prologue, l. 33.

Epilogue

It is our fear, dread sovereign, we have been
Too tedious; neither can't be less than sin
To wrong your princely patience. If we have,
Thus low dejected we your pardon crave:
And if aught here offend your ear or sight,   5
We only act and speak what others write.

The Prologue to the Stage, at the Cockpit

         We know not how our play may pass this stage,
*Marlowe But by the best of *poets in that age
         The Malta Jew had being, and was made;
 *Alleyn And he then by the best of *actors played.
         In *Hero and Leander* one did gain   5
         A lasting memory; in *Tamburlaine*,
         This Jew, with others many, th'other won
         The attribute of peerless, being a man
         Whom we may rank with (doing no one wrong)
         Proteus for shapes and Roscius for a tongue,   10
         So could he speak, so vary. Nor is't hate
 *Perkins To merit in *him who doth personate

Epilogue

2. *can't*] i.e. can it.
6.] See Introduction, pp. 39–41.

The Prologue to the Stage

5–7.] Marlowe gained fame through *Hero and Leander*, Alleyn through his acting roles, including Tamburlaine and Barabas. Q has colons after 'memory' and 'many', and some 18th c. scholars mistakenly assumed Heywood to be asserting that Marlowe was the author of *Tamburlaine*, which was published anonymously. The right punctuation was first given by Robinson. Heywood seems to think that the non-dramatic *Hero and Leander* gave more prestige to Marlowe than his plays.

10. *Proteus*] a sea god who had the power of changing his shape, described by Homer in Book IV of *The Odyssey*; Bennett refers to Spenser's *Faerie Queene*, III.viii.30 ff. The allusion is a compliment to Alleyn's virtuosity.

Roscius] Quintus Roscius Gallus (d. 62 B.C.) was the most famous Roman actor of comedy. His name was later used to refer to a great actor in tragedy as well as comedy.

12. *Perkins*] Richard Perkins (d. 1650) was a versatile actor who played many leading roles on the later Jacobean and Caroline stage. He seems to have been a personal friend of Heywood's. (See Bentley, *op. cit.*, II, 525–8).

Our Jew this day, nor is it his ambition
To exceed, or equal, being of condition
More modest; this is all that he intends   15
(And that too at the urgence of some friends):
To prove his best, and if none here gainsay it,
The part he hath studied, and intends to play it.

Epilogue

In graving, with Pygmalion to contend,
Or painting, with Apelles, doubtless the end
Must be disgrace; our actor did not so,
He only aimed to go, but not out go.
Nor think that this day any prize was played;   5
Here were no bets at all, no wagers laid.
All the ambition that his mind doth swell
Is but to hear from you (by me), 'twas well.

14. *condition*] character, temperament.
17. *prove his best*] do as well as he can, put himself to the test.
gainsay] oppose, hinder.

Epilogue

1. *Pygmalion*] in classical myth the legendary King of Cyprus who fell in love with his own statue of a beautiful woman (see Ovid, *Metamorphoses*, Book x).

2. *Apelles*] a Greek of the earlier 4th c. B.C., the greatest painter of antiquity. John Lyly presented him on the stage in his comedy *Campaspe*, published in 1584.

4. *outgo*] surpass, excell.

5. *prize was played*] Bennett points out that this is 'a metaphor from the fencing-school: to engage in a contest or match', and quotes from Robert Greene's *Quip for an Upstart Courtier* (London, 1592), B3*v*, 'like the Usher of a Fense-schoole about to playe his Pryse'.

6. *wagers*] Collier notes that 'wagers as to the comparative merits of rival actors in particular parts were not infrequent of old', and cites Dekker's *The Guls Horne-booke* (London, 1609), p. 36, and a wager in which Alleyn himself was involved (see *Henslowe Papers*, ed. W. W. Greg, London, 1907, pp. 32–3).

APPENDIX B

Lineation

I have noted here all departures in this edition from the lineation of
Q, but have not attempted to record all the relineations made or conjectured by other editors and scholars. The large amount of mislining does not, I think, necessarily indicate textual corruption. It
appears that the compositor had difficulty with scenes in prose or
mingled prose and verse, and frequently set prose as though it were
verse, in lines that do not fill the full width of his measure, with a
capital letter at the beginning of each line. Nearly three-quarters of
the instances of mislining recorded below are of this type. Other
oddities of mislining may be due to the use of cast-off copy (see
Introduction, p. 39).

[I.i]
71–2. And . . . Alexandria ?] *Dyce; one line in* Q.
[I.ii]
68–70.] *Shone;* First . . . be / Leuyed . . . one / Halfe . . . estate. Q.
73–4.] *Shone;* Secondly . . . become / A Christian. Q.
119–22.] *Dyce;* Out . . . thus / To . . . not / Thy . . . righteousnesse,
Q.
200–2.] *Spencer;* I, I . . . patience. / You . . . want. Q.
276–7. Why . . . house] *Penley; one line in* Q.
289–90. Tush . . . mean'st] *Dyce; one line in* Q.
304–5.] *This ed.; one line in* Q.
[II.i]
46.] *Penley;* Here, / Hast thou't ? / There's . . . more. Q.
[II.iii]
36–7.] *Broughton;* Now . . . Serpent / Then . . . foole. Q.
41–3.] *Broughton;* I . . . harm / I . . . sindg'd. Q.
54–5.] *Dyce;* I . . . the / White leprosie. Q.
70–1]. *Collier; one line in* Q.
98–100.] *Dyce;* Come . . . price / Of . . . much ? Q.
113–14.] *Dyce;* What . . . hast, / Breake . . . thee. Q.
118–19.] *Broughton;* A . . . vanity / If . . . well. Q.
121–3.] *Collier;* Some . . . colour / Of . . . goods. / Tell . . . well ? Q.

125–8.] *Broughton;* So . . . sickly, / And . . . day / Will . . . one /
    That's . . . leaner. *Q.*
167–8.] *Dyce;* Faith . . . *Ithimer,* / My . . . please. *Q.*
204–5.] *Dyce ii; one line in Q.*
220–1.] *Dyce;* Oh . . . Diamond / You . . . of ? *Q.*
360–1.] *Cunningham;* You'll . . . Iewes / Enow in *Malta Q.*
367–8.] *Van Fossen;* Faith . . . this / You . . . so ? *Q.*
377–8.] *Broughton;* Feare . . . he / Shall . . . him. *Q.*

[III.i]

17–22.] *Broughton, Penley;* Faith . . . Gardens / I . . . house / Where
    . . . I / Clamber'd . . . taking / My . . . tooke / Onely . . . man. *Q.*
24–5.] *Penley;* Looke . . . away: / Zoon's . . . keep'st, / Thou'lt . . .
    anon. *Q.*
26–8.] *Collier;* O . . . is / A . . . hundred / Of . . . Concubine. *Q.*

[III.iii]

1–3.] *Shone;* Why . . . neatly / Plotted . . . and / Flatly . . . beguil'd.
    Q.
9–11.] *Broughton;* Oh . . . subtil / Bottle . . . had *Q.*
20–2.] *Collier;* Why . . . it, / And . . . *Mathia. Q.*
35–6.] *Broughton;* A . . . sport / With . . . then ? *Q.*

[III.iv]

39–41.] *Broughton;* Who . . . and / Throw . . . any / Thing . . . sake.
    Q.
56–7.] *A. Wagner;* Well . . . brought / The . . . too ? *Q.*
58–9.] *Broughton;* Yes . . . deuil / Had . . . Ladle. *Q.*
64–6.] *Broughton;* Why . . . rice / Porredge . . . plump, / And . . .
    aware. *Q.*
106–7.] *Broughton;* What . . . of / Rice . . . it ? *Q.*
111–12.] *Broughton;* Here's . . . of / Flanders . . . powder. *Q.*

[III.v]

26–7.] *Reed; one line in Q.*

[IV.i]

12–14.] *Reed;* And . . . hard / By . . . Monks. *Q.*
18–20.] *Reed;* No . . . *Hebrew* / Borne . . . *diabola. Q.*
40–1.] *Reed; one line in Q.*
141–2.] *Collier; one line in Q.*
153–5.] *Broughton;* Nay . . . leane / Vpon . . . Bacon. *Q.*
161–3.] *conj. Bullen;* Oh . . . conuert / An . . . treasury. *Q.*
167–8.] *Dyce; one line in Q.*
179–80.] *Broughton;* Good . . . but / You . . . escape. *Q.*
192–3.] *Broughton;* Fie . . . when / Holy . . . another. *Q.*

[IV.ii]

6–7.] *Scott;* I . . . of / The . . . world. *Q.*

9–11.] *Scott;* That . . . such / A tall . . . you. *Q.*

18–23.] *Reed;* Vpon . . . the / Gallowes . . . a / Fryars . . . hempen / prouerb . . . mercy / Of . . . where / He comes. *Q.*

24–41.] *Broughton;* I . . . as / This . . . was / About . . . his / Hempen . . . if / Hee . . . whither / He . . . haste: / And . . . fellow / Met . . . and / A . . . he / Gaue . . . *Bellamira,* / Saluting . . . make / Cleane . . . that / I . . . is; / It . . . in / My . . . me / Euer . . . such / Loue . . . now / Would . . . her. *Q.*

43–4.] *Scott;* Gentleman . . . a / Poore . . . gone. *Q.*

46–7.] *Broughton, Oxberry, Penley;* Agen . . . sweet / Youth a letter ? *Q.*

48–9.] *Reed;* I . . . my / Self . . . seruice. *Q.*

54–6.] *Broughton;* I'le . . . to / Make me hansome: / Pray . . . discharg'd. *Q.*

59–60.] *Broughton, Penley;* Nay . . . me; / Sweet . . . sake: *Q.*

62–4.] *Broughton, Penley;* If . . . it; / But . . . doe / Their . . . earth. *Q.*

69–70.] *Dyce;* But . . . were / Reueal'd . . . harme. *Q.*

71–3.] *Broughton;* I . . . more, / I'le . . . too. / Pen and Inke; / I'le . . . strait. *Q.*

80–2.] *Broughton, Penley;* I . . . this / Shall . . . so. *Q.*

110–13.] *Reed;* At . . . turnd / Aside . . . thus; / Told . . . me. *Q.*

118–19.] *Broughton, Penley;* The . . . thus: / Here's . . . not ? *Q.*

121–2.] *Reed;* But . . . giue / Me . . . for't. *Q.*

124–6.] *Broughton, Penley;* Sirra . . . crowns, / And . . . hau't. *Q.*

135–6.] *Broughton;* That . . . lips. / What . . . me ? / It . . . Starre. *Q.*

138–9.] *Broughton;* Oh . . . one, / That . . . afore / We wake. *Q.*

[IV.iii]

24–5.] *Broughton;* Oh . . . see, / There's . . . letter. *Q.*

26–8.] *Broughton;* Might . . . him / Come . . . streight. *Q.*

30–1.] *Broughton;* I . . . dine / With . . . poyson'd. *Q.*

35–6.] *Broughton;* Or . . . window: / You . . . meaning. *Q.*

58.] *Broughton, Penley;* Soone . . . Sir: / Fare you well. *Q.*

65–6.] *Broughton, Penley; one line in Q.*

[IV.iv]

14.] *Broughton;* Doe . . . know, / He's a murderer. *Q.*

19–20.] *Broughton;* I . . . he / And . . . Fryar. *Q.*

22–3.] *Broughton, Penley;* We . . . shall / Be for me. *Q.*

34–5.] *Broughton, Penley;* Prethe . . . me / The . . . there. *Q.*

53–4.] *Broughton, Penley;* You . . . of / My Window. *Q.*

62–3.] *Broughton, Penley;* 'Tis . . . vpon / Pickled . . . Mushrumbs. *Q.*

64.] *Broughton;* What . . . this ? / The . . . doe. *Q.*

67–8.] *Broughton;* The . . . Elder / When . . . himselfe. *Q.*

70.] *Broughton;* A . . . is; / Whether . . . Fidler ? *Q.*

74–7.] *Broughton;* No . . . now; / Bid . . . same / Token . . . *Bernardine* / Slept . . . clothes, / Any . . . it. *Q.*

[v.i]

12–14.] *Penley;* Who . . . Gentlemen, / Poyson'd . . . Nuns, / Strangled . . . what / Mischiefe beside. *Q.*

16–17.] *Shone;* Strong . . . my / Lodging . . . all. *Q.*

28–30.] *Broughton;* Gilty . . . *Mathias* / Were . . . *Abigall*, / Forg'd . . . challenge. *Q.*

32–4.] *Broughton;* I . . . it ? / Marry . . . the / Nuns . . . daughter. *Q.*

[v.v]

58–9. Ay . . . attend.] *Dyce ii; one line in Q.*

The staging of *The Jew of Malta*

The original staging of the play cannot be easily reconstructed. Many essential stage directions are missing from the quarto, and if the analysis of the text given in the introduction is correct, those that do exist are brief authorial notes written *before* production, which would need to be expanded and modified as the first production got under way. Obviously some kind of upper level was needed for II.i, where Abigail throws money down to Barabas, for III.ii, where Barabas watches from above the duel between Lodowick and Mathias, and for v.v, which opens with Barabas standing in the 'dainty gallery' mentioned at v.v.33. There appear also to have been 'discovery' scenes, where a curtain covering a recess or enclosure is drawn to reveal a character inside. I.i opens with the stage direction *'Enter Barabas in his Counting-house, with heapes of gold before him.'*; it is unlikely that Barabas was in full view of the audience while the prologue was being spoken, and probably at the end of the prologue 'Machevil' drew a curtain which disclosed Barabas sitting at a table with his ledgers and piles of coin in front of him. At IV.i.140 the sleeping Bernardine is revealed, though unfortunately the quarto has no stage directions at this point, while at v.v.62 the cauldron into which Barabas has fallen is *'discovered'*. Scholars have recently become increasingly sceptical about the existence of an 'inner stage' in the Elizabethan theatre, and it has been suggested that there was nothing more than a shallow 'discovery space', masked by curtains, not more than a foot or two deep. This would be perfectly adequate for the 'discoveries' in I.i and IV.i, where nothing more complicated is involved than Barabas seated at a small table, and Bernardine (presumably) lying asleep on a bench. It is not so clear, however, that the 'discovery space' would be able to cope with the elaborate stage business at the end of the play when Barabas falls through a trapdoor in his gallery into the boiling cauldron below. One problem that arises here is to know how literally we should read such lines as v.v.1–3 and 32–6; do they describe something that was actually erected on the stage, or are they there simply to stimulate the audience's imagination, as is the case at v.i.86–94, where no attempt would have been made to construct an actual 'sluice' on stage? My own feeling is that we are dealing here with a special and possibly unique case, and I would suggest (though it must be emphasised that this is sheer hypothesis) that a wooden 'house' or booth was constructed on stage at the beginning of v.v, with a trapdoor in the roof, space inside for the cauldron, and curtains in front which could be pulled aside to disclose Barabas. It is true that no evidence has yet been discovered to prove that booths were ever used on the Elizabethan stage, and normally the erection of a booth would be a clumsy and inconvenient distraction for the audience, but the fact that Marlowe brings on two or more carpenters as characters in the play, and has Barabas *'with a Hammar aboue, very busie'*, suggests that he was aware of this and was trying to incorporate the construction of the booth into the action of his play. (It is, of course, just possible that the booth, if there was one, was in position throughout the play, and could therefore be used also for the 'discoveries' in i.i and iv.i, but this seems very unlikely.) Furthermore, Henslowe's description of the cauldron among his stage properties as being specifically 'for the Jewe' (see Introduction, p. i) suggests that there was something special about it (perhaps it was unusually large), and I would argue that Marlowe intended this whole piece of stage business to be as realistic and spectacular as possible. With the ordinary resources of the Elizabethan theatre the actor playing Barabas would have needed to mime his fall, as there was no trapdoor above the 'discovery space'; he would then have had to run downstairs and climb into the cauldron before being 'discovered'. This would entail an awkward delay of several seconds, but with a booth containing a trapdoor in the roof the whole thing could be done quickly and efficiently. I assume here that Marlowe wanted the fall of Barabas to be clearly visible to the audience, and this would not have been possible without some special arrangement. There may also have been a simple wooden ladder (the 'homely stairs' of v.v.58) attached to the side of the booth, ostensibly for Calymath to climb, but in practice used by Barabas and the carpenters. This whole interpretation is, I must repeat, purely theoretical, but it seems to me to cope with the problems involved more satisfactorily than any other theory, and it rather contradicts Glynne Wickham's conclusion ('Notes on the staging of Marlowe's plays', *Shakespeare's Dramatic Heritage*, London, 1969, p. 130) that Marlowe avoided complicated machinery because it was not available in the public theatre of his day. One further point about staging needs to be mentioned. In his article 'Elizabethan stage practice and Marlowe's *The Jew of Malta*', *Renaissance Drama*, n.s. IV (1971), 93–104, J. L. Simmons argues that at v.i.58–60, where the quarto has only the simple stage direction '*Exeunt.*', Barabas's 'body' would have been thrown down from the stage into the yard of the theatre where the spectators stood. Calymath and his army would then enter, also in the yard; Barabas would creep underneath the stage with some soldiers into the back of the theatre, and then re-enter on the main stage with Ferneze and the knights as captives, to be met by Calymath, who has jumped up from the yard on to the main stage. Simmons also proposes that the quarto's 'Truce', at v.i.86, should be read as 'truss' (an architectural term referring to a load-bearing framework or projection), and that in using it Barabas points to the wooden supports under the stage. Simmons's interpretation of v.i is ingenious, and may seem no more theoretical than the booth proposed above, but there is a case for arguing that in comparison it makes a far larger number of inadequately proved assumptions about the way the Elizabethan stage was used, and there is really very little in the text or stage directions of the quarto to justify it. In addition, it is unnecessarily complicated; the problems of staging v.i can be solved in simpler and more conventional ways (see v.i. 59.1n.). But some readers may feel that the same can be said for the cauldron scene, and all theories about the staging of the play will need to be rigorously investigated in the light of our general knowledge of the Elizabethan stage.

Glossarial Index to the Commentary

Words and phrases are listed in the form in which they occur in the text. An asterisk before a word indicates that the note contains information supplementing that given in *O.E.D.* This index also contains cumulative entries listing biblical allusions and proverbs or proverbial phrases (see under 'Biblical' and 'Proverbs').